THE STREET OF
DISILLUSION

by

HARRY PROCTER

Revel Barker
Publishing

First published in 1958 by Allan Wingate, London.
This edition published by Revel Barker Publishing, 2010

ISBN: 978-0-9563686-7-6
Revel Barker Publishing
66 Florence Road
Brighton BN2 6DJ
England
revelbarker@gmail.com

Harry Procter worked as an errand boy and in a shoe shop in Leeds while studying English and learning shorthand at night school in order to achieve his first ambition, to become a reporter on his local paper, the *Armley and Wortley News*, at 16.

At 18 he was appointed chief reporter of the *Cleveland Standard* in Redcar, North Yorkshire, and moved from there to the Middlesbrough office of the *Northern Echo*.

Laid off during an economy drive, he returned to Leeds and joined the *Yorkshire Evening News*.

He was offered holiday relief work for a week on the *Daily Mirror* in London, where he was taken on the staff and achieved his second ambition – to work in Fleet Street – at 22. After the outbreak of war he volunteered for the RAF and then returned to newspapers as a war correspondent for the *Daily Mail*, where he worked for eight years before joining the *Sunday Pictorial* (now the *Sunday Mirror*).

The Street of Disillusion covers his experience as a reporter up to the time he left Fleet Street, and has become a classic book about newspapers and journalism.

The legend
By Revel Barker

It is a disappointing sign of the laziness of what used to be called Fleet Street that journalists – whose craft, after all, is the use of words – when looking for an adjective to describe any former colleague (or, at least, any one that they actually remember) are frequently content to reach for 'Legendary'.

Future generations may debate whether more recent names (Harry Evans, say, or Keith Waterhouse or David English) deserve the epithet. Meanwhile the newspapermen in living memory who can fairly and honestly be described in that way can probably be numbered in single figures.

Arthur Christiansen, long-serving editor of the *Daily Express* (The World's Greatest Newspaper) in an age when editors would rather be seen dead than on the telly – although, remarkably, he played himself in a British movie, *The Day The Earth Caught Fire*, in 1961 – and Hugh '*Publish And Be Damned!*' Cudlipp might be the only Fleet Street executives on the list. Bill Connor, 'Cassandra' of the *Daily Mirror* (The World's Biggest Daily Sale) would surely be on it; James Cameron, who is remembered and revered long after his paper, the *News Chronicle*, has folded and been forgotten, Hannen Swaffer and Duncan Webb (the *People*) and Vincent Mulchrone (*Daily Mail*) would probably make it.

Sir Linton Andrews, editor of the *Leeds Mercury* and the *Yorkshire Post* (1939-60), founder member and then chairman of the Press Council, an acknowledged expert on the Brontë family of authors, was certainly a famous name among journalists (by no means confined to the provinces) during the period covered by this book. But it's a fair guess that his name has been forgotten, even in Leeds, now...

And then there's Harry Procter.

Twenty-five years after he had left the *Sunday Pictorial* people were still talking about him in The Stab In The Back, the *Mirror* pub that hadn't even existed during his days on the paper, and in El Vino, the Fleet Street watering hole. They carried their Harry

5

Procter stories – about how they'd worked with (or, more likely, against) him – like a badge to signify that they too belonged to a special generation of newspaperman; that they, too, were part of the folk tale that was Fleet Street in its rapidly disappearing glory days.

The problem was that they didn't tell the stories half as well as he related them in his own book.

Harry Procter believed that reporters on rival newspapers hated him for his consistent string of scoops. That isn't the way they saw it. Or, anyway, not the way they remembered it. Certainly, they feared him – and the most disheartening thing a journalist on an opposition paper could hear on a job was that the *Daily Mail* (or, later, the *Sunday Pic*) was sending Procter along to cover it. And, worse, reporters on his own paper must surely have resented the fact that, after they had failed to get a story, their editor would despatch his 'ace reporter' to sort it out in full confidence that he'd return – and quickly – with the goods.

It wasn't so much hatred, then, as approbation. And yet there was no secret about his technique. While whole teams of experienced reporters pussyfooted around on the periphery of a situation trying to find a way in to the story, Harry Procter got off the train or out of the car and stormed straight to the centre of it. Then he went to the phone with his copy and also, frequently, with the assurance that a full statement or confession, signed on every page by the elusive interviewee, was on its way to the office by registered post.

Anybody with what his old Mum would have called 'the nous', and with the self-confidence of a reporter who didn't count the word failure in his vocabulary, could have done the same.

Harry Procter's Street was a period piece that is totally unrecognisable today. Apart from the simple fact that it was an age packed by scoops – most of them home-grown, generated by contacts and conversations in the newsroom or in the pub, and never bought in from agencies or public relations people – it was a time capsule that can be opened only by reading this book.

New kids on the block who are on first-name terms with everybody from the Chief Reporter to the Editor (capital letters people, in his day) and even with the proprietor will smile at the way reporters addressed everybody higher up in the pecking order as Sir – even if they didn't respect, like, or agree with them.

They will doubtless guffaw at the idea of phoning in to ('politely') *ask permission to speak to* the Assistant News Editor, then say, 'Sir, I have a story to offer, would you be kind enough to tell me when I may dictate it?'

Or to plead: 'I wonder if can dictate at once, because, Sir, if you will forgive the phrase, it is rather hot stuff.'

It was, indeed, hot stuff and an altogether different world. But it was an era in which newspaper circulations were growing all the time.

In the end, it all became too much for our hero. He grew weary of writing the sordid details of murders and of exposing scandals and begged to be taken off crime and allowed to write light stories – what he called the 'corn'. But his boss Colin Valdar, and his boss's boss Hugh Cudlipp wouldn't let him. How could they, when every story he wrote increased the sales of the paper?

He tired of intruding – even when, as was usually the case, he was invited to intrude – into private grief.

Even his mother, who had set him off as a youngster on the road to Fleet Street, thought he had eventually taken a wrong turning. His wife despaired of disapproval from the neighbours about the yellow-press stories and death-cell revelations he was writing (but how would they know, unless they were among the millions who paid to read his articles every Sunday…?)

He was also (although half a dozen threats of libel writs ensured that he didn't go into it in any depth in this book) clearly frustrated and dejected by the unsupportive and carping attitude of his immediate boss, Reg Payne, who criticised his stories but always used them.

His health was starting to suffer. Nowadays it would almost certainly be diagnosed as depression, but an over-indulgence in booze and cigarettes (occupational hazards in a generation of journalists that rarely lived to enjoy retirement), the adrenalin highs created by a relentless chasing of exclusive stories, lack of sleep on out-of-town overnight jobs, and rarely seeing his young family meant that, having reached Fleet Street at 22 he was burnt out before he was 40. And eventually that became his ticket out.

'If this is Fleet Street, it's time I left it,' he wrote.

He returned to the north, to Manchester, and back to the *Daily Mail*. His disillusion with the great game in which he'd had such high hopes and made himself a household name provided the obvious title for a book.

He sent the manuscript to Philip Gibbs, author of *The Street of Adventure* – the book that had inspired him as a teenager – and Gibbs, by now a publisher, read it 'with very great interest and with admiration', wrote to the author saying he had done 'magnificently well as a journalist', and published it.

Harry Procter didn't live much longer. The former virtuoso in the art of wheedling confessions and revelations from people who were otherwise afraid to speak, the man who had imposed himself between the King and the US President when they held 'secret' talks on an American warship, died of lung cancer in 1965 aged only 48.

But he had quit at the top, while still Fleet Street's most famous 'ace reporter' and while the catch-phrase, applied to anybody with a story to tell, was still 'Tell Harry Procter about it'. Thousands did.

And that's why he was, and is, a legend.

Leeds-born Revel Barker was a reporter on the *Yorkshire Evening Post* at 17 and on the *Daily Mirror* at 20 and then moved to do investigations and exposés for the *Sunday Mirror*. He spent 27 years with the Mirror Group, retiring as managing editor, and now publishes books about journalism.

To Doreen

who gave me courage to tell this tale

'I do believe that as circuses, newspapers will die.

We have to return to our role of providing information.'

SIR WILLIAM HALEY,

Editor, *The Times*. June, 1957.

Chapter One

In the drab cellar-basement of a large Leeds store, a sooty-faced fifteen-year-old boy sat reading a book.

He sat before an open chimney where a great fire blazed away from its never-ending fodder of empty boot and shoe boxes. His seat was an old fitting-stool, the type used in footwear shops.

Great brown rats squeaked and ran about the cellar, for this four-storey building was near the Leeds City Market where vermin thrived by the million. The engines which drove the old-fashioned hydraulic lift moaned and grunted only three yards behind him. The noise of the traffic of a busy bustling city poured through the narrow, slit ventilator.

Oblivious to the noise, the rats, or the soot-filled air, the boy read on, hungrily absorbing every printed line.

No blood-curdling thriller this boy's book, no cheap romance. He was reading *The Street of Adventure,* by Philip Gibbs.

Fleet Street! Lined with great buildings in which millions of copies of newspapers were printed every hour of the day and night... where ace reporters raced for taxis, where editors shouted into telephones, where vans sped off laden with printed pages which would bring excitement to the millions and heartbreak to the few... Fleet Street... Adventure...

The boy's eyes shone. He was many miles away from Leeds.

Down the iron spiral stairway which led to the cellar came the robust panting body of the boss. He peered suspiciously as he reached the floor then, aided by the noise, tip-toed forward slowly until he was right behind the seated, long-haired boy.

'Reading again!' he thundered. 'Caught you red-handed this time, my lad. You're sacked!'

The startled boy leaped from his seat. And, as insults and curses were showered upon him, he placed his book gently on the fitting-stool, then silently began to take off his work-stained overall.

Seizing the book the manager started at its title.

'And what rubbish are yer reading this time?' he demanded.

The boy shrugged. 'It's just a book about Fleet Street. A book about newspaper reporters.'

'Fleet Street indeed,' roared the manager, brandishing the book like a weapon. 'And why the 'ell, I asks yer, should yer be reading a book abaht Fleet Street when yer supposed ter be sweepin' this cellar?'

The boy grinned, tolerantly. 'Because I'm going to work in Fleet Street, some day,' he said. 'Because I'm going to be an ace-reporter. Because one day you're going to see my name in big black letters across the front page of a national newspaper.'

The manager who, let's face it, had had his patience sorely tried by this lad many times before, puffed and shook his head. 'Lad!' he said, in his good broad Yorkshire, 'you're ruddy barmy, that's what you are. Never before 'ave I 'ad a lad in this shop whose head was filled with such rubbish. Go and get yer cards. Yer sacked!'

That boy was me. And I can faithfully report that, a few years later, when I next met this loud, boisterous, but good-hearted manager of the main branch of the Public Benefit Boot Company Limited, he was delighted to see me. And he was delighted to tell me he had often read my name in big black letters across the front page of a national newspaper.

'But who would 'ave thowt it?' he asked me, then. Well, who would?

When I worked as errand boy, lift-boy, and char-boy in that shoe-shop, I was paid ten shillings a week. It was the hardest work I was ever to do. Later, when I was earning a four-figure salary as one of Fleet Street's ace-reporters, when I owned my own car, when I talked with kings, politicians, murderers, film stars, and famous people from every walk of life, I often spared a thought for that dark cellar where I sat and dreamed great dreams. Most of them came true.

But at the shoe-shop they did not go in much for dreams. I used to start work at 8am by lifting the heavy shop gates into the lift and conveying them down into the cellar. My next task was to get down on my hands and knees outside the shop and scrub the mosaic paving until it shone. Thirty yards of brass work at the foot of the outside windows was my regular third assignment, then back indoors to polish the old mahogany lift and the lift shaft. About

10am I was allowed a mug of tea, but I had to drink it alone in the cellar. Then came the task I always thoroughly enjoyed – that of burning in the great fireplace the hundreds of empty shoe boxes – empty from the previous day's sales. In those days there was no paper shortage.

While the fire blazed I was supposed to be sweeping the cellar, and my orders were to do it at speed so that I could wash, smarten up, and drive the lift for the rest of the day.

I have kneeled, and scrubbed, and polished, outside that shop in Kirkgate, Leeds, when it was so cold that my fingers could not feel the wash-leather, when it was so hot that I worked in trousers and shirt.

But it never troubled me. My dreams were made of stern stuff. No young boy embarking upon, or hoping for, a professional career, could have had more discouragement, more advice to stop dreaming, more alternative suggestions for a future working-life. But I was deaf to it all. Everyone told me it was impossible, people with wisdom and knowledge kindly pointed out that my education and social position in life made it absurd for me even to hope. I did not hope. I just KNEW.

As an errand boy I must have read *The Street of Adventure* about twenty times – the book had a very special spell for me, as you shall learn.

My career as a journalist was started by my mother, an old woman, now aged eighty, who still lives within a mile or two of the house where she was born. Aided by her heavy Yorkshire accent (Shakespeare's language she calls it) she is a greater talker than I will ever be a writer. She raised a family on a thin purse: four sons and one daughter. I was her youngest child.

My schooldays were happy, but uneventful. I was bright at one subject only, a subject then named 'composition'. At the age of ten a story in my English book was read out to the entire school, and this happened several times later. In my fourteenth year I was running the magazine of the Wyther Park Council School, Bramley, Leeds.

At the end of my fourteenth year all the boys who were leaving school were recommended for jobs in offices, shops, and factories but my scholastic record was not deemed high enough for such a recommendation. My mother led me to school-teacher Arthur Cox, a man who had always taken a kindly interest in me.

She asked the teacher what job he thought I might be suited for. 'He might make a journalist,' ventured Mr Cox.

'A what?' cried my mother, who had certainly never heard of such a thing in her life. The teacher explained.

That evening, just after tea, my mother settled herself down in her favourite chair and stupefied her large family by announcing: 'Our Harry's going to be a journalist!'

My father, a retired school attendance officer with a rich Yorkshire humour, began to laugh out loud. And I, who for hours had been making strange guesses as to whatever on earth a journalist might be, and had by now an unspoken horror that it had something to do with railways, waited in dread for an explanation.

'I'll bet he doesn't even know what a journalist is,' sniggered my father from above his *Sporting Pink,* and I meekly confessed that I didn't. But my ignorance neither deterred nor worried my mother in the slightest – nothing in the world ever could.

'Well, then it's high time he found out,' she said, snappily, 'because it's a journalist he's going to be. Teacher says as it's the only thing he'll ever make.'

And thereupon she picked up a copy of the *Leeds Mercury* and gave me my first course in journalism.

'See here,' she said. 'This is a newspaper! Journalists are men who write things in newspapers. Look there "by *Leeds Mercury* Reporter". Now, the man who wrote that is what you're going to be – a journalist. Now then...'

At great length she continued. W L Andrews (now Sir Linton Andrews, chairman of the Press Council) would have been amazed could he have been present that day and heard my mother explain from her newly acquired knowledge just how his newspaper was produced.

'From now on you never go out without a pencil and some paper in your pocket,' my mother commanded, and since that day I do not think I ever have. 'Keep your eyes and ears open, write notes about everything you hear and see. What interests you and me interests everybody, always remember that.' It was wonderful advice.

My father, who at this time had already experienced twenty-five years of being daily amazed by my astonishing mother, did wonder a little about how she would accomplish launching me as a writer for the Press.

'How can you?' he ventured, timidly. 'His handwriting is terrible. Nobody can read what he writes.'

'Then he shall type what he writes,' said my dauntless mother. A few months later she bought me an old Salter typewriter for 35s. It was the first typewriter she ever came within a yard of, but she taught me to type.

Shortly after my fourteenth birthday she scrubbed my face and neck, bought me a new white collar and, bedecked in my Sunday best, I was sent off to storm the offices of the *Armley and Wortley News* and demand an interview with the editor – Miss Constance Goodhall, wife of the man who pioneered road safety in this country.

I can never forget the kindness of Connie Goodhall. I was just a little boy from a council school who sincerely believed that writing was his vocation. I had no introduction, I had nothing to recommend me other than a few untidily scrawled articles in a school composition book. She could have been forgiven had she refused to see me.

But she sat me down beside a cheerful coal fire, gave me tea and biscuits, read my dog-eared school books and persuaded me to talk. She was a very beautiful woman. In addition to editing two local newspapers she had a home to run, and had many social interests, but pleasantly she gave me her time.

And she said to me: 'You will be a journalist. And I am going to help you. I want you to go to night-school, learn shorthand, then come back to me in one year's time. Then I will give you a job...'

When the time came for me to leave, she scribbled on a piece of paper and handed it to me.

'Here is the name of a book I want you to read. It is a book which will teach you about journalism.'

On the tramcar home I opened the note and read it. It just said *'The Street of Adventure,* by Philip Gibbs.'

The following day I went to the Kirkstall Public Library and borrowed the book. Later I bought a copy for myself. As I have said, I must have read it at least twenty times in the next two years.

But I had to get a job. A radio and gramophone shop in Armley Town Street wanted an errand boy. They took me on at 7s 6d a week, and for a fortnight I pedalled a tradesman's bicycle collecting and delivering wet radio batteries. In my second week I slipped on the frosty road while carrying a large battery, smashing it to pieces. I was quietly fired on the spot.

'Strong Boy Wanted' it said in the window of a cut-price grocery store in the Kirkstall Road. And for months I delivered groceries, pulling like a horse at a wooden bogey with two small iron wheels. In the afternoons I weighed sacks of flour into stones and half stones. Customers gave me coppers as tips. I noticed pretty girls as I slugged my loads of groceries about the cobbled streets of Kirkstall, but they did not notice me. I hoarded shillings to buy myself a decent suit, never daring to wear it, but telling myself it was for the day, months ahead, marked on the calendar with a cross. At night, tired and aching, I went early to bed, to read about Fleet Street.

The year passed. And, without a letter of warning, I went again to the offices of the *Armley and Wortley News* to claim my heritage.

I had learned shorthand. I had studied English at night-school. I had read *The Street of Adventure*. Now I was to receive my reward.

'I have called to see Miss Constance Goodhall, please. I saw her a year ago and she told me to come back after twelve months!'

They were very polite. Miss Constance Goodhall, they explained, had left the *Armley and Wortley News*. But I could see Mr Alan H Simpson (now Major Alan H Simpson, MBE, Chief PRO. Northern Command) who was the Editor.

Alan was subbing copy when I entered his room; he barely looked up. He was sorry there was nothing he could do.

I turned and ran from the office.

My mother asked: 'Did she give you a job?' I couldn't answer.

Later a friendly letter came from Alan Simpson, who had phoned Connie Goodhall to ask why I had called.

'Honestly, Harry,' he wrote, 'journalism isn't worth the candle. Take my advice and forget it.'

And down to Leeds central I went to search for another errand boy's job. They hired me at the boot-shop.

The best thing about it was that the hour I had to spend burning empty boot-boxes and sweeping the dismal cellar was an hour for concentrated, undisturbed, thought.

'Nobody's going to help you,' I eventually decided. 'You've got to do it yourself.'

I discovered the address of Mr W P Riley, then Chief Reporter of the *Armley and Wortley News*. I called to see him at his home and told him the lot. 'Tommy' Riley listened. And he gave me a piece of wonderful advice.

'There is a key which will open for you the door of any newspaper office,' he told me, solemnly. 'That key is a b----y good story. You can write it on embossed paper, you can have it neatly typed on foolscap, you can scribble it on a sugar bag. But if it's a good story, the paper you send it to will want it. And if they want your stories they'll want you.'

I have used this method for every job I have ever obtained since. It has never failed. It cannot fail.

Back in the boot-shop I sat down and wrote a story about my daily life and labours. I put it all down, about scrubbing the mosaic entrance, polishing the brass, driving the lift, making the tea, running the errands. And I posted my story to the *Leeds Mercury*.

About one week later I was sitting at the kitchen table having breakfast. I was holding a pint mug of tea, staring dreamily at the table-cloth.

Ours was a typical Yorkshire table-cloth. The joke about them in Leeds in those days was: 'My pal Bert came to tea the other day and spilled his cup all over the clean table-cloth. I wouldn't have cared, but we hadn't read it.'

The table-cloth I stared at was three days old – I had not read it. And there it was before me, covered with crumbs, tea-stained. My story. It was my first story to appear in print. The man who is now Sir Linton Andrews saw the story, liked it. He himself wrote the inset which appeared above it:

'We always like to know what the young people are thinking,' read the inset. 'Here is the utterance, clearly sincere, of a young errand boy in a large Leeds Store.' This was followed by my own story, word for word.

Proudly I showed it to my family. Proudly I hurried to the house of my former school-teacher to flaunt the cutting. School-teacher Cox seemed just as happy as I.

'You may be in Fleet Street, some day,' he said, and his eyes were as wide open as though he had said: 'Some day you may become Prime Minister.'

I went along to the offices of the *Leeds Mercury* and asked to see Mr Andrews, the editor. I was granted an interview with the commissionaire. So I popped into a telephone kiosk, looked up the editor's private address, then caught a tram-car to Headingley, in those days the most exclusive Leeds suburb. And eventually 'WLA' – that was how Sir Linton Andrews was then known – told his French maid to invite me into his study.

Linton Andrews was an outstanding man, even in those times. He had a national reputation as a journalist of the highest integrity, and the daily column he wrote, headed 'WLA', was as popular in Leeds as Cassandra's is today in London. He told me kindly that I could have a few minutes only of his time. I told him a few minutes was all that was required; for, after all, all I wanted was to ask him to make the errand boy whose story he had published into a junior reporter. My request appeared to amuse him, and he laughed, kindly.

'I admire your tremendous enthusiasm' he said. 'But a journalist must be an educated man. You go along to the Leeds University, then, in a few years, you may make a reporter.'

But for an errand boy earning ten shillings a week, a university course was not possible.

I decided to take Tommy Riley's advice. I decided I would send the *Armley and Wortley News* so many stories that it would be too expensive not to have me on their staff.

I asked my father; 'What was Armley like when you were a boy? What were the schools like? How has it all changed?'

My father told me of the Armley and Wortley of forty years before. I wrote it up, and the *Armley and Wortley News* splashed it.

My mother sent me to see an old man who was a geologist, with the comment: 'There's a good story in every old man.'

He told me all about his dream journeys, deep, deep down under the local High Street, and Alan Simpson gave me the feature page for the article I wrote. Several other stories were accepted by the local paper.

I got bolder. Every night I spent at my typewriter. For fun I decided to type a letter to the managing director of the Boot and Shoe Company, for whom I worked, offering suggestions as to how his main city store could be improved.

To my astonishment the managing director was so impressed by my letter, sent anonymously, that within a few days he paid the store a visit in person. As I drove him and the manager up in the lift I saw that the great man was holding my letter.

He toured the shop. 'I agree with the writer of this letter,' I heard him say, and I laughed secretly, wondering whether he would agree if he knew it was written by the little boy who was driving the lift.

At the cost of many hundreds of pounds, my ideas – ideas sent by the errand boy to the managing director in secret – were adopted.

With a pride I dared not share with anyone I watched the workmen install the new system I had suggested. But I was fired before I could really judge whether the improvements were worth the money.

I refused to take another job as errand boy, feeling certain that I could make at least ten shillings a week as a free-lance journalist. I was wrong for, although the odd story and paragraph were accepted by the local paper, my writings did not pay. But shortly after my sixteenth birthday Alan H Simpson offered me the post of junior reporter on the *Armley and Wortley News.*

I now know that I had W P Riley, the Chief Reporter, to thank for this. He had strongly urged that I be given a chance. I was extremely grateful to him, and I remember wondering then how I could ever repay him.

Fifteen years later, when I was a highly-paid reporter on the London *Daily Mail,* I received a telephone call from Riley.

He was speaking from a kiosk outside the *Daily Mail* office. Would I see him? He told me he was in trouble. He had that day used all the money he had in the world to fly from Guernsey to London, hoping to find himself a job.

'But the big worry is, Harry,' my old chief confided, 'that I have left my wife and two small children sitting in the lounge of the Guernsey airport. I had hoped to get enough money in London to wire them their fare to follow me.'

I returned to the *Daily Mail* office, made a few telephone calls, and within three hours I had Tommy's wife and two children safely installed in my own home at Beckenham, Kent, where they all stayed until Tommy found himself a journalistic post in London.

It was a wonderful thrill for me to be allowed to repay, in a small way, the man who gave me my first start in journalism.

Tommy Riley trained me with care. At first the only tasks he gave me were to make 'local calls', a round of vicars, clubs, local societies. But as my confidence grew he gave me bigger assignments, and very soon I was holding my own as a valued member of the staff.

They changed the name of the paper to the *Leeds Guardian,* and gave it a sudden new look which shocked the old regular readers. It was here I saw my first 'exposure story' – I never dreamed then that later on I was to become one of Britain's best-known experts on newspaper exposures and that my name would be feared by every scoundrel and confidence trickster in the land.

But this exposure was a much gentler affair, an attack on the committee of a local carnival held annually to raise money for the hospitals. It sold a lot of papers, but the advertisers did not like it. They withdrew their support, and very soon my colleagues and I all received notice and the paper was sold for as little as £100 to a Mr Cyril Licence, the proprietor of a local newspaper at Wetherby.

The new owner-editor told me that I was to be one of the only two reporters he intended to re-engage.

He was bluntly honest about why he had reached this decision. I was the lowest paid reporter.

'I have little money,' he told me. 'But I want to bring the old paper back, and revert to the old title of *Armley and Wortley News.'*

He, and I, and a young reporter named Arthur Merrill, turned out the paper from the front parlour of the owner's modest Armley house. We posted our 'copy' to Wetherby where the paper was printed.

The first week the new owner put out a news bill, 'T'Owd Paper Back Again' This bill inspired me to write a ballad on the headline, and the following week I saw my first published effort at rhyme. The first verse was:

T' owd paper's back agen.
Good news for Armley men.
Handy size for wrapping fish in.
Takin' home your favourite dish in
Tidings glad for Armley men
T' owd paper's back agen.

Fifteen verses followed, but I am sure the first one was the best of them all. I wrote it as a joke, I offered it for publication as a joke. I have never got over the shock of it being published.

But, despite my poetic efforts, I was not to serve 'T'owd Paper' long. Two weeks later I was fired because I could not afford to buy a second-hand bicycle in order to ride round and find the news. Colleague Arthur Merrill had a bicycle, and he stayed on.

For the next few months I took a university course – at the University of Life. I left Leeds, without money, with only a small attaché case, and literally took to the road. I slept in hedges, in haystacks, cheap lodging houses. Sometimes I went for days without food, but it never troubled me much. I was fascinated by the people I met in all the strange places my rovings took me; poverty and hardship did not bore me. I took on all kinds of temporary jobs; at fairgrounds, with canvassing teams, as a street photographer. All the time I kept on writing, and my experiences allowed me to write some articles for *The World's Fair.* They published my first short story entitled 'On the Knocker'.

Then one day I heard of a job going as Chief Reporter of the *Cleveland Standard,* at Redcar, Yorkshire. I arrived at the office armed with a Redcar story, and was immediately hired.

I was eighteen years old. The *Cleveland Standard* paid me 30s a week, but the paper taught me something of every facet of newspaper production. I was reporter, sub-editor, acting-editor for a while, and in my spare time I touted advertisements for the commission they brought me. Sometimes, on this happy little newspaper, I had to take a spell setting up type on the 'lino'.

We printed on an old 'flat bed' which was forever breaking down. We had no folding machine, but children from a nearby school were allowed to leave early to help us fold the papers. One Friday night I astounded Redcar by bringing out a late night 'special' of the local election results. Not only did I have to print that special edition, but I raced down the local High Street, shouting it, and selling it.

I was very poor in Redcar, but I was extremely happy. If life has taught anything at all, it is the great truth that money and happiness are not dependent on each other – are not really connected. I have been immensely happy drinking champagne in Paris or Rome, but also I have been hilariously joyful with only a few coppers in my pocket.

In the post of Chief Reporter on the *Cleveland Standard,* I found little financial reward, but it was rather wonderful being a big fish in a small pool. Everyone in Redcar knew me, I had many friends and few enemies. And I had power.

Power is an exciting thing. And, really, there is little difference in the enjoyment of the power wielded by that great newspaper giant Hugh Cudlipp, who runs the *Mirror* group, and the power of the editor of a local newspaper in a small town. The thrill is just the same.

In Redcar I had to do all the major reporting: the council meetings, the police courts, funerals, weddings, inquests. And, in addition, I made it my business to turn out a bright, human story every week.

When short of a special human interest feature, I had to pull one out of the fire. One week therefore I went careering round the wall of death on a motor cycle, an experience which gave me a novel feature-article by weekly paper standards. Also this story brought me my first mention in a national newspaper trade journal, which printed a picture of me on the wall, captioned 'The Reporter Goes Round and Around'.

And I began to know the pulse of this small, coastal town, a pulse which said, at every beat, 'The Season, The Season, and The Season'. Redcar lived for its holiday season, the time when day trippers and holiday-makers flocked to its glorious stretch of golden sands. The winters were merely a long breathing space for the people of Redcar – a waiting time. I learned to know that a rainy Easter – just darned bad luck to the average town dweller – could mean ruin to some of the small tradesmen who were now my friends.

'The Season?' said one such man to me. 'Aye, it was on a Wednesday last year.'

I knew the grim tragedy behind his simple pun.

In Redcar I wore my first evening clothes, full tails and white bow. I had to represent the *Standard* at the Cleveland Hunt Ball, held at the exclusive Coatham Hotel, Redcar. The suit and shirt were borrowed from an amateur pianist who did not happen to be playing that night.

I remember strolling nervously on to the powdered dance-floor of the Coatham Hotel, feeling as awkward and as uncomfortable as if I had worn chain mail. To make matters worse I suddenly realised that I had never danced a step in my life. Panic seized me. I just stood, and stood. I looked magnificent, my shirt and tie were spotless, my suit was immaculate. Yet I felt like a tailor's dummy, and I was just as motionless. The head-waiter approached me.

'What shift are you on, chum' he asked.

My first impulse was to choke him, slowly, in full view of all the elite of Cleveland. But I hurried to the office of the hotel manager, a man I knew well, and, with peacock-like dignity, demanded an apology.

The manager sent for the head-waiter.

'Mr Procter,' said the head-waiter, 'I didn't make a mistake. But seeing you standing there like a statue for almost an hour I got scared that one of the guests might go up to you and say: "Get me a scotch and soda". Then you would have been upset.' I burst into a fit of laughter, and the three of us had a drink.

At nineteen I had a really lucky break, the luckiest break of my career. I happened to meet the prettiest girl I ever saw in the whole of my life. She, the silly girl, fell in love with me, and then I bullied her into marriage. Not only did I get myself a wonderful wife, a loyal friend, and a wise counsellor for life, but I had the luck to marry a female Peter Pan. Today, after producing six children, she looks just as young as my teenage daughters. Weary of the question which has dogged our lives: 'What is a girl as young as you doing with this old gentleman?' I introduce her to strangers as my daughter, and this saves them bewilderment.

Shortly after my marriage I took a job on the Middlesbrough reporting staff of the *Northern Echo,* where I toiled from 10 a.m. until midnight six days a week.

The *Northern Echo* was a gentleman's paper. When an *Echo* reporter of those times raced to a telephone kiosk to phone over a 'scoop', he did not shout: 'Give me the desk!'

Instead he would politely ask permission to speak to the assistant news editor, and say, 'Sir, I have a story to offer, would you be kind enough to tell me when I may dictate it?'

It was for the dignified *Northern Echo* I obtained my first murder 'scoop', a 'scoop' any national paper – I now know – would have paid £500 for.

An attractive Middlesbrough girl had been murdered in far-away London, and the story was so crammed full of sex, romance, and mystery, that all the national papers sent their star reporters to Middlesbrough to get stories and pictures from her parents.

I was overawed when these great men from Fleet Street appeared in my Middlesbrough 'local' and began to wave large whiskies in front of my humble glass of mild ale. But I was determined that I would beat them all. They had high-powered, chauffeur-driven cars, I had only a bicycle. It was pouring with rain.

This was the first story I ever 'tied-up' – a phrase which means not only getting the story, but also making it impossible for any other reporter to get it.

About nine o'clock that night, after a hard and slogging day, I was given the full, exclusive story, and also every picture in the house of the glamorous creature whose life had ended so tragically. Flushed with success I drove off into the rain, propped my bicycle outside a telephone kiosk and phoned my night-news desk.

'Excuse me, sir,' I said, the rain pouring from the brim of my hat, 'But I have got an exclusive story on the murder. I wonder if can dictate at once, because, sir, if you will forgive the phrase, it is rather hot stuff.'

I felt extremely nervous about office reaction to my 'scoop', for I secretly held the view that in reality the *Northern Echo* chiefs regarded exclusive stories as 'rather vulgar' – stories to be avoided whenever possible.

Very humbly I outlined my story to the Chief Reporter.

'Good gracious,' he said, rather reproachfully. 'Do you know, I think I shall have to mention this story to the Chief Sub-Editor. You may dictate it now.'

Mention of the Chief-Sub-Editor frightened me, for, although I knew about the existence of such a god-like being, this was the first time anybody had actually spoken of him to me direct.

After dictating my story I spoke again to the Chief Reporter. 'Procter,' he told me, 'you are a fortunate young man. I am absolutely amazed, but the truth is that the Chief actually wants to speak to you personally. Now you just stay where you are, because you are going to be transferred to the Chief.'

Such an honour frightened me to death; I almost put down the phone and ran for it.

Over the telephone came the slow, solemn voice of the Chief Sub-Editor. To me it was like being in telephonic touch with Heaven.

'Young man,' he said, 'I have read your story with interest. But I am informed that this story is exclusive, and that you are the only reporter to get it? Is this true?'

The tone of his question sounded as though I had been caught out in some dirty deed.

'Yes sir, it is true.'

'Humph! And I am also told that in addition you have got, exclusively, all the available photographs of this unfortunate young lady?'

'Yes sir, I have.'

It was like giving evidence at the Old Bailey.

'Humph! Well, if that is so, tell me young man, how soon can we expect the pictures to be in this office?'

I was even warming to him a little by now. And with almost a suggestion of gaiety in my voice I told him, 'Oh, but sir, I have fixed that. You will have them in thirty minutes. I am going to leave my bicycle at a garage and get a taxi straight to Darlington with the pictures. In fact sir, it is all arranged and I...'

A sound like a pistol shot came from the receiver.

'A what? A taxi? Young man, have you suddenly lost your senses? You have the impudence to address me and inform me that, although there is a perfectly good train service between Middlesbrough and Darlington, you...'

I remember thinking that any national paper would have hired a helicopter to hover above me and collect the photographs. I remember feeling the rain running down the back of my neck. I remember thinking of my bicycle. But I do not remember thinking of my wife and baby.

Into the telephone I spoke three short words. They were words certainly not suitable for a young reporter on the *Northern Echo* to utter to the Chief Sub-Editor.

I ought to have been fired with ignominy. But they splashed my story on page one, with the exclusive pictures. I was never forgiven, of course, but I was not dismissed.

I had learned a lesson that night which I should have remembered all my life. A lesson I should have taken with me to Fleet Street. 'Scoops', exclusive stories, pay no dividends at all to the reporter who gets them. In Fleet Street, particularly, the worst thing a reporter can do for himself is get a 'scoop'. I have had hundreds of 'scoops' in my time, murder 'scoops', political 'scoops', war 'scoops'. And to any young reporter who may read this I say 'If you ever get a 'scoop' throw it away.'

A reporter who gets an exclusive is hated by most other reporters on the job. He is also hated – and this is more important – by most news editors other than his own. And news editors have long memories.

The best loved, most popular reporters in Fleet Street are the ones who never get exclusive stories, who never offend the opposition, who never write a single line that could be envied by any other member of their profession. I know Fleet Street probably as well as any reporter alive today, and I know this to be true. It is the quiet, mediocre, never-set-the-Thames-on-fire reporter who is really popular in what Sir Philip Gibbs has called *The Street of Adventure'*. Ask my good friend and colleague Duncan Webb, who has had more 'scoops' in Fleet Street than any man but I. He will agree with me.

An exclusive story may delight your own news editor just for a night. But a week later try and get a job from the opposition news editor who had his knuckles rapped because of your exclusive. This is a lesson which ace-reporters in Fleet Street never learn.

But the *Echo* 'scoop' which almost got me fired was not my only one. Searching for apartments for my wife and myself, I was sent to the house of an unemployed Middlesbrough gardener – a man with a large family and an empty pocket. He was a quiet, simple man, and he was glad to rent me two furnished rooms.

One morning he stopped me in the hall of his house, flicked the braces which ran over his thick, flannel shirt to his shabby trousers, and nervously inquired:

'Are you a newspaper reporter, sir?'

'I am,' I told him.

'Now that's interesting' he said. 'It is quite a coincidence having a newspaper reporter living in my house, for I have a sort of story for the papers. You know how poor I am, and you know we've three kids and it's only a week off Christmas. Well, it looked as though we were going to have a very thin Christmas indeed.'

I was a little irritated, for I was in a hurry to get to the morning session of the Middlesbrough Police Court. But the unemployed gardener was so meek and humble that I had not the heart to brush him off.

'I have just had a telegram from Littlewoods,' he said. 'I have won £30,000 in the football pools.' And he showed me a telegram from Liverpool.

'Congratulations,' I said. And I wrote down his full name, the names and ages of his children, and thanked him for this item of news.

It was not a big news item to the *Northern Echo*. But I wrote a paragraph and threw it, with other news paragraphs, into the copy tray.

A small paragraph appeared the following morning headed 'Windfall for Unemployed Middlesbrough Gardener'. This paragraph was spotted by the local evening newspaper; they sent a photographer to the house, and that afternoon I saw a picture of my landlord, his wife, and their children, in the late editions.

I was interested, but only casually, for these things mean little to the busy reporter.

The following day a message was brought to my desk saying that the unemployed gardener was waiting to see me down in the hall.

I got the shock of my life when I saw him. Not a vestige of the shabby, nervous, unemployed gardener remained. He was wearing a dinner-suit, with white shirt and bow tie. He had an expensive, tall, silk hat on his head. He carried a smart cane walking-stick.

But most impressive of all, he was wearing a silk-lined cloak. And outside my office waited a luxurious motor-car with a uniformed chauffeur at the wheel.

'I must buy you a drink,' said my landlord.

Mesmerised by the splendour and the sudden change I let him lead me into a nearby hostelry where, beaming with benevolence, he called, 'I am Mr----, the man who's won £30,000 in the pools. Drinks all round...'

This man was news. Gone was the awkward shyness of the unemployed Middlesbrough gardener. Here, it appeared, was a man born to spend and spend and spend; to spend glamorously, dramatically, and recklessly.

I hurried back to report to my Middlesbrough chief. He felt it was not a suitable story for the *Northern Echo*, and I was hurried off to some routine assignment. But by evening my ex-humble landlord was the talk of the town.

Bedecked in all his splendour he was going from hotel to hotel, shouting about his good fortune, ready and willing to treat any man or woman who would accept his favours.

His pockets were stuffed with money. And no millionaire ever enjoyed money as did this father of three.

He had gone, it transpired, to a tailor, and offered double money for a suit, shirt, and cloak, to be made at once. He had hired a car and a chauffeur. He had ordered a new motor-car. He had ordered a new house to be built just outside Middlesbrough on the condition they began work on it at once. He ordered new furniture, radios, jewellery, and in his great car he went careering around the coast; Redcar, Saltburn, Marske. Feted everywhere as a great sport, a jolly good sort, and a very nice bloke indeed.

All the world loves a spender. And within days this man had a host of friends.

Back at my rooms my wife had a strange tale to tell me. The wife of Middlesbrough's most popular man was having a thin time of it. She complained that since the newspaper story she had barely seen her husband, nor had any of the small children.

'I wish he'd never won the money,' she sobbed to my wife.

Late that night he arrived home with a load of champagne, whisky, gin and beer, placed them in his drab, bare kitchen, and decided on a private party.

His wife began to cry. His children began to cry.

Their tears, it appeared, astounded him.

'Haven't you seen my picture in all the papers?' he challenged.

'Aren't you proud of me? I am a famous man, and a very rich man, too. This will be the best Christmas of our lives.'

'Not if you are not at home with me and the kids,' protested the poor wife. 'I wish with all my heart you had never won the money.'

'What?' This, it seemed, was too much for him to bear.

His good spirits turned to anger and bitterness. Tears, alcoholic tears, began to flow down his flushed face, and pulling out a bunch of pound notes he flung them on the kitchen fire.

'All right,' he shouted. 'If you don't want the money I'll burn it.'

I had the torturous experience of watching good, crisp pound notes blazing away in a kitchen grate.

Several of his friends rushed forward in horror. With difficulty he was prevented from burning a second bundle. The next morning one national paper carried the story of my landlord burning pound notes.

I phoned the story to my office, but my paper was not interested. But as fantastic day followed fantastic day, even the dignified *Northern Echo* decided they could not ignore my landlord, and I was asked to write an 'inside' story.

But I got an inside story I could not print. It was a story which made me most uneasy.

Another tenant of this house where I lived, a travelling salesman, came to me quietly to ask my advice.

'You know the day the story and pictures first appeared?' he said. 'That night he came to me and asked me what a cheque for £30,000 would look like. You know what a simple sort of chap he was in those days? Well, to amuse him, and at his request, I wrote out a cheque for £30,000 on one of my own small cheques from my cheque book and I haven't had it back – he says he's lost it.'

I was sitting by the fire of my rented room when I heard this news, but suddenly I began to feel very cold. I went and confided this story to my Chief. He took me along to the Chief Constable of Middlesbrough, the late Mr Donald Heald, who promised to make a few inquiries.

The gardener announced that he was to be presented with his cheque on the stage of a local theatre, by a Mr Smith who was travelling especially from Liverpool for this purpose. The gardener, with friends, attended the theatre. The presentation was to take place on the stage. I was sent along to cover the story.

Mr Smith did not arrive. The gardener left his seat to visit the cloakroom, and returning he made what I considered a shattering statement.

'I have met Mr Smith in the cloakroom, and he has quietly presented me with the cheque. I am too shy to go on the stage. Here is the cheque, look at it.'

It was a small cheque from a private cheque book, written out in ink. I hurried off to the Chief Constable of Middlesbrough.

The amazing thing was that, despite all the publicity in the local and national press, no reporter had bothered to make a simple routine check with Littlewoods, asking if the gardener really had won a prize. The police made the check. Littlewoods had never heard of him.

That night the gardener hurried home, borrowed my best brown suitcase, and then vanished.

The following day I began to make the thorough investigation which I ought to have made days earlier, and by evening I had pieced together the amazing story of how my humble landlord had hoaxed the town.

When the photograph of himself and his wife and children appeared in the evening newspaper he had taken a copy along to a firm of moneylenders.

Had he tried to be clever he would never have got away with it. But, shy and nervous, in his dirty, shabby clothes, and with a white muffler about his neck, he had approached the moneylenders.

Smiling apologetically he had produced the newspaper cutting. 'Look, that's me and the wife and kids,' he had said. 'I'm the chap who's won £30,000. But, as it's almost Christmas, would it be possible for me to borrow a few pounds until I get my cheque – just enough to treat the wife and kids?'

Would it be possible? Get him a chair; get him a cup of tea at once. Possible? Dear Sir, we shall be delighted to lend you as much money as you wish.

The beaming moneylenders piled pound notes upon this shabby, unemployed, father of three. They would have advanced him £10,000 there and then in cash, had he asked them to. They stuffed the money into the pockets of his shabby coat, poured him more tea, and asked him to sign a form to repay them at generous interest.

Then they shook his hand and told him to call again at any old time if he wanted more pound notes.

The shabby gardener went along to another firm of moneylenders. He repeated his story; he produced the grubby newspaper cuttings. A similar reception was given him.

So that, when he appeared in his silk-lined cloak and his tall, top-hat, the unemployed father of three had possibly more money in his pockets than any man in Middlesbrough.

The police hunted far and wide, and eventually my landlord was found and arrested. Where was the money? He shrugged, he was the simple gardener again. Well, he must have spent it all. He certainly hadn't any of it left.

I next met him when he was in the dock at the Middlesbrough Police Court, and he gave me the old, humble smile. He pleaded guilty to all charges made against him.

In a written statement to the police he said he had been sending in football coupons for years.

When he told the reporter (me, he meant) that he had won £30,000, he really believed he had, he said. He had checked the copy of his coupon and found it a winner.

He had borrowed the money in good faith, he said, believing that fortune was to make him rich.

'Imagine my horror,' he told the police, 'when, a few days after all the publicity, I looked in the pocket of my old gardening suit, and found that letter inside. I had made out a winning coupon. But I'd forgotten to post it.'

He was sentenced to six months, and I recall that the Stipendiary Magistrate made some rather biting comments about moneylenders and the interest they charged unemployed gardeners who said they had won on the pools. He never returned my suitcase.

Chapter Two

As I have said, a reporter's life on the *Northern Echo* was very hard work. But it was very honest work, and very excellent journalistic training. The *Echo* was a newspaper where a journalist, if he so desired, could settle down for life, and raise a family in happy security.

But I had, unfortunately, read *The Street of Adventure,* and I regarded the *Northern Echo* merely as a journalistic milestone.

It is about 200 miles from the tiny office of my first weekly newspaper to the huge newspaper offices of Fleet Street; and to walk it would be tough going. But it would be easier to crawl from Leeds to Fleet Street than to do it the way I did. I made it much quicker than most reporters make it – than most of the comparatively few provincial journalists who ever do make it. To quote Tommy Riley, my first boss, again: 'There are two ways of getting on in journalism. One is by good luck; the other is by hard work. The second way is the surest.'

I just worked, and worked, and worked. In my youth I had no hobbies, I did not dance, I played no games. For me there were no working hours and non-working hours. I was never off duty. I lived for newspapers and newspapers alone, and although I adored my wife, it is amazing to me now that she could ever have borne the married life I made her lead. She saw me in the early morning for a brief twenty minutes as I ate my breakfast.

She could never include me in her private, social plans – she could never say: 'Next Tuesday we will go to the Joneses.' Even on my weekly day off she could never be sure of me; one exciting line in the stop-press of the evening paper and I would be off and away. It was all work and no play – if we met again before midnight, we considered it an amazing coincidence.

Even when our twin daughters were born I could not forget 'the news'. I was hard at it in the *Echo* office, pounding away at my typewriter, oblivious to the fact that my wife was in the

Middlesbrough Maternity Hospital expecting what I thought was 'a' baby.

Colleague Arthur Day answered the telephone.

I was blazing away at my typewriter, and a part of my mind which was not really me recorded his incredulous question as he spoke into the telephone.

'What? Twins? Twin daughters?'

Then he offered me the telephone. I glanced up, impatiently.

'Who is it?'

'It's the maternity hospital. They say your wife has just given birth to twins.'

I took the phone and rang off impatiently. 'Some clot of a practical joker,' I said, and went on typing.

Arthur Day phoned back the Maternity Hospital. It was true.

I finished off my story and placed it in the copy tray.

Then I phoned the hospital and talked with the matron.

'All the mothers in the hospital are having twins this week,' she said. And I became really interested.

My paper, the next morning, carried my story – 'Boom in Twins at Middlesbrough.'

Somebody gave me a poem, which I carried in my wallet for years. It was:

Who is the weary journalist? This is he.
Who's lucky if he gets to bed by three,
Condemned by all, to the uttermost perdition
Because he's missed the Hebrides edition.
Who is the weary journalist? This is he.
Who on the merest pittance has to dree?
His thirst is weird, because the Banks of Dee,
Have bred cashiers, devoid of kindly senses,
Who want receipts attached to his expenses.
Who is the weary journalist? This is he.
Who plans a column splash, and writes that 'we,
Are able to reveal...'
Then wakes to see,
Plus all his pains, ad infinitum,
Some hell-bent sub. has cut it to an item.

Who is the weary journalist? This is he.
Who starts to plan a comprehensive spree,
By taking some Delilah out to tea,
Then hears her mother warn her amorous daughter,
'Be careful dear, he's only a reporter
...who lives in sin, and dies in Leyton
But gets a human story out of Satan.'

In Middlesbrough I used to wonder about the man who wrote that poem, for the printed cutting had his name on it – Montague Smith.

Years later, on the *Daily Mail* Montague Smith became a close colleague, a dear friend, and the godfather of one of my children.

It was in Middlesbrough that I met the amazing W P Hurst, now chief administrator of the PDSA. He was then a humble superintendent of a small PDSA clinic, but it was easy to recognise in him the seeds of great ability. Now, when I watch his weekly animal programme on television, I remember those far-off Middlesbrough days when both of us were unknown, but where both of us had faith in ourselves and each other.

Bill Hurst, strangely enough, taught me much about journalism, and I, strangely enough, taught him something about animal welfare.

I was sent to see him by my chief, and instructed: 'Write a small paragraph about this poor chap's animal clinic and try and get it in the paper, Councillor So-and-So wants to help him.'

I fell for Bill's charm at once. Instead of a paragraph I wrote a whole page feature, and sent it off to Darlington.

Learning of this my Middlesbrough Chief was furious.

'What a crazy thing to do,' he said. 'I tell you to write a paragraph and you write a book. The only way to save you from being fired is for me to phone up the Chief and apologise.'

He phoned up the Chief and he was told that they had received my voluminous report on the animal clinic. They were using every line of it as the main feature article, with a photograph of Bill Hurst operating on a monkey. They had a special bill out the following morning.

Bill Hurst was jubilant. He had been sent from London to open up north east Yorkshire and, although he had worked like a slave, his activities had caused virtually no interest. Now 'the power of the Press' had come to his rescue.

Together we worked out several schemes for publicising the PDSA. I taught him that to go to a newspaper and ask for a publication about his work was the worst thing he could do; instead he must get the newspapers to come a-chasing him.

Somehow or other we managed to get someone to bring an alligator with a pain in its tummy along to the clinic, and somehow or other the newspapers heard about it and sent reporters and photographers along. Bill gave the alligator a very special and a very large, pill – I always swore it was a tablet of soap but he has always denied this. It made the headlines. More and more publicity followed, and the PDSA flourished. The unknown Middlesbrough superintendent now budded forth as an organising genius, promotion followed quickly, and it was not long before he was at PDSA headquarters in London.

Bill Hurst did not forget my help, and in return he took an active interest in my career. An intellectual, a well-read man, he taught me many things, introduced me to literary feasts from his own well stocked library, polished my Yorkshire rawness, convinced me of the value of a good tailor.

But, best of all, when hard times came in Middlesbrough, when the future looked black and hopeless and Fleet Street seemed impossible, he helped me to keep my faith in myself.

And soon I was to appreciate his help.

The HP instalments on my furniture were always paid weekly, but often, due to my laziness or to my work, they were a day, or two days, late. I had paid the instalments for more than a year, and the furniture was soon to become my own.

I left home one morning leaving a happy wife, busy with her children in a well-furnished, well-run house.

When I returned she was sitting on the floor, weeping.

The house was empty.

The salaries of local reporters in the provinces in those days did not run to private telephones. So that, when two broad, unshaven men arrived at the house with a van, forced their way inside, and began to move the furniture, she could not phone me.

Within thirty minutes they had cleared out my home. Their excuse, legal in those days, was that the weekly instalment due the day before had not been paid. And when she offered them the money they refused to take it.

I hurried at once to see my friend the Chief Constable of Middlesbrough, Mr Donald Heald.

'Possession,' he told me, 'is nine points of the law. They have the furniture now. You can fight a court action, but I think you will waste your money.'

I returned to my empty house, to my heart-broken wife.

We were glad we still possessed the perambulator, for our twin babies were sure of a bed. We decided to sleep on the bare floor.

And then one of those truly wonderful things happened, one of those wonderful experiences which have made it impossible for me to ever lose my faith in people – my love of people, and my conviction that most humans are essentially good.

A knock came at the door. A man and woman, two people we did not know and had never noticed before, had brought us a bed and a mattress. They asked no questions. The woman had seen the van arrive, had watched the men move out our furniture.

'I always believed that they had to leave you a mattress to sleep on,' said the woman, simply. 'But it seems I am wrong.'

They brought in the bed and mattress, and then, without waiting for our thanks, they went off to their home.

We did not even know their names.

The next day I managed to buy a second-hand table, an old chest of drawers. Within a few weeks we had sufficient furniture to make life tolerable.

That was not all.

The excellent job I had performed as a reporter, the hard work, the exclusive stories, were unimportant now, it seemed. A week before Christmas I saw the customary parcels arrive – presents from the firm to the staff. A box of cigarettes to all smokers, a box of chocolates to non-smokers. I picked up my parcel.

'Put it back,' said an executive, rather roughly. 'There's an economy drive on, we're cutting down, and there's a letter there giving you a week's notice. So you're not entitled to your Christmas present.'

Bill Hurst proved himself a true friend that week.

We closed up the house, disposed of the second-hand furniture, and Bill took us all into his home for Christmas, and thanks to him it was a very merry Christmas after all.

We stayed on for the New Year festivities, and we could have stayed longer, but we were unwilling to impose upon his friendship. He saw us off on a Leeds-bound train at Middlesbrough station.

'Do not worry, Harry,' he said, as he took my hand through the carriage window. 'I am certain you'll bob up again.'

I have been bobbing up again ever since.

Chapter Three

Jobless, penniless, but as confident as ever, I returned to my home town, Leeds, which natives fondly call 'Old String o' Beads.'

I installed my wife and babes with relatives, sorted out a selection of my best newspaper cuttings and placed them in a small case, then started on foot for Manchester – the London of the North. I hitch-hiked across the Pennine Range.

I knew no one in Manchester, I had never been there but my reasons for going there were obvious. In Leeds there were only two newspaper offices, in Manchester there were many.

I pawned every article of value except my best navy blue suit and two clean shirts. These were not retained as luxuries but as vital tools of the trade – I had to look prosperous.

I tramped from newspaper office to newspaper office. Dozens of news editors read my book of cuttings, several were favourably impressed. But times were hard, generally, in those pre-war years. Many journalists, solid, experienced men, were unemployed. At least a dozen eager, willing scribes rushed for every vacancy.

Reluctantly, but with no bitter feelings towards life, I sought out the huge Salvation Army hostel and asked for a bed.

I had about one shilling and ten pence in my pocket. I sat down at a rough table side by side with tramps, pick-pockets, hawkers, and human scarecrows. I felt tired out, and sad. But I was also ravenously hungry.

For five pence I was able to buy a kipper, a mug of tea, and a slice of bread. Seated among the men whom the world had forgotten I ate my supper. The Street of Adventure had never seemed farther away.

I did not mind eating with men who were shabby and poor, who were ill, lonely, and unimportant to the world outside. But I did object to the ones who were dirty. The unwashed ones, the smelly ones, the ones with filthy table habits. Against these I had a legitimate grouse.

I counted my coppers. I discovered that even the Salvation Army hostel had its social barriers; single, private cubicles were four pence more than the communal wards.

I was three pennies short of privacy.

On the wall of the communal lounge was a notice which read:

'If you are in need of spiritual help, ask for an interview with the Superintendent.'

Above it was a bigger notice announcing 'GOD IS LOVE.'

I searched my conscience. No, I was not in need of spiritual help.

But I was in need of three pence to pay for a private cubicle. Both needs were important, I told myself.

I was given an interview with the superintendent.

'How can I help you?' he beamed.

'By loaning me three pence,' I told him. 'I won't waste your time, I don't want to criticise your hostel, but I just can't face up to sleeping in a communal ward! And I'm three pence short of a private cubicle.'

This superintendent was a most discerning man. His eyes roved my appearance, my polished shoes, my well-pressed suit, my clean white shirt.

'Who are you?' he asked.

'I'm just a man looking for a job.'

'I will get you a job.'

'Not the sort of job I am looking for; as a matter of fact I am a newspaper reporter who's down on his luck. Let me owe you three pence for a private cubicle, that is all the help I want.'

This superintendent had a way of talking which I just could not get around. Gladly, he said, he would allow me to owe him three pence, but the debt, he argued, would also cost me a part of my manhood.

'Go and sleep in the communal ward,' he urged, 'surrounded by your brothers. You are a writer, think of the rich experience it will be for you. Some day you will write a brilliant article about the night you slept in our communal ward.'

Well, I never did, and I do not intend to now. The night I spent in that communal ward was sleepless, uncomfortable, depressing, and disgusting. I have far more cheerful things to write about. The only lesson it taught me was that I ought to have had more sense – I ought to have slept in the clean, healthy privacy of a field.

Why lodging in the open air should be an offence against the law is a mystery which has baffled me ever since that night.

Early the following morning the superintendent sent for me. 'I see you have not washed or shaved,' he said.

'I certainly have not,' I answered. 'If I washed in that communal toilet of yours, and used the filthy sackcloth towel hanging on the roller, I would never wash again.'

He took me to his private apartment, loaned me his bathroom and towels. I was his guest for breakfast.

'Ask no questions,' he said, later, 'but come with me.'

He hustled me into a small car, and went beetling off into the Manchester streets.

'Where are we going?'

'Never mind. You shall learn.'

To my horror I discovered we were driving slowly down Withy Grove, Manchester, which could be called the Fleet Street of the North.

The car stopped. 'I can't go in there,' I said. 'I was in there yesterday.'

'I insist that you follow me.'

My only concern at that moment was my fear of hurting his feelings – after all, his intentions were good and honest.

The superintendent was, I discovered, a personal friend of Mr Terence Horsley, then a highly paid executive of Kemsley Newspapers.

Terence Horsley, it appeared, had slept at the Salvation Army hostel some years before – not from necessity, but to get a story. Terence Horsley, apparently, had not noticed the dirty, sackcloth towel, the constant abuse of the wash basins, and he had written a praiseworthy piece. Hence the great friendship which had blossomed between him and the superintendent – a friendship which the Salvation Army chief now believed would gain me a post on Kemsley Newspapers. They talked first of all in private, then they talked in front of me. Then Terence Horsley (he was killed later in a gliding accident) said he would like to interview me privately.

The Salvation Army chief's eyes sparkled with expectancy, and bowing and beaming, he retreated backwards through the door. And I was alone with the great executive.

Terence Horsley eyed me in silence from across his great desk. He lolled back in his chair and clasped his fingers.

'Aren't you damned well ashamed of yourself?' he said. 'You, a journalist, a member of the fourth estate! And sleeping at the Salvation Army hostel.' He made a clicking noise.

'I am thoroughly ashamed of myself,' I said. 'So ashamed, Mr Horsley, that tonight I shall come to your house and ask you for a bed.'

His eyes flickered. Then the coldness left his face and he chuckled.

'OK,' he said, 'Let me see some of your cuttings.'

He liked my cuttings and he said so.

'You are just the type for the *Daily Express,*' he said. 'A bright writer with the new angles.'

'I went to the *Express* yesterday. I saw the Editor, Mr Percy Elland, but he told me he did not think I could master the *Express's* capitated style of writing…'

'What?' said Horsley. 'What the devil is a capitated style of writing?'

'It means a story that grows to a head,' I said. 'I didn't know either, but when I left I went to the public library and looked it up.'

Terence Horsley could not give me a job – there were no vacancies, he said. But he gave me some space work, and allowed me to be paid for paragraphs on acceptance. Which meant a clean bed and at least one meal a day.

Then, from across the Pennines, carried on the never silent tom-toms of newspaperdom, came important news. There was a vacancy on the *Yorkshire Evening News* at Leeds – a reporter had been fired. Already several unemployed Manchester reporters had struck their tents and gone to Leeds.

But to me the news was an answer to my prayers. I knew I would get the job – all I had been praying for was a genuine void on some reporting staff – a vacancy. For it was hopeless to try and join reporting staffs already overcrowded.

I jumped on a Leeds bus.

'Look, chum,' I said to the conductor. 'I want to go to Leeds and I haven't got the fare. But I've got to get there quickly because I want to get a job. Can I give you my name and address, and I'll pay when I can?'

'Sit tight, lad,' said the conductor. 'I've been on the dole myself.'

I arrived in Leeds. A quick reconnoitre of the position told me that about forty experienced reporters had already applied for the vacancy – these were the bad old days. Mr T A Stott, the News

Editor, was considering the applications and would make the final decision.

I decided that to apply for the job would be a sheer waste of time. The words of Tommy Riley echoed in my ears: 'A good story is a key which will open the door of any newspaper office…'

I jumped on a Hunslet tramcar. I had to get a story, a good news story, and I had to get it quick. It was no good waiting until I heard of a story.

The truth was, I knew that in every town and city good stories are lying undiscovered – going to waste. The *Yorkshire Evening News,* the *Yorkshire Evening Post,* the *Yorkshire Post* and the *Leeds Mercury,* were all employing trained news-finders to dig out these hidden nuggets and bring them into the office. I knew that all the normal news channels would be fully covered by staff men – for instance, it was no use going to the police station.

I remembered my early training on the *Armley and Wortley News* – how I made about a hundred calls a week collecting paragraphs. Hunslet had been one of my districts.

That old trail of 'local calls', I felt certain, if followed long enough, would yield me a story.

I called on a Hunslet vicar; a club secretary; an animal clinic; the Hunslet Engine works.

By evening, I had two, good, hard news stories. I went home, typed them out, then slept like a babe.

At nine the following morning I was at the entrance of the *Yorkshire Evening News,* asking to see Mr T A Stott, News Editor.

Instead they sent a reporter down to see me – Arthur Haddock.

I handed him my two stories. 'Like to offer you these,' I said. He read them. He took me upstairs, put me in the waiting-room, then returned with Mr Thomas A Stott in person – the News Editor.

'I like these stories,' said Tommy Stott. This was the first time I had ever met this great Leeds journalist. He wore a brown tweed suit, he was rather stocky, and his face had a mournful shape. You might have taken him for a monk, a country rector, but never a news editor. Later I came to know he was one of the best evening paper experts in the land.

'Yes, I do like them,' he added. 'I'll use one today and one tomorrow.'

'Tomorrow I will bring you two more,' I said.

'If you like I will bring you two good stories every day.'

Tommy Stott was interested. He asked me questions about my experience.

'Would you like a staff job?' he asked. 'We have a vacancy at the moment. Did you know?'

'No!' I lied, wanting to be entirely dependent on my plan.

He went off and had a chat with the editor. He came back and took me into the reporters' room.

'This is Harry Procter,' he introduced me, 'Our new reporter. He'll be starting at nine o'clock on Monday.'

My success on the *Yorkshire Evening News* was remarkable. I was one of the youngest of a first-class team of journalists – and yet, within months, I was the star.

But during the first week I was a bundle of nerves, and made a mess of every job I did because of a feeling that the job was too big for the experience I'd had.

On the Friday Tommy Stott called me over and said: 'You have done so badly that I really ought to fire you, you know. But the reason I am not going to do so is because I think you're a good reporter. Now, you think there is a difference between reporting Middlesbrough Police Court and reporting Leeds Assizes, but they are really just the same. The bigger the job, the easier it is. Any reporter can do big jobs; it's the little piddly ones which are difficult. Now, if I try you for another week, will you promise to take one piece of advice?'

I promised.

'Every time I send you out on an assignment I want you to say this little phrase to yourself over and over again: "I will crash through this, I will crash through this".'

Tommy Stott was a good, religious man. Another type of man might have used a ruder word than 'crash' when recommending the little pep-phrase. But I understood.

It worked like magic. I 'crashed' through every assignment I was given. I went racing about Leeds and Yorkshire, chasing the news, quickly adapting myself to the new lightning pace of evening paper work.

The provincial evening papers are much faster than the London ones. Their reporters are trained to work at a speed which would make the average London man sick with giddiness.

Often, Tommy Stott has rushed over to my desk and said: 'Procter, it's past 12 o'clock, but I must have this story by the 1-10 edition...'

And he meant it. The story might be a train disaster, a pit strike, a threat to put a penny on the local rates. If a *Yorkshire Evening News* reporter was given his assignment at 9am he was lucky – he had four hours to get, write and then dictate his story. The reporter whose assignment came at mid-day had to really make things blaze.

The high-speed training stood me in good stead, later, when I came to Fleet Street. Most opposition reporters had to sit down and write their stories after they had got them. Not I. A minute after my final inquiry I was always able to go straight to the telephone and dictate the complete article. And rarely did the Fleet Street sub-editor vary it much.

This ability of working at great speed I owe to Tommy Stott. From his teaching and training my mind became like a tape-recorder – it wrote the story mentally as the facts were being collected. This knack was of tremendous value later when, as a Fleet Street man, I was able to pull off national and international 'scoops'. It often assured me a first edition 'beat'.

The *Yorkshire Evening News* paid me well, and for the first time in my life I was comfortably off. I was able to rent an attractive house with a large garden, furnish it fully, and spend a little more time with my wife and babes.

My only problem in those days was the problem I have suffered from all my life. The problem of SUCCESS. It is just no use pretending that people like SUCCESS. They hate it. For instance:

On the *Yorkshire Evening News* I had a page-one story almost every day of my life. Sometimes I have seen that evening paper carry two lead stories – one on each side of page one – and both mine.

My success was so complete that my fellow reporters called a meeting and decided to make a protest to the News Editor. Arthur Haddock led the petition.

'We all wish to protest that you are favouring Harry Procter,' they told Tommy Stott.

'You are giving him the biggest breaks, the plum jobs, every day. We think you are being unfair.'

Tommy Stott was livid with rage. Not because of me, but because he had been accused of unfairness. As I have said, he was a God-fearing man, a journalist of the very highest integrity, and he put honesty and principle above all else.

'I will give you your answer to this accusation' he thundered. 'But on one condition. Procter must know nothing about it. Come to me in the morning.'

Arthur Haddock, who was one of the senior reporters and a first-class journalist, reported to Tommy Stott at 9.30 the following morning. This was the time at which the News Editor usually 'marked the diary', put the initials of reporters against the news assignments for the day.

'There is the diary,' said Tommy Stott to Haddock, 'now look at it and tell me which is the plum job for the day, which is the best assignment'

Arthur Haddock pointed to an entry. 'Right,' said Tommy Stott, and he placed Haddock's initials against the plum.

'Now,' Stott continued, 'which is the most miserable assignment on the diary for today. Which is the "crap"?'

Haddock pointed to another entry.

'Right,' said Tommy Stott, and against this entry he wrote the initials HP. 'Now, away you go.'

Looking at the diary, and knowing nothing of this scheme, I was rather crestfallen to see that my job for the day was to get a report about the felling of a large chimney at Kirkstall forge.

In newspaper offices news is weighed and valued like sausages.

'Three lines in the gossip if you're lucky,' said a fellow reporter when I told him my assignment. But I liked page one. I made many inquiries, and I found that the chief reason the huge chimney was to be felled was because experts had decided it would be a dangerous landmark in the event of war; it might help enemy bombers to slaughter thousands of citizens. To Leeds this was important news.

I wrote my story. Arthur Haddock wrote his story.

The 1-10 edition came upstairs. I was glad to see my story about the chimney splashed on page one.

Haddock's story, the plum, was a paragraph on an inside page.

Tommy Stott took the paper to reporter Haddock. He pointed to the two published articles. 'There is my answer to your accusation that the News Editor of this paper is not impartial. Arthur,' he added, 'you are one of my best and most valued reporters, but if you ever accuse me of unfairness again I shall fire you.'

Arthur never did. He came over to me in the afternoon and congratulated me on the story.

'Page-one-Procter' he grinned, and we were good friends ever after. In fact it was Arthur himself who first revealed to me the story of the protest.

Sometimes I worked too fast, even for the *Yorkshire Evening News.*

I remember speeding off in a newspaper van to a dangerous bend on which a young motor-cyclist lay dead.

The police took the driving licence from the dead man's pocket, and gave me the name and address inside. I phoned over a small story which caught the first edition. It was published. Half-an-hour later the Press Association sent a story over the 'tapes'. But their story had a different name for the victim, and a different address.

Tommy Stott prepared to fire me, for on the *Yorkshire Evening News* inaccuracies were never tolerated.

I rushed round to my 'dead' man's house, and the 'dead' man himself opened the door.

'You must tell me the truth,' I implored, 'and tell me it quickly, otherwise I'm going to be fired. I have reported that you are dead – killed in a motor accident at 7 this morning. Now why was the victim carrying your driving licence?'

Reluctantly he told me the truth. His friend had been married only two days before. He had loaned his friend his motor-bike, and also his driving licence in case he was pulled up by the police. His friend did not have a driving licence. Yes, he knew what he had done was wrong, but he had merely wanted to help a young bridegroom. Now that young bridegroom was dead.

I raced to the telephone. I phoned over this tragic, but moving, story of how the wrong man's name had been published earlier, how the police themselves had reported the dead man's wrong name to their headquarters. It was a 'scoop'. And it caught the 1-10 edition.

Of course my second story was a complete vindication of the alleged inaccuracy of my first. And to have a front page 'scoop' was nicer than the sack.

But another thing happened that day, a far more important event in my journalistic career.

I was sent by relatives to break the news to the young bride – to tell her that her bridegroom was dead.

When I met her, a young, happy, radiant girl, I funked my task.

I decided that the job of breaking such news should be done by an expert. I took her along to the police station. A gruff, busy sergeant was behind the desk.

I explained my reason for bringing her along.

The police sergeant gazed at the radiant bride who did not know she was a widow.

'Are you Mrs....?'

'Yes, I am.'

'Is this your husband's wallet?'

'Yes, it is'

'Well, he's dead. He was killed in a road accident this morning...'
She fell backwards and fainted into my arms.

Now it is not my business to criticise that police sergeant. Many would say that this method of breaking the news was the best one. But since that day I have always felt it my duty to try and ease the burden of people suffering from grief or tragedy – people I have met through my work.

Since then I have often had to be the bearer of bad news, but never again did I shirk my duty.

After all, I am a specialist – a specialist in people. I like to feel that I have always shown kindness and love to those in trouble – honest, decent people I mean, not crooks and murderers. I have lived with tragedy continuously for twenty years, but I am certain there is not a man, woman or child in Europe, who ever objected to the way I handled them in their grief. They may have objected to my published story, but never to my interview. The *Sunday Pictorial* paid me the highest money I ever earned mainly because I am a specialist in handling people. In every town and city of the British Isles I have friends – people who remember me kindly. I won their friendship by simple friendliness, not by cash.

Of course, it has not all been tragedy, thank goodness. There has always been a lighter side, a brighter side.

The *Yorkshire Evening News* story I best remember was the one I wrote headed 'The Comedy of Alf the Innocent'.

Alf was a Leeds grocer, honest and upright, a man who wore his best blue suit, his brown shoes, and his grey cap, on special occasions only. Alf was not a talkative fellow, but he was respected by all who knew him.

The greatest day of Alf's life came during my Leeds reporting days. He was called to serve on the jury at the Leeds Assizes; a great honour; a great event; a day to be remembered.

And obviously a day on which Alf must not only look his very best, but be his very best. A day on which his conduct and his manners must be impeccable. A day about which he could talk for the rest of his life, therefore nothing should be allowed to mar, or blur it.

My first meeting with Alf is a moment I shall cherish for ever, perhaps it is one of the richest moments of my life. I was sitting in the Press box and Alf suddenly appeared in the grim, iron-railed dock, pale and obviously puzzled. But he gave the Judge a noble look as they ordered him to face 'His Worship'.

Before the Judge stood the be-wigged clerk of the court.

'Alf Blank,' he thundered, 'you are hereby charged with burglary by night, breaking and entering, and carrying burglar's tools. What say you to the charges?'

It was perhaps the only moment of his life when Alf lost his normal composure.

'Me?' said Alf. 'Me, do things like that? Now see 'ere, there must be some mistake. 'Cos I'm on t'jury.'

I persuaded Alf to tell me his tale.

'It was just that I didn't want to make a fool of myself,' he explained to me. 'Yer see, I've never been called for t'Jury before, I didn't want to show myself up.'

Alf's sincere anxiety about not letting down the side had, it appeared, caused the trouble.

He was sitting outside in the hall of the court when a policeman called out; 'Alf Blank.' Alf jumped to his feet, smartly, and the policeman beckoned. 'Come with me,' said the policeman.

Down to the cells below the court they led Alf, who gazed around him in wonder. This was a treat he had never expected, he had never known they took jurymen to see the cells.

'Empty your pockets, and off with your clothes,' said a policeman.

'Really,' said Alf, 'do yer mean it?'

'Now then, get on with it, and less chatter.'

'Really' said Alf, as he parted with the gold watch and chain which hung from his waistcoat. 'Really,' said Alf, as he took off his clothes and allowed them a down-to-the-last-stitch search. 'Really, I never knew yer did all this to a chap. I shall certainly have summat to tell my mates tonight.'

I told his mates for him, through the medium of my newspaper. I explained how, just by coincidence, another Alf Blank had been invited to the Assize court that day. Not to serve on the jury, but to serve a long sentence in prison after standing his trial, for this other Alf Blank was a wrong 'un.

'But it gives yer a laugh,' said Alf as the policemen apologised to him and brushed his blue suit with their hands. Last summer, when I had to serve as a juryman at the Maidstone Quarter Sessions, I remembered Alf.

There were some first-class journalists in Leeds in those days, reporters who had never read *The Street of Adventure,* who were, therefore, content to spend their lives serving the extremely high standard which is Yorkshire provincial journalism.

There was the man they called 'The Swaffer of the North', the only man I ever knew who could be in two places at once. His speciality was to cover events happening both in Leeds and Sheffield.

He was a first-class reporter, and a very good writer, but News Editor Tommy Stott solemnly warned him that the next time he arrived in the office later than 9.15am he would be fired.

The following morning he arrived at 10.10am.

'Now Tommy,' he said to the News Editor, before the News Editor, who had been boiling for thirty minutes, could say a word.

'Now Tommy, don't blame me. I woke up bright and early, I had loads of time to catch my bus, I even took a stroll round the garden after breakfast. But when walking for my bus, and just as I saw it coming, I happened to glance down and see my shoe-lace was undone. Now, Tommy, that was a fortunate thing you know, my spotting that loose shoe-lace. Had I not noticed it, and ran for my bus, I might have tripped and broke my bloomin' neck. And if I'd have had six months in hospital all because of...'

Tommy Stott walked away in silence, dejected and defeated.

'He just takes the wind out of my sails,' he said, sadly. Another morning the Great Reporter came in late again.

'This time,' said Tommy Stott, 'I refuse to even listen to your explanation. This time...'

'But Tommy,' cried The Great Reporter, 'What could I do? What could you do? There my wife goes off early shopping, leaves me in bed, and forgets to unlock the bedroom door. I tell you, Tommy, that any other man but me would have been a prisoner all day, locked up in his own bedroom and as surely a prisoner as though he were locked in Armley Gaol. But not me, Tommy, I thought of you, I thought of the paper. So I sat glued to the window-frame for more than an hour until the window cleaner…'

And the next time, he said: 'Now Tommy, I am not late this morning, technically speaking, I am not late at all. In fact I'm early. I arrived in Bond Street with twenty minutes to spare, jumped off the bus with time on my hands. And then, good gracious, I realised I'd forgotten to put my vest on. Now Tommy, icy cold weather like this, it was my duty to you and this paper to…'

That Great Reporter! He had been fired on the *Yorkshire Evening News,* he had been fired on the *Yorkshire Evening Post.* But he was such a great reporter that they were continually re-hiring him, both of them.

His writing was so colourful, so rich in poignancy, that no one in the *Yorkshire Evening News* office even wondered which reporter would be sent on the Saturday to cover the baking of the Denby Dale Pie. It was obviously an assignment for the Great Reporter.

Now in Denby Dale, Yorkshire, that year, they had built a huge brick oven in the open air, and they were to bake a giant pie. The pie was to be sold in portions to the crowds, and all the profits were to go to the local hospital.

Here was, indeed, a tale to be told, a tale which would need the turning of many a phrase. Obviously the man for the job…

But News Editor Tommy Stott did not share the unanimous feeling about who should cover this gay assignment.

'I will frankly tell you I am worried about sending you to Denby Dale,' he told the Great Reporter. 'I know you will write a brilliant, descriptive story, if you go, but I also know that tomorrow is Pontefract races and all week I have been waiting for you to make some excuse for getting the day off.'

The Great Reporter had never looked more hurt in his life.

'Tommy,' he said, 'what a terrible insinuation to make. And you knowing that I've given up backing horses forever, and have no more interest in Pontefract races than you have in the chorus at the Leeds Varieties.'

He was sent off to cover the baking of the Denby Dale Pie. Now, on evening papers, for regular, organised, news events, the reporter is given a typed list with the times of his telephone calls, and also the specified number of words required on each call.

Young reporters gathered round the copy-taker as the Great Man's first 'take' came over.

It was a brilliant piece of reportage. He told of the great, hot oven, the huge pie. Of how he and the crowd sniffed the air delightedly, so fragrant, so delicious was the smell of this mammoth baking. He painted the scene with the brush of genius; he described the gay crowds, the happy children. His first 'take' was rushed into page one.

His second 'take' came dead on scheduled time. More exquisite colour, more detailed reporting of this happy day. Straight into page one it also went.

By the time the main edition went out on to the streets, it carried his superb description of how delicious was the actual taste of the pie, he told of how the people had waited in calm and ordered files to buy their portion, of how the pie was cut, and served, of how delicious was the gravy.

Yes, The Gravy. He was putting through an additional account of how well the gravy suited his personal palate, when someone rushed in with a copy of the opposition evening paper.

Their main lead story told of how the Denby Dale Pie had burst its oven banks, how the boiling gravy had flooded the watching crowds, how many had been taken to hospital, and how some were seriously injured.

Of course, there were some who accused the Great Reporter of being at Pontefract races when this terrible accident, this big news story, broke.

This, of course, was mere suspicion. It was never proved.

I am told that, some years before my time, a well-known woman novelist disappeared. After days of anxiety she was found wandering in Harrogate, and it was explained that she had been suffering from loss of memory. A London paper offered a large sum of money to any reporter who could gain for them, exclusively, a personal interview. The Great Reporter phoned over to London a graphic, personal interview with the woman.

'There'll be trouble,' said one of his friends, 'when she denies she ever saw you.'

The Great Reporter rubbed his chin.

'If she has forgotten her meeting with me which took place while she was suffering from loss of memory, her illness must be more serious than I feared,' he said.

He was just one of the fine characters I knew and loved in Leeds. In Fleet Street I have known and loved some pulsating and interesting men. But the provinces are not so dull as Fleet Street would have one believe.

It was great fun in Leeds, but I was getting to be an old man by the conceptions of age I then held – I was almost twenty-two. It was time I trod the pavements of the Street of Adventure.

I wrote to the *Daily Mirror* and asked them for a job on their London reporting staff. I phoned the *Mirror* several stories, which they used. And one day a telegram arrived from Mr Donald Mackenzie, their London News Editor.

The telegram announced that if I could get a week's leave of absence, he would give me a week's trial on his staff.

Fate took a hand. I got the leave of absence sooner than I expected.

The Editor of the *Yorkshire Evening News* was Guy Schofield, former Chief Sub of the London *Evening Standard,* later Editor of the *Daily Mail.*

He joined the *Yorkshire Evening News* when I was firmly established there, and within a few weeks he sent for me to say he was particularly pleased with my work. On the fourth night of the Leeds Tattoo, held at Roundhay Park, I was sent along to see if I could get some new angle on what, by that time in the week, was old and stale news. Each night previously a different reporter had been sent, but only straight-forward descriptions of the programme had been published.

These were the days when Hitler was big news, when the Dictator of Nazi Germany was casting a dark shadow over all the world. Daily we were reading of his great armies, his tanks, his guns, his huge military parades.

Searching for a new angle as I watched British troops give their brilliant display, I wondered how our soldiers really did compare with the Germans.

I went hunting through the crowds, feeling certain that among the many thousands there to see the show, there must be at least one German.

I found a German schoolboy. He was in England on a holiday on the schoolboy exchange system. He sat spell-bound, watching our soldiers. Then he clapped his hands on his knees and shouted 'Hurrah! Hurrah!'

I talked to him, and wrote a story called *The Tattoo Through the Eyes of a German Schoolboy*.

Guy Schofield told me he liked it very much, and he expressed the hope that I would write more features.

I enjoyed writing features, I had many signed features published in those days. But the features editor, with kind intent, would sign them 'John England'.

'Harry Procter is no good as a by-line,' he kept saying. 'It is too ordinary a name. You must change it.' I swore I never would, and I've had the name on a thousand front pages since.

I explained this to Guy Schofield, and he promised that if my features were as well written as the Tattoo article, he would sign them with my name.

From that day I began to take special care with my writing.

I remember writing one colourful story, sending it in with pride, then seeing the Chief Sub-Editor, Mr Shawcross, charge angrily into the reporters' room, waving my piece in his hand.

'I refuse to allow one of my subs to touch this copy,' he cried, and flung it into Tommy Stott's waste-paper basket. Tommy Stott quietly retrieved the story, said nothing to me, but walked along to the Editor's room.

'Excuse me sir,' he said to Schofield, 'but one of my reporters has written a story which Mr Shawcross says he will not allow his subs to touch. I wonder whether you would look at it, sir?'

Schofield read the story, then pulled out his blue-pencil. 'Well, Mr Stott,' he said. 'We won't worry Mr Shawcross. After all, I was a sub before I was an editor, so I'll sub it myself.'

Things, it seemed, were going well. But, let me repeat, beware of 'scoops'.

One day I went along to the Leeds University and obtained an astonishing story from the students – for although I had not been able to take Linton Andrews' advice and take a course there, I was always welcomed by the students who were my friends.

For many years the city of Leeds has held its annual 'Rag Day', when the university students run amok and raise money for the hospitals. For years a feature of 'Rag Day' had been the 'Rags Revue', a gay, saucy, stage-show put on by the students.

The 'Rags Revue', I was told, had been suddenly cancelled, because the girl students of the Leeds University had decided that it was wrong for girl students to kick and show their shapely legs in public – even for charity.

I made the 1-10 edition. My story went page-one, and the opposition, the *Yorkshire Evening Post,* were caught unawares and could not catch up. They phoned the *Daily Mirror* in London, gave them the outline, and they went to town on the tale.

About a week later my student friends came to me with another 'beat'. A number of girl students had decided they could not let down the hospitals. They were willing to kick their legs for charity. The show was saved.

I held the story over for the following day, so I could collect pictures of the girls who were willing to show a leg. I interviewed every girl but one.

I published all the pictures of the girls I saw, and they brought me one of the girls I did not see. They assured me that she had told them she was willing to join the show. I published her picture and her name.

But, I was wrong. She was not willing to kick her legs for charity, and she made a written objection.

I had made a mistake. Reporters cannot afford to make mistakes; most British newspapers insist that accuracy must be the golden rule. I ought to have checked, and double-checked. I admitted I was wrong.

Editor Schofield, quite rightly, took a serious view.

'I left London to create the finest evening newspaper in the world,' he told me. 'You are one of my most valued reporters, but I will not allow inaccuracies. I am going to suspend you for two weeks.'

And he did. The next day I kicked my heels around the house, angry only with myself. And then I remembered the telegram from the *Mirror* News Editor.

'Fleet Street,' I told myself, 'here I come!'

Chapter Four

I left King's Cross Station, walked into Bloomsbury, entered an Italian cafe in Coptic Street and ordered a cup of tea. 'Where can I rent a room?' I asked the proprietor, Primo Oddie.

'Here,' he said. 'For 25 shillings a week.'

That night I walked down the Street of Adventure for the first time in my life.

I woke early the following morning. I walked down Holborn, turned into Fetter Lane, entered the imposing office of the *Daily Mirror*.

I produced my telegram. I went up in the lift with a man about my own age, named Norman Hare. We eyed each other in silence.

We did not know it then, but there was one job going on the *Daily Mirror*. Norman Hare and myself were, that week, to be each given a trial on the *Mirror* reporting staff.

The plan was to let the best man win.

Into the waiting room came Bill Webber, an assistant news editor. He took Norman Hare into the corridor outside, gave him a piece of *Press Association* copy fresh from the wire machine, told him to go out and try and get a story.

Then he turned to me. 'Here is your assignment for today,' he said. He gave me a clipping from an evening paper which announced that a man had hanged himself on a lonely watercress farm.

'It isn't much of a break for my first day in Fleet Street,' I said. 'It's up to you,' said Bill Webber.

The investigation I made that day on the lonely watercress farm was so thorough that I do believe I could have reported how many watercress leaves were thriving there. But I could not find a story. It was a sad, dull event, of no interest to a newspaper reader – devoid of glamour, sex, or romance. I phoned over a story as green as the watercress. It was never used.

All day Tuesday I sat around the reporters' room, ignored by all.

In the evening I went for a beer in Peele's tavern, and there saw

55

Norman Hare, obviously as lonely as myself. We tried to cheer each other up. We had one thing in common, both of us had thick Yorkshire accents, for although he was born in the South, he had been reared by a Yorkshire mother just as broad of accent as myself.

On the Wednesday morning I got the clear hint that my trial was at an end – they had decided I was of no use to the *Mirror*. Just how and why I do not know, for I had done no work. But this busy, bustling office had no time to really ponder about whether a lad from Leeds, with corn in his hair, might or might not be of value.

A girl reporter smiled at me, kindly. 'So you're from Yorkshire, are you?' she asked. 'Do you find that the pavements tire your feet down here?'

'We have a few pavements in Yorkshire,' I said. 'It's not all ploughed up, you know.'

Bill Webber whispered to me: 'You'll be paid a week's wages, you know. And if you're short of train fare, we'll give you a ticket back.'

I said to him: 'I'm not going back.'

In walked George Greenwell, a *Mirror* photographer.

'Blasted jobs I get,' he moaned. 'Sheer waste of time this, sent off to photograph a fat couple. They won't even spare a reporter to go with me on this damned thing – that's what they think of it.'

I reached for my hat. 'I'll go with you,' I said, 'I am a reporter in a sort of way.' He was glad of my company, at least, and allowed me to travel with him in his car.

'Hopeless, this job,' George explained. 'They're peep-show folk you know, just like the bearded ladies. They won't touch it – why waste my time.'

'They will touch it,' I said quietly. 'Not only will they touch it, they'll splash it. Because I've decided it's time I stopped sucking my thumb and got round to a spot of work. I don't care if they are circus people, pygmies from darkest Africa, or people from another planet, I'm going to write a story about them and the *Mirror* is going to use it. A few pictures from you might help.'

We found our fat couple living in a caravan. I made a quick inquiry from them, then called George Greenwell over for a private conference.

'Now look,' I said. 'These people do hope to get into some small show as a fat couple, but I'm going to forget that, are you?'

I continued: 'I am not writing a story about two fat people in a peep-show. This couple have just arrived from Australia; they've only been married a few months. So far as I'm concerned they're here honeymooning in England. They are the World's Heaviest Pair of Newly-Weds. And they are News.'

George Greenwell immediately became enthusiastic. This gigantic pair of honeymooners weighed about eighty stone between the two of them. Theirs was a true-love story, I decided – so true that if they hadn't had the good fortune to meet each other they'd have remained single all their lives.

I set about fact-finding. My bridegroom was so immense that the only part of his wedding trousseau he was able to get ready-made were collar studs and boot-laces. On the ship that brought them over, there was no bridal bed big enough, or strong enough, to hold them, so they slept on the floor.

The heavyweight lovers could not find a honeymoon hotel in London – there wasn't even a floor strong enough to take their weight, let alone a bridal bed.

George Greenwell did a magnificent pictorial job. I went back with him to the office, commandeered a typewriter, and wrote my piece.

I led off: 'The World's Heaviest Pair of Newly-Weds are Honeymooning in England.'

I reported to the news room, where they were astonished to see me around. I went over to Donald Mackenzie, the News Editor.

He looked up at me. He had a thick, phoney American accent. 'Hello,' he said. 'Oh yes, you're the boy from the sticks. Well, it's been a change for you down here, I suppose.'

'Excuse me, sir,' I said, 'But would you do me the favour of reading my copy?' I put my story on his desk.

He looked irritated. 'Yes, son, later. Busy now, boy.'

I walked back into the reporter's room in disgust. It seemed that, at long last, my magic key had found a door it could not open. I lolled back in a chair and lit a cigarette. The Street of Adventure, I thought sardonically.

Ten minutes later Donald Mackenzie came puffing into the reporters' room. He held my story. 'Son,' he said. 'This stuff is marvellous. I'm holding it over until tomorrow and I'm going to give you the entire middle-page spread. Mrs Watson, my secretary, is typing you out a letter of appointment. Son, I think you're good.'

I walked over to Peele's tavern to drink a silent toast to myself. In walked Norman Hare. He looked sheepish and embarrassed. 'Poor devil,' I thought. 'And he's not a bad bloke at that. Still…'

I bought him a drink. We both talked awkwardly to each other. We were both embarrassed. Eventually I could stand it no longer.

'Look, cock,' I said, and handed him my letter of appointment.

'Terribly sorry and all that, but let's be pals and have a drink.'

Norman clutched my letter eagerly. His face lit up.

'Hell,' he said. 'Congratulations! I'll buy you a drink, then you can buy me one, for just look at this.'

And he tossed a white envelope on the counter. It was a letter of appointment, word for word, exactly the same as mine. Only the names were different.

I grabbed his hand and grinned. 'Hell, and I thought…'

'And so did I.'

He and I had a rare old party that night. We have been staunch friends ever since.

That Friday, when I opened my pay packet, I felt like a millionaire. Nine pounds, nine shillings, for one week's work. It was big money in those days.

I wrote a letter to Editor Guy Schofield, thanking him for all his encouragement, explaining to him that I did not wish to return to Leeds, and asking would he allow me to leave without notice. I told him, writing with a chuckle, that if he wished, I would return to Leeds at the end of my suspension period, and work for him for a month.

He wrote me a warm letter back.

'I am glad to hear you have decided to push the boat out in Fleet Street,' he wrote. 'I am sure you will do well.'

The same week I received a letter from my old News Editor, Thomas A Stott. I have treasured it all my life.

'This is a sad, yet pleasant task,' he wrote. 'The sadness lies in the fact that I have lost you – a lad I liked, and whose qualities were a never-ending source of admiration to me. The pleasure, of course, lies in the fact that you have got a full man's job in the very heart of journalism. Early in your stay here I noted your peculiar and all too rare qualities – the natural ability to write a colourful story, and your amazing tenacity.

'A man who goes out of the door after a story and leaves behind a confidence that he will get it, is a great asset to a Chief – and you were such a man to a remarkable degree. I have said to John M and to Haddock (the two senior reporters) too, many a time, "Old Procter is on the trail after so and so, and he'll get it – he never fails." That is a man after my own heart, and I take this opportunity of thanking you for the work you have done and the wonderful stories you have written… I shall never forget HP.'

His PS reads, 'I enclose a testimonial, I wish I could have made it even better.'

I have received many testimonials in my time, but I have never been prouder of a reference than the one my old Leeds Chief sent to me. Never once in my life have I ever shown it to a potential employer, never once have I used it for the purpose for which it was intended. But I knew it would, and still would, get me a job on any newspaper in the world.

It reads:

> *To Whom it May Concern*
> My experience of Mr Harry Procter extends over far too short a period – less than two years. Yet in that time he has given a satisfaction greater than is usual. In thirty-four years experience in journalism and twenty-two years as a Chief Reporter and News Editor, I have rarely been so pleased with the work of a reporter.
>
> I have certainly had no experience of a man who could write, and write at a speed, a more colourful story. When only a few facts have been available, he has transformed them into a bright and masterly article.
>
> He seemed equally at home on ordinary interviews, mystery stories, crime, fires, smash and grab, train smashes, romances with a big news interest, etc.
>
> I never knew him return and report failure. And that is a wonderful recommendation for any reporter. His tenacity – he never gave up a trail – is one of his greatest qualities.
>
> His departure from the *Yorkshire Evening News* to go on a national paper was a distinct loss to me. Yet I always knew his qualities would sooner or later cause him to make such a move.
> *(Signed)* Thos. A Stott,
> News Editor.

I walked down the Street of Adventure – the happiest and proudest young man in the world. To me, at that youthful and energetic age, Fleet Street represented the beginning of all things, the end of all things, the meaning of all things. In Middlesbrough I had boasted to my colleagues: 'By the time I am thirty I will be a Fleet Street Reporter.' And here I was eight years ahead of schedule.

When I look back now, with my wisdom, with my experience, with the cynicism which Fleet Street gave me, and – yes, let us confess it – with my disillusions, and think about that young Yorkshireman who walked down Fleet Street all those years ago, I would say that, in my professional opinion, he had the world at his feet.

He was a fairly good-looking lad. He was as fit as a young ox, he was a moderate drinker, an indifferent smoker. He was trained to the hilt, as a solid, all-round reporter; trained to write straight-forward, simple English, to report the truth – and only the truth – accurately, swiftly, certainly. He was capable of tackling any assignment, which, even in this world hub of journalism, could be offered to him. He was a good reporter.

What use did Fleet Street make of this young man's body, mind, soul, ability? And, equally, what use did he make of Fleet Street?

These are questions to be answered not by me. I am merely the reporter now, telling the tale fully and, I hope, fairly, presenting the reader with the facts. The reader must decide upon his own answers.

Fleet Street, I then expected, was to be the testing ground for all of my previous hard work and effort.

I remember standing enthralled before the Edgar Wallace Memorial, a simple plaque at the corner of Fleet Street and Ludgate Circus, reading with reverence that glorious epitaph: 'He Died a Good Reporter.' I remember offering a silent prayer in front of that memorial that I might be able to uphold the standards of journalism required by Fleet Street.

A few years later, when I was a full-blown member of that rollicking, swashbuckling haven of hard-drinking, the London Press Club, I dared not have talked to my fellow members about that night of dedication. I think they might have laughed.

But that night I glowed with a humble pride in Fleet Street, and in being one of its fellows. And I went off to my Bloomsbury bedroom early, to brush up my shorthand.

I need not have bothered. For, within a month, I discovered that at least one thing the *Daily Mirror* were not paying me for, was my ability to take a shorthand note.

Chapter Five

The great Fleet Street office I now found myself working in was the most efficient, clock-like, industrial hive I had ever seen. To use a phrase, then unheard of even to the *Mirror,* 'it went like a bomb'.

It was a machine of great power, a machine which knew exactly what it was doing every hour of the day and night. It could be a ruthless machine.

It had no time at all for failures, or even second-raters. It wanted the best – the very best. There is a story told in Fleet Street of how a reporter, after being fired, borrowed six children and took them into Lord Northcliffe, thereby regaining his job.

A man whom the *Mirror* did not want could take twenty children plus his aged grandparents, into the office, and he would not produce a single tear. Geraldine House, I found, was very efficient, but very tough!

Continually, I found, the *Mirror* was trying out young journalists from the provinces – there was a constant flow of new faces. Very few survived their trial – very few were good enough.

The *Mirror* wanted Sex. It was not hypocritical about its needs – it was perfectly honest to both its employees, its readers, and its advertisers. Sex, the *Mirror* discovered, sold papers – papers – papers by the million. Hard news was merely the third course. The strip 'Jane', the *Mirror* discovered, could sell far more papers than an article by Dr Albert Schweitzer.

Perhaps you do not approve but, if so, please don't blame the *Daily Mirror.* The *Mirror* group, like every other industrial group in the world, is out to make a profit on selling yards of paper with black ink on it. If the millions did not want to buy these yards of pulverised wood-pulp, the *Mirror* group would pack up shop at once.

Had I stayed on at my shoe-shop and sold shoes all my life, I would have sold the shoes the customers liked and wanted. Had I tried to sell shoes the public did not want – merely because I thought the shoes were better for their feet and their souls – I'd have starved. I do not want to be the judge, but here is one fact I will present to the jury.

Supposing the *Daily Mirror,* the *Sunday Pictorial, Reveille,* and the *Woman's Sunday Mirror* decided tomorrow to say to their critics: 'We think you are perfectly right. We are going to close down at once. Hugh Cudlipp is going to dedicate the rest of his life to mending fishing nets in Cornwall, our Editors and Managing Editors, and Assistant Editors, all wish to enter monasteries. We were wrong, forgive us, goodbye.'

What would happen then? I can just see the rush of those pious, *Times*-reading, church-going, non-smoking city financiers swarming down Ludgate Hill to buy up the stock. I can picture those sweet and gentle ladies, raised on shooting sticks, breast-fed on boiled toffee to avoid contact with the vulgar things of life, diving into their stockings in great haste to invest their savings in the new company – a company hurriedly formed to provide a commodity for the millions, which the *Mirror* group had withdrawn.

I remember the surprise I got on one of my earliest Fleet Street assignments. The News Editor tossed over to me a reader's letter, with a faded cutting attached to it.

A twenty-year-old girl had written to the *Mirror* enclosing a cutting from a twenty-year-old church magazine. She explained that on the day she was born in an obscure, Hertfordshire village, a baby boy was also born. Their names had both been sent to the local Vicar for insertion in the 'Birth' column of his parish magazine. By mistake the names had appeared under the 'Marriage' notices instead; the magazine inaccurately recorded that the boy and girl, only that week born, had been joined in Holy Wedlock.

Quite an amusing letter, I thought, well worth ten lines in 'Live Letters'. But to my astonishment, I was told to hire a taxi at once, hurry off to Hertfordshire, find both the girl and the boy, and phone over a nice hot story for the first edition'.

'And you can let it run,' they added, as I left. A Fleet Street phrase I now know to mean: 'You can go to town on it.'

I was very puzzled as I hurried off to Hertfordshire. Could this be news, I wondered, as I re-read the cutting on the train? I found the girl and interviewed her, recording in my notebook her light-hearted remarks about her early 'marriage'. Then I found the boy.

I interviewed them separately because they now lived several miles apart. They told me they had only met each other once or twice in their entire lives. Other than the joke in the church magazine – a joke their families had always shared – they had no interest in each other.

I wrote a good, bright story, giving the facts, blowing on them a little, perhaps – as one does with cinders to make them glow – but keeping to the facts.

'What the h--l is this?' the night news editor bellowed into the telephone. 'We expected a bright piece!'

This 'rocket' shook me. I stammered and stuttered nervously, saying I had done my best. Then, timidly, I listened to the words of the night news editor.

'When are they getting married?' he asked. 'We want to lead off by saying that the boy and girl who were married in the week they were born are now to be really married in church! The same village church, of course.'

'But they're not getting married, sir!' I ventured. 'They barely know each other, and they've each got a boy and girl friend of their own.'

'What the h--l do you think we sent YOU down there for?' came the reply. 'You b----y well talk them into it. Give them a fiver apiece if you like, but they damn well'll have to get married. And for Gawd's sake hurry, you've already missed the first edition.'

I was learning fast. The next morning we carried the story about the forthcoming 'marriage', a nice bright intro, thinning down to the joke about the parish magazine.

I finished the assignment about 1-30am. I roused the sleeping taxi-driver I had hired at the local station. He was an old man, partly deaf, and by now he was rather weary of running me about Hertfordshire, and waiting around.

'Take me to London,' I said. 'There are no more trains.'

'Too far,' said the tired old man.

There were several pounds on his clock; he was tired, but I was exhausted.

'No London, no money,' I told him bluntly.

In the middle of a pine-clad road his taxi broke down. He took a tube out of the engine, blew down it. The taxi went. This happened three times. The fourth time the halt was a longer one, and, anxious to stretch my legs, I walked up the road. I heard the firing of the taxi's sparking plugs, and looking back, I saw the old tub jaunting merrily off towards London.

I was alone in the wilds of Hertfordshire, at 2am.

Cursing at the whispering pine trees I walked down the road. Thirty minutes later a heavy lorry pulled up and gave me a lift.

Five miles further we were stopped by a police cordon, and a policeman flashed his torch into my face.

'That's him!' shouted my old friend the taxi-driver. 'That's him who bilked me. Said he was a Fleet Street reporter, he did.'

I was hauled off to the police station. A disgruntled explanation, a showing of my Press card, a telephone call to the *Daily Mirror.*

The police were bitterly disappointed I was not the criminal they had hoped to capture.

'Pay the man,' they said.

'I refuse to pay him a blasted half-penny until he gets me to Bloomsbury and carries me up to bed.'

The police shouted this into the half-deaf ears of the taxi-driver. He drove me home; and I gave him a generous tip, getting a receipt for my expenses.

I flopped down on my lonely bed. I was a Fleet Street reporter who had just carried out his first assignment as a marriage-maker, and I had darn well caught the second edition at that. But the following morning I was hauled before the desk for missing the first.

When I look back upon this first attempt at marriage-making, I have no remorse. For when I think of the lives I have turned upside down since then, in order to provide bright headlines for the breakfast table, I realise that this incident was mere child's play. The real thing was to come.

The *Daily Mirror* applied the same 'get the story' standard to their own staff if by chance they became news.

My wife takes a small size-two in shoes, and during the war years this size was almost impossible to buy. She used up her reserves, and then toured Oxford Street. Her plight became desperate, she was almost barefoot.

I decided to spend a day off searching for a pair of size two shoes. I went from shop to shop, but my wife, with the stubbornness typical of all small women, refused to wear anything less than a three-inch-high heel. The quest seemed hopeless.

Then in the window of a shop in Shaftesbury Avenue, I spotted a pair of tiny, black, court shoes, with high heels. I pulled the salesman outside, and pointed to them.

'What size are they?'

'Size two, sir.'

'I'll have them'

He removed them from the window, was beginning to wrap them, when the manager came over. 'You can't sell those,' he said. 'Size twos are very hard to come by these days.'

Turning to me he said: 'Sorry, sir, but I make a point of holding back the odd pair of size two shoes I get for an old customer who can't wear anything else but twos.'

'What do you think my wife can wear?' I protested. 'A pair of Alpine skis?'

He refused to budge; we had quite a row.

I hurried back to the *Daily Mirror* office, picked up my phone and, as a private person, complained to the Board of Trade. The official was sympathetic. He asked for my telephone number, and the name of the shoe-shop.

Twenty minutes later a most apologetic shoe-shop manager phoned me. He was terribly sorry, he said. He had received a call from the Board of Trade, 'and he now saw the problem in an entirely different light.'

'I will send the shoes to you at once,' he said, and he did. I phoned my wife with the wonderful news that she could WALK out with me again.

A colleague heard it all. He mentioned it to Ted Castle, Assistant Editor.

Ted said: 'Write it! I'll give it page one lead.'

I wrote: 'This is the modern version of the fairy story Goody Two Shoes. A suburban housewife plays the principal part, a tired husband is Prince Charming, and there's the Board of Trade in the role of fairy godmother...'

Hoping to avoid a scene with my wife I used her maiden name. Ted Castle spotted this in the proof and changed it to her real name.

'No newspaperman, or his family, have a right to expect special privileges when they themselves are news,' he said. He was right. I arrived home rather late, but, like the Greeks, I bore my gift in hope.

'I've a good mind to throw the shoes at you,' said my wife. 'Who sent the photographer? A photographer's been here from the *Mirror* wanting to take a picture of my legs – just my legs and feet! Would you really have your own wife's legs pictured in the *Daily Mirror?'*

The story ran page one. But no picture!

About this time a song was all the rage. *The Love Bug Will Bite You if You Don't Watch Out.* I was sent to interview a 'student of bugology', a young man who claimed to study bugs and insects. His story was that he had been carrying some bugs in a test-tube while travelling on the top deck of a bus. The bugs escaped, he said, and one severely bit the leg of an attractive young lady sitting next to him. She screamed, he apologised, they talked. They had fixed the wedding date, they both told me. The story went page one.

I told my news editor I had discovered that the 'student of bugology' was also a drummer in a night club, that the girl bitten by the love-bug was a hat-check attendant.

'Don't worry, son,' he said. 'Give them a fiver apiece and get them to sign. It's a d----d good story.'

But I was certainly tasting SUCCESS. The *Mirror* told me they were delighted with my work. They told me I had the right flair, the bright style they required, and that I never returned to the office and reported failure. I have often reported that stories did not exist, that facts supplied by contacts were untrue, that men accused of being scoundrels were honest in reality. Where the story existed I have always brought it back – no one in Fleet Street will challenge this.

For the first time in my life I had a bank account – I was actually saving money. My wife and children, in Leeds, were receiving a generous allowance. My private needs were few, I paid for my room, I had three good meals a day. My pleasure, my fun, came from my work.

The only problem I had then was a misunderstanding about my married status. In Leeds Press circles the story went that the *Mirror* would not employ married men – and so on my first day I had told them I was single. In the first few days I realised that what I had believed was untrue, but I was afraid to confess my mistake.

My wife, therefore, on her rare visits to London, had to be introduced as 'my girl friend from Leeds', which, naturally, infuriated her. I confided my problem to Norman Hare, and he urged that I should make a full confession to Dot Watson, the News Editor's secretary.

'Ma Watson' as we all called her – and as they still do call her – was, and still is, an angel-on-earth. She knew every private worry and personal problem of the entire reporting staff. She mothered us all, the women reporters just as much as the men, and she shielded us constantly. And yet I was afraid to unburden myself to her.

Early in 1940, when I volunteered for the Royal Air Force and was accepted, Mrs Watson asked me questions about my private life – had I a mother or father to support?

I blurted out the whole truth.

'You clot!' she said. 'What a stupid boy you are.'

Then she asked me for the names of my wife and my children. And all through my two years of service with the forces, the *Daily Mirror* made the same, generous allowance to my wife and children that they made to the wives and children of all their reporters; they were always willing to pay the best price per pound.

I saw the *Daily Mirror* put on battle-dress and organise for war. She did it with the same, perfect, clock-like precision, which hallmarked everything I ever saw her do.

Whether showering blessings, exposing injustices, firing executives, or selling sex to millions, the *Mirror* was – and still is – always exact and sure. That's why they make money in Geraldine House.

On the day war broke out, Donald Mackenzie, News Editor, and R T Suffern, Managing Editor, marshalled their forces.

I was ordered to my post outside the Houses of Parliament at 10am on that fateful Sunday.

There were great crowds there. It was a brilliant day, the sky stretched out above Big Ben with barely a cloud to be seen. The faces of the crowd were tense and anxious. The minute hand of Big Ben slowly approached 11am – zero hour.

Would it be war?

I phoned over a story about the thousand anxious eyes which watched Big Ben. Then I looked into the sky, an empty sky.

The sirens sounded. People panicked. Most of us expected that in seconds the empty sky would be filled with Hitler's *Luftwaffe*. Nobody screamed, nobody shouted, but people began to push and run. I was bowled over on to the grass verge in Parliament Square. I was frightened.

I hurried down the tube. An angry official down there told me,

'You shouldn't be here. We've locked the gates, because we don't know what will happen to tubes in an air-raid.'

I stayed on to wonder what would happen.

The 'All Clear' came. I returned to the office and sat down with my colleagues in the reporters' room.

That reporters' room has now vanished, so has the 'News room'.

Since then the *Mirror* has swept the walls away, and made one great operation room for editors, sub-editors, reporters – the lot.

But I fondly remember that room as it was that day. It was the last time I ever saw the *Mirror* pre-war reporting team together.

Within a few days we were all scattered about the country. I was sent to Dover to wait for Hitler there. Friend Norman Hare was despatched to the East Coast. Suffern and Mackenzie studied the map of Britain with care.

Had Hitler ever landed he would not have caught the *Mirror* napping. It is unlikely he could have surprised our troops – but it is certain he had no hope of missing the *Mirror's* first edition.

I kicked my heels in Dover. A few shells! One middle-page spread about a singer called Kay who was entertaining the boys in a Dover pub – 'OK For Troops' went the bannerline. But lots of boredom.

I was called back to London. That night I went into The Cottage Club in Litchfield Street, before the war called, unofficially, 'The *Mirror* Boys' Club' because we all went there. It was almost empty, there was not one face I knew on the front-side of the bar. I had a few beers. I had never felt more utterly miserable.

They packed me off to Birmingham to take charge of the *Mirror's* Midlands office. Now this was fun.

The *Mirror* wanted a bright Midlands edition. Ted Castle was now the London News Editor, and his eye was as keen and as enterprising concerning the provincial offices as it was concerning his London Staff. Ted wanted results, and nothing but results. He got them.

He wanted at least one bright story a day from me. Usually he got it. And the Midlands circulation soared.

In Birmingham I worked with one of the most lovable and fascinating characters I ever knew – old Dave MacLelland, one time star-photographer of the *Daily Mirror*.

He was by no means a young man when he came up from London to join me in the Birmingham plan – but he had more virility, more enthusiasm, than most younger photographers I had known. The taking of a straight picture bored him – he would refuse to do it whenever he could. He was an artist – and still is – and he loved being an artist.

He spent hours in the cold at Dudley Zoo taking dozens of pictures of a sea-lion, because he wanted to get exactly 'an expression I saw on its face this morning'. He got it.

He had been all round the world for the *Mirror* group as a young man – he had travelled on horse-back in far distant lands, his expenses in gold sovereigns stuffed into the old-time leather money-belt he wore.

He was a bald man, the only bald-headed man I ever knew who was proud of his baldness (I had never met Yul Brynner). On assignment, when our interviews were commencing, he would raise his hat and announce: 'I'm an old bald-head, don't mind me.' No one ever mentioned his baldness to him, because he always mentioned it first.

He once told me that, while covering a political meeting of national importance, he and the other photographers were snooping about on tip-toe taking pictures of the principal speaker.

'Out with the bald-heads,' thundered the politician, 'out with the bald-heads.'

Dave, in front of the audience, put his hat on. The laughter crippled the meeting, and, he says, almost changed the Government.

I had to be extremely careful in what I said to 'Old Dave'.

One night in Birmingham I met a man with the longest and most magnificent moustache in the world. Gently, sensing his pride, I asked permission to write about it, permission to let a photographer make a news portrait of it. The man was not keen, but I gently persuaded him to agree.

I gave Dave the man's address, and off he went, keen as a razor blade. He returned, dejected, to say he had been thrown out.

'You said he was sensitive, but I did not realise he was as sensitive as all that,' said Dave.

Before calling on the man Dave had gone to a pet shop and bought a budgerigar. From a hobbies store he had bought an eighteen-inch strip of balsa-wood – the man's moustache was eighteen-inches from tip to tip. He had asked the man if he could tie the balsa-wood to each end of the moustache and perch the budgerigar in the centre.

'Mind you,' said Dave, 'it would have needed a lot of waxing.'

I could never get up early enough to beat old Dave.

One day, short of news, I saw a paragraph in the evening paper saying that an old stage elephant had died. She was buried, without honour, in a farmer's field.

I phoned up the owner and asked him about the elephant's early life.

'She was a dancing girl,' I wrote in my story, 'born and bred among the glitter of the footlights...But she died of a broken heart. For Daisy was the elephant who couldn't forget...'

I phoned my story over without telling Dave. He hated me to do stories without possible pictures, and I could not see an unmarked elephant's grave making a *Mirror* picture.

Ted Castle cried with joy about the story of Daisy, and gave it middle-page spread. Poor Dave got the wash-back at 7 that night.

'We must get a picture of Daisy the Elephant Who Died of a Broken Heart Because She Could Not Forget,' thundered the unromantic art editor in London.

I gently told Dave that the owner had left town, I had no clue where he might begin his search for a picture.

Dave returned to the office door after thirty minutes absence. He wired to London a photograph of Daisy.

'You know,' he said, as he showed me the picture after London had accepted it with thanks, 'Daisy looks just like any other elephant, doesn't she?'

Dave never gave me one dull day. In charge of the picture-wire-machine was a certain George Grundy, who loved Dave with all his heart, but pretended not to.

'I can never get Dave to buy me a drink,' he used to complain, 'unless I've bought him one first.'

It was a game they played with each other, a game they played with poker faces, but which they really loved.

I have watched the two of them stand for an hour, elbows on the bar of the little tavern near the Birmingham office, determined to stay thirsty rather than have the 'shame' of buying the 'first one'.

Dave loved to boast about how mean he was – in truth he was a generous man. In Birmingham they had three measures for beer – a pint, a half, and a third measure they called 'a stick'.

'Now what will you have a stick of?' Dave used to say.

An old Fleet Street shibboleth declares that no reporter is fully fledged until he's been fired ten times. But I am the only reporter who ever fired himself. And that was the fault of Dave MacLelland.

Dave and I were having a thin week without news, when one evening we learned that an old man in a county hospital had a remarkable hobby – he designed model houses of matchboxes.

His results were so beautiful and original that people wanting homes used his models.

Old Dave was thrilled by the possibilities suggested, of a colourful picture story, he always said that old men and old dogs make the best pictures, provided you can introduce glamour into the scene with them.

'Just imagine it,' he exclaimed, his eyes a-sparkle, 'the old man with snowy white hair sits in bed holding one of his model dream houses and a lovely young Irish nurse leaning over...'

It was my task to organise this picture and story. I phoned the hospital and was told to come along the following day when all arrangements would be made.

'Remind them that we shall want a smart nurse,' said Dave. They promised a smart nurse.

All was ready when we arrived. The old man's snow-white hair had been carefully groomed, and Dave was delighted with the aged invalid's photogenic possibilities. The little model house, with its red roof and green garden, was a delight. Dave, with the 'MacLelland leisure' which would drive any high-speed news photographer crazy, began to rig up his tripod and lighting effects.

'Where is the nurse?' he asked.

'Here I am!'

I turned, and to my horror, saw a tall, uniformed man with a black, walrus moustache.

He was smiling at us, showing his big teeth. His black shoes shone, his white shirt was spotless, and his uniform was immaculately pressed.

There was a very awkward silence. The male nurse, who stood six foot, and took tens in shoes, broke in.

'Matron gave me the morning off to tidy myself up,' he said shyly. 'I've had a bath and a hair-cut.'

'Psst!' said Dave, turning white. His brief remark I knew meant he was saying to me, 'For Gawd's sake do something! If have this monster in my picture, both it and I will be ruined forever. I must have a pretty, glamorous, lovely Irish girl, dressed like a nurse, in my picture. And it's all your bloomin' fault.'

The big male nurse was getting angry at the awkward silences. He was beginning to blush. I pushed him forward.

'Take him, Dave,' I said.

And in Dave's ear I managed to whisper: 'For Pete's sake take his picture, or there'll be a riot. This is the greatest moment of his life.'

Dave cursed me silently, and in my ear he whispered, 'All right! But while I stall for time GO AND GET ME A GIRL.'

Dave posed up the big male nurse, and I, realising for the first time that we were in a male ward with all-male nurses, walked out of a French window and hurriedly crossed the lawn.

I stepped into the women's ward, and spotted a beautiful young nurse with black eyes and black hair. It was obvious at a glance that the fairies on the Emerald Isle were eating out their hearts at her absence.

'You'll do,' I told her at once. 'Come with me quickly and have your picture taken for the *Daily Mirror.*'

She was interested – what girl would not be? – but fearful. 'Will matron approve?'

'She will love it.'

As I smuggled her into the all-male ward I saw that our friend with the walrus moustache was still posing by the bed of the invalid, his arms folded, smiling away for all he was worth, while the white-faced Dave clicked the shutter of his plateless camera.

Tears of joy came into Dave's eyes as he saw the pretty Irish nurse. In a few seconds he had her posed at the bed-side, and was soon clicking merrily away at her and the aged invalid. She gave his camera radiant smiles, and he was happy.

And then I noticed a new expression on the face of Old Walrus. His black moustache was drooping. He was hurt.

This was more than normal jealousy. It appeared that he was even keener than we had feared on having his picture in the *Daily Mirror* and, being no fool, he was guessing the truth.

Suddenly he gave a grunt, and said snappily: 'She has no right to be in here. This is a male ward.'

And turning he walked away, without stopping to ask for copies through the post.

'Enough, Dave,' I whispered, sensing danger. 'Pack up and let's get moving.'

At the lodge gates a porter barred our path.

'Are you from the *Daily Mirror?*'

'We are,' I said.

'Matron wants to see you at once.'

I have had much experience of hospital matrons. They are wonderful women, we could not do without them, yet I never knew one who could not paralyse me with fear. But this one was exceptional. Dave still insists she was eight feet high. She seemed to fill the whole room. Nothing had been said, but my legs were giving way, and Dave's teeth were chattering.

'You have defied me,' she thundered. 'For the first time my authority has been usurped.'

That was a mere beginning.

We had no defence. But even if we had it would have made not the slightest difference. This was a court of justice as stern as any Assizes. We stood and trembled as the great voice boomed on.

In came the witnesses and gave their evidence. First the male nurse, Old Walrus himself, who had phoned the Matron to tell her of our terrible deed. He was regretting it now, and shook at the knees as he gave his evidence.

Next witness was the little Irish nurse. She had never been inside the Matron's office before, and she was in abject terror. Tears flowed down her sweet cheeks; her anguish gave us a strange courage. Had we not been guilty we would have pleaded so for her sweet sake.

'Have you anything to say as to why you thwarted my authority, broke my rules, disorganised my hospital, and committed the crime of taking a female nurse into a male ward?'

Dave tried to speak, but could not. I managed to cough out in a whisper, 'Nothing, Matron. Except we are very sorry.'

'Sorry! It is no use being sorry. You must both be dismissed at once as a disgrace to your profession. I shall phone your office and speak to the chief. Who is in charge there?'

I saw my first gleam of hope.

'Really Matron, you would not think of...'

'His name, at once? I demand your chief's name at once? Who is in charge of your Birmingham office?'

'Well Matron, if you really insist, the man in charge is Mr Harry Procter, but...'

'Don't 'but' me! Mr Procter shall be informed at once of your disgraceful conduct. I shall speak to Mr Procter personally, and right away.'

As we stood in shamed dejection she phoned my office. She asked for Mr Procter. A junior there confirmed to her that Mr Procter was in charge, that he was out, and should be back within the hour. She assured the junior she would phone again. And then, with an assurance that we need expect no mercy, she dismissed us.

We never spoke on our way back to the office. Prompt on the hour the telephone call for Mr Procter came though.

'Harry Procter speaking,' I purred into the telephone.

'Ah, Mr Procter,' she said. 'Forgive me for troubling you, I know you must be a very busy man. But I must bring to your attention the disgraceful conduct of two of your staff, a photographer and a reporter...'

It took her twenty minutes to outline the whole, damning case. I never interrupted. I sipped my tea and listened, the white-faced Dave at my side. I did not attempt to hurry her.

When she had finished I said: 'Matron, I am terribly shocked to hear this. The two men concerned have returned to the office, and I will see them myself, personally. Will you phone me back in twenty minutes?'

For twenty minutes we drank our tea. The phone rang. 'Matron,' I began. 'I have seen the two men personally. They admit their guilt. I am most grateful to you for bringing this unfortunate matter to my attention. I have fired them... fired them on the spot...'

'They deserve no less, Mr Procter.'

'I entirely agree with you, Matron.'

'Goodbye Mr Procter, and forgive me for taking up your valuable time.'

And that was how I fired myself. And also fired one of the best picture artists Fleet Street ever saw.

A week later the matron phoned Mr Procter to tell him in a friendly and charming manner about a very good story at her hospital. I sent two local men to cover it.

Chapter Six

I enjoyed Birmingham. As you will have gathered I am a bit of an egotist and loved being my own boss, running my own office, projecting and developing my own ideas. I was able to rent a beautiful flat over a shop in Halesowen, one of Birmingham's loveliest suburbs, and there install my wife and babies. Days off, of course, were now impossible, I must be on call constantly, day and night. But Dave would sometimes come home for tea, then act as baby-sitter while my wife and I had a beer together.

But too many of my friends were 'joining up'. I could not walk ten yards in any direction without seeing a soldier, a sailor, or an airman.

One day a news assignment took me to the recruiting office of the Royal Air Force in Birmingham. I walked out of the building, looked over my shoulder, then walked back.

'Will you take me?' I asked. 'I can ride a bicycle, so I can learn to fly a plane.'

I had a medical, said all my goodbyes, and was bustled off to Cardington Receiving Unit.

They gave me a test, a paper test. As I sat at a desk with a pen in my hand I got the old jitters I suffered as a child at school on exam day. Trigonometry, geometry, were just words to me, and I failed.

I was told I would be returned to civilian life, but in a few months, when the training machinery now being created was established, I would be recalled and reconsidered.

This was too much for me to bear. I had been given a party in my home town, Leeds, and cheered off to fight for my King and Country.

I had been given another farewell party by my friends in London, a third by my friends in Birmingham.

I explained it all to an understanding Wing Commander.

'I shall have to return all their beer, sir,' I said.

He was helpful. 'What about photography?'

I shrugged: 'Well, I've worked for the leading picture paper, the *Daily Mirror.*'

He let me have a go, and although I made a reasonable show of handling a camera, I was useless at developing and printing in the darkroom.

'I just can't go back, sir,' I pleaded. 'Another man has been moved up from London to Birmingham to take over my job. I shall look a fool.'

'You're a journalist! Why not be a clerk? We're crying out for clerks at the moment, because administration must be built up before we can build up air squadrons!'

I firmly refused: 'Couldn't stand the shame of it, sir. Joining the Royal Air Force in war time and pounding a typewriter?'

'Look' he said, 'Take my advice. At the moment the fact is that we have got far more volunteers for aircrew than we can accept – we haven't the facilities for training them. In six months time the position will be very different. Sign on now as a clerk, stay with us and do a good job, then in six months we'll re-muster you to aircrew? How's that?'

I agreed. And the next day they gave me a uniform.

They sent me, and a hundred others, to Morecambe for our square-bashing, and drilled us from 8am to 6pm in a sweltering sun. I was immediately singled out as 'the awkward recruit' of the squad – there must be one in every training squad or the instructor's pantomime patter could not go on – and I was made a fool of every day. Our corporal instructor irritated me by making corny jokes I had heard my father tell when he talked of 1916.

'Procter! I told you to present arms, not climb up your ruddy rifle!'

The Flight Sergeant used to shout: 'Come out, that man there with the little moustache,' and this always won him a big laugh. So I shaved it off.

He was raving at having his best comic line robbed from him by my action.

'So you think you can hide by shaving it off?' he glared. 'I'll keep my eye on you.' And he did.

I shared a billet with six other airmen – run by a typical seaside landlady, struggling to make as big a profit out of the RAF as she had previously made out of her seasonal visitors.

She fed us mainly on lettuce, which she grew in the back-garden.

We were so ravenously hungry that we bought hot pies every lunch-time and parked them on the plates with the lettuce, hoping to shame her. She never made a comment.

'Let me organise this,' I boasted. 'It is no good moaning; let us make a complaint through the proper, normal, channels. I've been reading King's Regulations. We all complain together, officially, to the corporal, then on it goes to the Flight...'

We made an official complaint. The following day there was lettuce for lunch – but when we returned for tea I was the hero of the war.

Tea-time only! A lovely sirloin steak for each of us, fried fresh tomatoes, succulent chips, a jar of mixed pickles, bread and best butter, a pot of steaming tea, and a plate of cakes and buns to follow.

'It's worked,' I cried. 'What did I tell you?'

'Jane-Man, you're certainly no fool,' they said – they called me the Jane-Man because they knew I was a *Mirror* reporter.

We were beginning to stuff the nice paper napkins provided, down behind our blue shirts, when a voice we all knew yelled: 'Attention!'

It was the 'Flight'. With him was a Wing Commander, sent along especially to be sure that our official complaint was officially and fully investigated.

We stood up, stiff and silent. The Wing Commander stroked his moustache, sniffed, let his eyes rove fully over the crowded table.

'Steak!' he yelled. 'Fresh fried tomatoes! Chips! Cakes and buns!' Then his shoulders trembled and he blew through his teeth.

'And mixed pickles! So this is the food you complain of. You impudent, ungrateful...'

He certainly gave us a rollicking.

And before he left he warned us: 'If ever I hear so much as a squeak or a squawk from any of you ungrateful ----- again I'll have the lot of you court martialled.'

The following day the food was worse than ever, and the landlady was jubilant. 'Complain again,' she crowed, 'if there's anything you don't like.'

The corporal told me: 'Procter, take a bit of advice from an old airman which is not in King's Regulations and Air Council Instructions. Never complain!'

Poor fool! I did not take the advice.

Our training ended, I was sent to No 16 Maintenance Unit, newly opened at Stafford, where I was at once made personal clerk to the commanding officer, Group Captain Green.

He was a very nice gentleman. He told me: 'AC Procter, I am lucky to have got you – a Fleet Street journalist – as my clerk. Work hard and you'll soon have promotion.'

Everybody in the Air Force had the idea that journalism, newspaper reporting, writing feature articles, equipped a man to be a clerk – to shuffle green index cards, to keep files, to write letters which always started: 'Sir, I have the honour to request...'

Yes, the Group Captain was a kindly man; within three days he decided to get himself a new personal clerk, and he never said an unkind word to me.

A Wing Commander collared me. 'I understand,' he said, and he did. 'You are no clerk, but you are a master of English and spelling. I shall put you in charge of correspondence.'

He was delighted the following day to be able to bring back one of my letters in which I had used manoeuvre twice, but spelled it wrongly, and differently each time.

'There you are, there you are' he nodded, gaily. 'Fleet Street reporter, but you can't teach me to spell.' He was so delighted with me at that moment that if he could he would have made me a sergeant.

At Stafford I lived in a tent with Peter Cole, an airman with a public school education, and Arthur Spiller, a huge, gawky Cockney, from London's East End.

One night Cockney Spiller pulled out a photograph of a very beautiful girl.

'By Jove!' exclaimed the educated Peter Cole, 'but what a really lovely girl.'

'Take yer dirty paws off it,' said Spiller. 'She's mi cousin who's in America she is. Never seen her, she's never been over 'ere, but we often writes, see?'

'By Jove' said Public Schoolboy Peter, entranced. 'I swear I will marry that girl some day, I swear I will. I'll make you a bet...'

'Geronatofit! She wouldn't marry the likes of you, she'll want a bloke who can work for his living, not sit preening himself an' wearing them there 'orrible green silk pyjamas you wears. There is one thing, cock, as you'll never know in this world, and that's the name and address of mi cousin in America.'

A few years later, when I bumped into Arthur Spiller in – of all places – a Fleet Street pub, I asked him: 'What happened to old Green Pyjama Peter?'

'Him?' said Arthur, almost spilling his pint. 'That b-----d! Do you know what he did to me? Pinched mi bloomin' picture of mi cousin in America, an' with 'er name an' address on it, an' all. Gets posted to Canada, looks her up, bloomin' well marries 'er, he does.'

It was true, as I later confirmed when I met Peter Cole.

There was lots of fun at Stafford, and I ought to have been happy. But often I felt a clot when, while pounding a typewriter, a Spitfire zoomed overhead.

I applied for re-muster to air-crew. It was refused on the grounds that my work at No 16 Maintenance Unit was too important to be broken.

Then, very foolishly, I became awkward about the matter. Eventually I got to the Air Candidates Selection Board.

'Can you ride a horse' asked a piece of top brass. 'Ever been fox-hunting?' He was disgusted to get a 'no' to both questions.

I was moved to a Group Headquarters in Leeds, where I was placed in charge of the records and progress reports of young airmen undergoing training as pilots. I had to keep the records up-to-date.

To me this was a heart-breaking job, a job which led to trouble.

Each airman's documents were tagged together in correct order. The first document gave the U/T Pilot's name, number, and an answer to the printed question, 'Occupation in Civilian Life'. The rest of the papers gave the marks the airman had received for trigonometry, mathematics, and actual flying.

The last document in the bundle had three printed lines:

Recommended for a commission…
Strongly recommended for a commission…
Not recommended for a commission…

I used to play a little game with myself. If the first page entry said: 'Occupation in Civilian Life, Baker's Roundsman', and the airman had top marks in all subjects, I would bet myself a shilling he was 'Not recommended for a commission'.

If the first form showed him to be a young man of birth, 'Occupation…gentleman…' even though his marks were low, I would bet myself he was 'Strongly recommended for commission' – 'a born leader of men'.

I usually won. Remember this was in the early days of the war, when the Royal Air Force was being run by the old-time, peace-time gang, who believed that a man with no experience in horse-riding, fox-hunting, or shooting-stick-sitting could never become a commissioned officer in the Royal Air Force.

Men like Sir Winston Churchill, Lord Beaverbrook, and others, changed all that – made bus conductors into Wing Commanders – and built up the greatest Air Force the world had ever seen.

I had the shameful experience of seeing the old snob commanders running things. I kept a private record of these things, produced some startling statistics, and showed them to a Wing Commander, giving my comments.

A few weeks later they posted me to Orkney Island.

On Orkney Island there was nothing to do, not even work. We were so bored that we actually played hop-scotch and other games of our childhood. After some months of this I began to have real fears for my sanity.

Two or three stories from Orkney Island began to appear in the *Daily Mirror*. The Station Warrant Officer openly accused me of being responsible, pointing out that an airman had no right to write to the press. I shrugged my shoulders.

'All our mail is censored, an officer reads all my correspondence.'

There the matter was left to rest. The stories, of course, were light, bright, human stories – not anything of a military nature or of importance to security.

My camp was at Skae Brae, in the centre of the Island, three miles from the nearest village tavern. One day, feeling too adventurous for my surroundings, I hitch-hiked to Kirkwall, entered a large Nissen hut, and saw a bored airman lying on his bed, staring at the roof.

'Hello Arthur!' I surprised him, and he literally leapt like a trout. It was Arthur Day, a reporter colleague with me on the *Armley and Wortley News* and later a colleague on the *Northern Echo*. My appearance at his bedside on that far off island gave him a shock he never fully recovered from.

'When you go home to Leeds, Harry,' he pleaded, 'if you see my mother, don't tell her just how ruddy awful it is on this island, please. I don't want her bothered...'

He was much better off than I. He had buildings to look at, a cinema, two pubs; WAAFs to watch down the streets. I had nothing but tree-less hills, huts and sheep.

Dejectedly he showed me a parody which summed up the situation, written by some wit before he went mad:

This ruddy isle's a ruddy cuss,
No ruddy trains, no ruddy bus,
And no one cares for ruddy us.
OH ruddy Orkney.
All ruddy mud, no ruddy drains,
No ruddy fun, no ruddy dames,
We lads forget our ruddy names.
OH ruddy Orkney.
Oh everything's so ruddy dear,
A ruddy bob, for ruddy beer.
And is it good? No ruddy fear.
OH ruddy Orkney.

'Well, you got to Fleet Street,' he said. 'How was it?'

I told him about Fleet Street. This solid, Yorkshire journalist (when I last heard of him he was on the *Yorkshire Evening Post)* was surprised at some of the tales I told.

One day, while working in the orderly room, I was asked to 'post' eight clerks to the North of England. In the mood of a man buying a ticket for the Irish Sweep I wrote my own name and number on the signal back to records. Before the Orderly Room Sergeant realised just what had happened, I was on the boat for Thurso.

My new station was better. I was now a clerk in an HQ staff. My job was to organise billets, canvass billets for WAAFs, appease angry landladies.

This, once again, was a job with people, a job requiring the handling of people, and very soon the young billeting officer was eager to leave everything to me. I could charm down the tempers of even the most outraged landladies.

They would storm my office and say: 'Those two WAAFs! Get them out of my house at once.'

And often the landladies would leave my office agreeing to take four WAAFs from our next intake.

One day I was hauled off before the Commanding Officer for refusing to salute a young flight lieutenant.

I was making one of those stands 'on principle', a foolish thing to do in the armed forces. There was a personal problem between myself and the officer. I sincerely believed – I am now sure, quite wrongly – that I could not respect him.

The CO listened patiently to my side of the story.

'But even if what you say is true,' he said. 'Your salute is to the uniform, not to the man wearing it.'

'Then, sir, must I salute every uniformed dummy I see in the windows of Montague Burton's?' I asked.

The Air Force won.

One day I saw a notice pinned under the Daily Routine Orders. It said that 'AC2 Blank, a former solicitor, is willing to give free legal advice to any airman in trouble.'

I recognised the name as that of a young solicitor I had known. I looked him up on the spot, we changed into civvies, got into his car, and went off on a spree to Scarborough.

On the way back, at about 2am, he and I were stopped at Filey, and placed under arrest.

The next morning we faced charges of wearing civilian clothes without permission, being absent from billets without permission, being out of bounds, etc. etc.

And AC Blank, the former solicitor, was not in a position then to give to me, an airman in trouble, any free legal advice.

I was sentenced to twenty-eight days detention. On principle – oh, just how many young and stupid hearts have suffered needlessly for two, those two, misunderstood words – I asked for a court martial.

They took me to a cell, the converted cellar-basement of the large boarding-house which was our headquarters. No mother hen could have cared more lovingly for her chick than did the Red Cap sergeant who was my gaoler. He gave me blankets, a mattress, cigarettes, books.

'Don't be a chump, Harry,' he said. 'You can do it on your head if you accept the CO's punishment. I'll look after you, you'll have everything you want. It'll be a nice rest.'

The flight sergeant in charge of the busy orderly room knew, just as well as I, how much paper work, how many working clerk-hours must go into the preparation and carrying out of a court martial.

On comparatively trivial offences they did not want to be bothered.

The 'Flight' himself came to see me, brought me a packet of cigarettes, talked to me like a fond father.

'Take your punishment like a man,' he said. 'If you go before the CO in the morning and say you have changed your mind, and now wish to accept his punishment, I can personally promise your sentence will be reduced to fourteen days. And look how snug we've made you down here.'

I took their advice. The CO announced that he had decided to reduce my sentence by half. I saluted, returned to my cell, lit a cigarette, and lolled on my comfortable mattress.

In came the Red Cap sergeant.

'Take that cigarette out of your mouth,' he shouted. 'Men, remove the mattress, and all but one blanket, these books should not be here, take away the prisoner's matches, cigarettes, shoe-laces, and braces...'

'Oh! Grandmother, dear,' I said to the Sergeant, 'how changed you are.'

I did not trouble to remind him of his loving promises of the night before. I just scrubbed out my cell on my hands and knees, scrubbed the wooden bunk which was my only resting place, ran up and down the local High Street at the double, his threats and curses ringing in my ears.

'Still, I might have got two years in the Glasshouse, had I gone forward for court martial,' I consoled myself that night, as I heard the key turn in the lock of my cell, leaving me alone to a blackness so dense I felt I could hardly breathe.

Two nights later I woke suddenly on my wooden bed and heard a strange whistling. It was a landmine, falling by parachute, and it sounded immediately above me. Then part of the ceiling fell on top of me. All the soot shot out of the chimney and choked the air.

The landmine had fallen about twenty-five yards away, completely wrecking houses, killing several of my fellow airmen.

I freed myself from the debris, and battered on the door of my cell. It was an hour before they remembered they had a prisoner locked away in the basement – but of course they were all busy trying to help badly injured airmen and civilians. I had a few cuts and bruises, but I could walk. When they released me I heard the Red Cap sergeant loudly reprimand my gaolers.

'You know regulations say that a prisoner's cell must be unlocked as soon as the sirens sound,' he said.

I was taken to hospital, a converted luxury hotel. My room overlooked the sea, I had a private balcony. I was never lonely because, according to regulations, a military policeman had to stay by my bed night and day.

The young RAF doctor, who called to see me each day, would enquire: 'Well, how is our murderer this morning?' I served the rest of my sentence in luxury, and thoroughly enjoyed it.

Back on my feet I at once demanded an interview with my CO. 'I'm sorry, sir, but I can't stand this any longer. There is a war on, I am a young, fit man, and I refuse to continue my service as a nursemaid to WAAFs. I want to join an air-crew.'

Off I went to Edinburgh to sit before the Air Candidates Selection Board there.

Things had changed since my last attempt. The Officers who now interviewed me cared nothing about either horse-riding, fox hunting, or bridge-playing – they wanted as many fit young men as they could get to join the ever growing army of flyers.

They tried their darndest to get me through.

At my verbal test a combat flying officer asked: 'You are flying a Spitfire at such and such an angle. The wind is such and such. Your speed is such and such, and your height is such and such. At such and such degrees, at your port-side a Fokker-Wolf comes straight at you and starts blazing away with his guns. What would you do?'

There was only one line of his question I could understand. So I answered: 'I should blaze straight back at him, sir.'

He smiled. 'That is just the answer I wanted,' he said.

But my knowledge of mathematics, trigonometry, and geometry was, frankly, nil.

The presiding officer told me, kindly: 'We would like to pass you, we can see by your record how restless you have been on the ground staff. We are certain you would make a first-class pilot, we are certain you would quickly learn to fly a plane. But once you got up there on your own, you wouldn't know where to go.'

Chapter Seven

I saw at once, and for the very first time, the reason I could never be a fighter pilot. The officer shook my hand and wished me good luck.

I had no more interest in my work; I was posted to Kirkwall, near Blackpool; I became sullen, aloof, unsociable. One day an officer asked me: 'What would you do if we let you return to civvie street'

I said: 'I would become a war correspondent.'

'All right then,' he said. 'We are going to let you go.'

To keep this promise I had to leave the *Daily Mirror,* and join the *Daily Mail.* When the *Mirror* had to decide which of two reporters should go with the American airborne Army on D-Day – young Ian Fyfe, or myself – they chose Ian. They told me it was because I had four children, and Ian – at that moment – was single.

I was miserable when I parted with Ian that night, shortly before D-Day – I bitterly envied him the American uniform he wore which I thought ought to have been mine.

Ian was a wonderful reporter, his background, his experience, his training – HIS PAST – were almost identical with my own.

As we parted he said, in his cocky, Scots way: 'I'll bet you a fiver, Harry, I get the first story back from France – I bet you I scoop the pool. I've got a marvellous idea, boy...'

I never learned what his idea was. He never reached France, his plane was lost over the Channel early on D-Day morning – so he never returned to the Street he loved so much.

The *Mirror* was very glad to have me back. Like all newspapers they had lost every reporter who was fit and well. These had been replaced by journalists with disabilities, some were even lame. So there was plenty of work for me to do in Geraldine House.

The *Mirror* now had returned to its former brightness. Jane was the darling of the Army, the Air Force, and the Navy, and the circulation was stretching the chains of the paper shortage to bursting point.

I took a flat in Lincoln's Inn Fields, five minutes walk from the office.

My ability to write a descriptive, human, story was now given full play in the many major tragedies I had to report.

The terrible bombings presented me with opportunities galore to write the 'human angle'.

A bomb fell on a dance floor, causing a heavy toll of lives among the dancers who died swaying to the rhythm of the band. I shared this story with all my contemporaries, but I was the only reporter who asked about the dance band.

I found that the dance band was led by a disabled youth who had been turned down by the forces – he had recruited his musicians from young men whom the forces had rejected on medical grounds. At long last, when I found his father, I was presented with the band's professional card.

'Joe So and So and His Boys. Blitz or no Blitz, We Play On'.

The story wrote itself.

Amongst the rubble of a blitzed council school I saw a young policeman, sweating with anxious haste, digging at the bricks, broken school desks and twisted steel.

The first body he brought out was of a little child – his own! Sticking out from a pile of debris I saw a fire-blackened school gate bearing the notice 'Infants Only'.

In every bomb disaster there were a dozen tragic, human stories.

Those were the ones I sought.

The *Mirror* was still bright.

I well remember Noel Whitcomb, the world's most famous feather fingered columnist, joining the *Mirror*. I was sitting in the reporter's room with colleague Arthur La Burn – later to become the author of best seller *It Always Rains on Sunday* – when cockney news editor Garry Ellingham ushered in two clean shirted, pink faced young men.

' 'Arry and Arthur,' gushed Garry, 'meet the two new boys, Noel Whitcomb and George Pollock.' We nodded.

'These two young lads', said Garry, 'are going to be reporters, but special reporters; in time I want all my staff to specialise. George here will specialise in radio notes and Noel here in swimming...'

'What shall I specialise in Garry?' I asked.

'Oh, we have something very special for you 'Arry, but go and get your tea now...'

As I walked out I passed the handsome Noel and sniffed the huge carnation in his button-hole. 'Take that out, chum,' I said. 'You'll not get away with carnations in Fleet Street.'

'I'll bet you I do,' said Noel. He has worn a carnation every day in Fleet Street since – it is as well known in Fleet Street as Churchill's cigar or Chaplin's moustache.

Later, on the *Daily Mail,* I was offered a story about a dog which was supposed to talk. We turned it down, the dog owner phoned the *Mirror.* They sent young Noel Whitcomb out on the story – the newcomer had not had a break so far.

I shall never forget the introduction Noel wrote on that story. 'I have just had a short conversation with a dog,' wrote Noel Whitcomb. That introduction made him overnight almost a star columnist of Fleet Street. I like his column, but he has never, in my opinion, beaten or equalled the story he wrote about the dog who could say 'I WANT ONE'.

I invented the phrase 'GI Joe'. When the first contingent of Americans arrived in London, my instructions were to grab the first American soldier to walk through the station barrier and hurry him off on a sight-seeing tour of London.

There was no pre-selection, I literally grabbed the first one. His name was Joe Davis, he was a former truck-driver from Minnesota.

He and I started the tour at 9am, following a prepared schedule: the Tower of London, the Houses of Parliament, the British Museum.

He was very quiet. At 12 noon he said to me: 'Sir, this tour is just swell, I'm enjoying it. But would it be OK for me to buy you a drink?'

We scrapped a visit to the London Art Gallery and an inspection of Smithfield Market. After a few light ales, Joe's shyness left him, and all I had to do to get my story was to write down exactly what he said. In my feature I called him GI Joe.

I began to specialise in writing stories obtained from the American forces.

One Friday I met a sobbing bride-to-be. Tomorrow, she said, was to have been her wedding day. She had bought her full bridal trousseau, white dress and veil, the wedding cake, the ring. Her wedding was all arranged to an American soldier at a tiny church near his camp in the wilds of rural England.

'But he overstayed his leave, and they've sentenced him to six months,' she sobbed.

I told her to pack all her wedding regalia into a suitcase and meet me at the station. I teamed up with Fred Cole, a *Mirror* photographer, and we took the bride and her trousseau to the American camp.

I dressed her with care in the beautiful white satin gown, fastened down her tulle veil with a circle of orange blossoms, arranged her bouquet of roses, pinned up her train.

And in all her bridal splendour I took her by taxi, right through the gates of the American army camp, and led her straight into the office of the commanding officer.

'Look at her, Colonel,' I said. 'Today is her wedding day. Are you going to be remembered as the man who broke her heart?'

The bride stood in silence, looking sad but beautiful. For ten minutes I pleaded for her happiness, with all the skill and eloquence I could muster. There was truthfully a tear in the colonel's eye when I finished.

'But what can I do?' he said, weakening.

'After all, the man is my prisoner. I am responsible for him. Military law says he must remain in my custody.'

'No one is suggesting you should break the regulations, Colonel,' I assured him. 'The bridegroom is your prisoner, he must remain in your custody. The church is only a mile away, the parson is waiting. Here stands the bride.

'All that I ask, sir, is that you go to the bridegroom's cell, handcuff him to you, take him into church and let the wedding go on. Then bring him straight back to his cell. After all, it is a very simple thing we are asking, it won't take up an hour of your time.'

For a moment I thought that all was lost. Then the bride began to weep, silently, sweetly. No hysterics, just a gentle trickle down her rosy cheek.

'Say, I'm new to this country. Tell me, what do you think a British commanding officer would do in the circumstances?'

'Colonel,' I said, determined to tell the truth. 'I can assure you that in these circumstances a commanding officer in the British Army would not hesitate in making an immediate decision.'

'OK,' he said. 'I'll go and get the bridegroom.'

He returned with the prisoner handcuffed to his wrist. Off we all went to church, cameraman Cole making the best of every blessed moment.

Inside the church the parson asked: 'Who is to give the bride away?'

'The colonel,' I said, and the colonel did. After the wedding the colonel allowed the bridegroom to kiss his bride, then marched him back to his cell.

We took our bride back to London in triumph. Cole and I had got exclusively one of the most exciting wedding stories of the year.

It was also a 'scoop' on the other side of the Atlantic, for I was allowed to send a copy of my story on to the *New York Daily News.* They were grateful.

It did not end there. I had, apparently, stirred the colonel's romantic emotions to such an extent that he wrote to the bride and told her that she could spend one hour a week alone with her husband while he was serving his sentence.

I wrote my second 'scoop' as 'The Honeymoon By Instalments', and again the American newspaper sent me its thanks.

I liked the Americans, and because I got on so well with them, they gave me many exclusive stories from their ranks.

I was certainly having luck in Fleet Street. But I nursed a secret grievance – that the Editor would not allow me to don a war correspondent's uniform and keep the promise I made to the RAF.

This was an important period in my journalistic career. I was being talked about now, not only in the *Mirror* offices, but in other newspaper offices in Fleet Street. Several flirtatious news editors were giving me the wink.

And a whisper was going about Fleet Street, a whisper which both angered and challenged me.

'Of course, Harry Procter does well on the *Mirror,* you know, but he'd be useless in solid journalism.'

I knew I could tackle any type of journalism. My training had made me just as able to report for *The Times* as for the popular papers. I knew I could do it, but I wanted to prove it to all in Fleet Street.

I was in doubt, and again Fate took a hand.

A girl in the provinces (I am not going to mention her name here because it would be most unfair to her) gave birth to triplets.

No reporter could find out who the father was. The *Mirror* had sent a girl reporter on the assignment but, curious about the father, they called her back and sent me.

I talked with the young mother. The argument I used was that she was being most unfair to the father of her children by hiding his identity. If she loved him – and I was sure she did – perhaps he would wish to announce with pride that he was the father. I urged that she leave the decision to him, that she gave me his name and address in confidence, and that I would not publish it without his permission. She must not let people think the father was ashamed of his children, that he wanted to have nothing to do with her or them.

'But he's proud of the babies, and he loves me;' she said. 'But you see, he is a married man. And also he is an American soldier.'

I was very interested. Already this story, without one hint of the father, had appeared in all the nationals.

I gave her my promise, and she gave me his name and address. He was stationed 200 miles away, but I left at once.

I met him in the early evening in the buffet of the local railway station. I was able to persuade him to let me publish the story, with his name and photograph.

What a magnificent story he gave me.

It was not only the facts which were so NEWSY.

It was the way this little, red-haired, American sergeant, told the tale.

At the time I took a full shorthand note of his conversation, which was so good that I dictated it over the phone to my office, verbatim, writing only an introduction. The story was enriched by his lively American humour, by his own natural phrases.

It was the best story of my life, so far.

He had a wife back home, he said, but on meeting the English girl he fell in love with her and wrote and asked his wife for a divorce. He was still hoping a divorce would be possible, and then he would marry the mother of his triplets.

On hearing that the 'baby' was to be born the sergeant went to his commanding officer – 'my boss' – and asked for special leave, giving the reason for the request.

'H--l,' said the boss. 'We're too busy to spare you just now, Sarge. Unless you think you can beat it there and back within a twenty-four hour pass?'

'Sarge' swore a solemn oath he would be back on duty within twenty-four hours. He arrived at the girl's home, to be told by her mother she was in the maternity hospital awaiting the birth.

'Now, did I need a drink, sir?' Sarge told me. 'So I says to Marm, 'Marm I certainly need a drink'. And she brought me a drink. A great pot of this stuff you folks call tea. Now, sir, that old lady is a nice old lady, and I was not going to offend this old lady, so I drank the tea. Then I went to the phone.'

He told of how he was informed that his girl had given birth.

'So I phoned up the boss man, and he says "Great work, Sarge. Now get on that bleedin' train and come back like 'ell as fast as you can!" Course I called back to tell the old lady, and told her we must have a drink to celebrate. So she goes and brings me another great mug of this damned tea, which I have to drink.'

He told me of how he phoned a second time to the hospital, and learned that he was the father of twins. Of how he phoned his boss.

' "Twins!" says my boss man, "now ain't that cute." And when I arsks him for a day's extension in view of the baby being two babies, he thinks it over and eventually he agrees. "But Sarge," he warns me, "if you're pulling a bleedin' fast one, it'll be the worst joke of your life. I'll have those stripes off your arm as fast as..."

'Honest boss' I says, 'it is the truth I'm saying.'

All this sudden excitement was rather much for the little red-haired Sergeant, and so, 'jest to take this 'orrible taste of tea off my tongue' he went into a nearby tavern and ordered an extra large Scotch. He had several more before closing time. He was swaying a little as he made his way back to Mum's house, but passing the phone box he decided to make a last inquiry about his girl and his twins.

'Triplets,' they told him, so he phoned again to his boss man.

'You drunken, red-haired liar,' shouted the boss man. 'Now I can see the whole thing was one darned frame-up. If you don't jump the next train back to camp I'll send a bleedin' escort for you.'

All the *Daily Mirror* were delighted with the story, particularly Garry Allighan, who was then News Editor. Ted Castle was by now Assistant Editor. 'They'll lead the paper with the story, Harry,' he said. 'This will get you your break as war correspondent.'

When I phoned Garry later, he was in tears. John Walters, recently arrived from America to take a newly created post cementing Anglo-American relations, had urged that the story might cause bad feeling against the American Forces in England. On these grounds he had the story killed.

But they had wired it over to the *New York Daily News,* who sent me a telegram saying: 'You have scooped the world.'

I felt so badly I could have jumped under a train.

That week, *World's Press News,* the trade journal of 'the print', published a story about my story, headed 'Great Scoop that Was Not Used'.

Guy Bartholomew, then the Great White Chief of the *Mirror* group, did not like the story in the trade paper – apparently he did not like great 'scoops' not being used. There was a rumpus.

Humbler executives looked at me sulkily. I was unpopular.

So I walked down Fleet Street, and called on Lindon Laing, News Editor of the *Daily Mail.* In my pocket I had a letter of congratulations signed by Garry Allighan dated the day before.

Chapter Eight

Lindon Laing was certainly one of the greatest newspaper men Fleet Street ever saw. He was a giant, both in stature and in ability. I never knew a man in Fleet Street more fiercely hated. I never knew a man in Fleet Street more passionately loved.

I believe it was G K Chesterton who wrote: 'There is a great man who makes every man feel small. But the real great man is the man who makes every man feel great.'

Lindon Laing fitted both descriptions. He could inspire a reporter with such confidence that the scribe would sincerely believe himself to be capable of any task on earth. He could make a reporter so terrified, so ashamed, that he wished he'd been born to Chinese peasants.

'No man ever lived who could bandy words with me, mister,' was his cry.

This huge figure rose from his desk, towered above me, his right hand in his pocket – a typical Lindon Laing pose.

'So you've come to see me at last, mister?' he grinned – he could have played Long John Silver superbly. 'Well, mister, I thought you'd be around as soon as you were fired!'

'But I have not been fired.'

'Don't worry about it – it makes no odds to me, mister. Even I was fired from the *Daily Express,* man. Forget it.'

He bobbed in and out of his office, then called a secretary. 'Type out the usual letter of appointment. His name is Harry Procter – with an 'e'.'

After the official ceremony of appointment was over, I tossed before him the letter from Garry Allighan.

'I don't believe in getting jobs with references,' I said. 'You say you don't believe I haven't been fired? Well, they don't write a reporter a letter of congratulations one day, and fire him the next.'

He read it and chuckled. 'Why didn't you tell me you'd not been fired?' he grinned, impudently. 'I've been and told the Editor you've just been fired. I'll take this in and show him and explain how you misinformed me.'

I did not want to work out the customary notice on the *Daily Mirror* so I decided I would organise my own dismissal. I returned to the office and pulled Garry Allighan's tie out. I began to speak my mind with deliberate foolishness, hoping that some executive would leap up in anger and say: 'Enough Procter! You're out!'

But I could not get the sack. In despair I barged into the private sanctum of R T Suffern, the Managing Editor, and squawked: 'I'm utterly fed-up. Why don't you fire me?'

But Suffern refused to give me the boot. Many years later when my baby daughter Phyllis had grown to twenty and was a reporter on *Reveille,* Suffern made amends by firing her because, amongst other things, they didn't see eye to eye about her hair style. I must admit that her notion that untrammelled hair was appropriate for the Blessed Damozel – which were my daughter's notions of a suitable coif for Fleet Street purposes – justified the action taken by the newspaper at the time.

'I refuse to look like a girl who has just come out of a slot machine,' she said. The years between must have hardened him.

It was Lindon Laing, the Fleet Street maestro, who taught me the art of exposure. Later on, as Chief Reporter of the *Sunday Pictorial* when almost every week a villain had to be unmasked, the Laing tuition gave me an advantage over most other Sunday newspapermen.

He taught me the power of hard facts. Facts were all he dealt in. He told me that if ever I could invent, from my imagination, a better story than the real truth, he would publish it, but not until. He taught me a thousand new tricks.

He taught me the trick of publishing exactly what people say – a trick as powerful as an atomic explosion.

When I exposed Jack Anstey, the Trotsky agitator, during my first week on the *Daily Mail,* I handed my story to Lindon, and he asked:

'But didn't you ask this scoundrel where his money comes from?'

'Oh yes,' I said, 'but he wouldn't tell me.'

'What did he say when you asked him?'

'Oh, he just made a silly remark. He said "You can tell your *Daily Mail* readers that every time Hitler raids London he drops me money in paper parcels".'

94

'Fine, mister,' said Lindon. 'Just put it in your story, exactly as the man said it.'

I thought then that no man in Fleet Street could teach me anything about how to present my facts in story form.

Lindon had an annoying habit of hovering about my typewriter if I was 'knocking out' a good story. He would peer over my shoulder in silence, read my introduction, then pop into his own room. He would return, impishly, throw a piece of paper on my desk, then run away.

On the paper would be a pencilled sentence – his own idea of a different introduction to the story I was writing. I would read the note and curse him violently, because the new introduction was always better than my own – therefore I had to use it.

He was a very vain man. He used to say: 'I would never send a reporter out on an assignment I thought I could not get myself.'

One day he sent me off to expose a rogue who was defrauding children having holidays abroad. Every newspaper in the country was out on this story, but I was the only reporter to get an interview with the man, an interview which confirmed many facts and produced a first-class tale.

I returned to the *Daily Mail* in triumph.

Lindon held out my story.

'What's this Harry? I told you I wanted a complete confession from this rogue, signed on every page. This is no use to me, mister...'

I exploded with wrath and hurt pride. 'I am the only reporter in England to get this, and you insult me,' I protested. 'What you are asking for is impossible, and you know it!'

'Impossible, mister!' he shouted. 'Come with me. If you don't know your job then I must teach it to you.'

He beckoned to reporter John Hall to join us. He never spoke a word on the car journey to the assignment.

He did not ask for an interview. He leapt up the stairs to the man's private office, opened the door, and barged in, John Hall and myself following nervously.

'What an outrage,' said the man. 'Get out at once or I will call the police.'

'Call Scotland Yard,' said Lindon Laing. 'Tell them that I am Lindon Laing of the *Daily Mail,* that I have bullied my way uninvited into your office, and that I refuse to go. Tell them also that I accuse you of being a rogue, a liar, and a cheat. And tell them it is high time they flung you into goal.'

The man was at Lindon's mercy from this moment on.

'Can I make a bargain with you, Mr Laing?'

'A bargain? Of course you can't, mister – how can a rogue make a bargain with honest journalists?'

He made a full confession of all his sins, allowed it to be typed, signed it on every page, handed it to Lindon Laing. Later Lindon Laing gave the statement to me with a first page introduction attached.

'There's your story, Harry. Take it to the subs, then come on and I'll buy you a drink. You've done a first-class story today.'

At first I feared Lindon Laing, then I admired him, but soon I loved him. He was my immediate boss – his instructions to me had to be carried out to the letter, but he was also my friend.

Lindon Laing had a 'news sense' which has never been equalled in Fleet Street's history. Why the *Daily Express* ever allowed him to leave them, cross the street, and join the *Daily Mail,* had always mystified me, for no journalist could ever be of greater value to a newspaper.

Hounding down a crook, exposing an injustice, he was as ruthless as the sword of Herod. But he would never allow a story or an investigation to harm or hurt an innocent, honest person. I was never once sent on an assignment by Lindon Laing of which any journalist could have been ashamed.

He was forever doing little acts of kindness in Fleet Street, carrying out secret schemes of benevolence; he genuinely hated the recipients of these favours to know about their source. Most of his good deeds were done in an intriguing secrecy.

Though tough, and noisy, menacing, and bullying, he was at heart extremely sensitive.

Before he was a news editor he was one of Britain's greatest crime reporters, and yet he could never stay in the Press box to see sentence of death passed on a murderer.

'There is no sense in hanging a man, mister,' he would say.

When the healthy, ruthless rivalry between the *Daily Express* and the *Daily Mail* was at its fiercest, the *Express* bought a helicopter to cover the news.

Quipped Lindon Laing: 'The *Express* may have a helicopter, but we've got a Harry Procter...'

He was a man who never ceased to amaze and astound.

One day a local correspondent called to see him to ask for a reporter's job.

Laing said to me: 'Like to see me appoint that young man news editor of the ----? I'll do it all from my desk here in the *Daily Mail*.'

He did it within a few hours. He sent the young man along to see the editor of the paper, told him exactly what to say.

'Mind you, mister,' said Laing, 'only say what I've told you to say, and only give the answers I've told you to give. Do as I say and tomorrow you'll be a Fleet Street news editor.'

'But,' said the incredulous young man, 'supposing they ask me a question that you haven't given me an answer for, what do I do then?'

'Then you don't answer it, you blithering idiot,' shouted Laing. 'You walk out, phone me from a kiosk, tell me the question, I'll give you the answer. Then you go back.'

And that is exactly what did occur.

The young man was appointed News Editor of the paper and at the salary the *Mail* News Editor had promised him.

Lindon was the son of a Durham miner. During the days of the great depression he decided to hitch-hike south and establish himself at Brighton. The two Brighton trunk murders, on which he 'scooped the pool' daily, made his fame, and Fleet Street called him. He was a Fleet Street reporter for a short time only, they quickly made him News Editor.

When he left Durham it was his dream to make enough money to buy his mother and father a small house in the south. This he did.

No reporter could have had stronger support from his News Editor than I had from Lindon Laing during my long years with the *Daily Mail*. I was indeed fortunate.

One day he bustled into the *Daily Mail* reporters' room, and gave me an order.

'Procter,' he said. 'Go home at once, take the office car. Stay home for a month, a week, a year if you like – your salary will be paid in full. You're working yourself to death, man, you're ill. You're one of my best reporters and I want you fit.'

He was a busy man but he came to see me regularly in hospital.

After some months I recovered, called on him and said: 'I shall be back on Monday.'

'That's fine, mister,' he said. 'You will be welcome.'

We never met again. A few nights later he missed his normal train to Brighton because he stayed behind to fight for a journalist who was to be retired on pension.

Lindon Laing stormed up and down the *Daily Mail* offices like an angry volcano.

'I won't have it,' he shouted. 'I won't have it. That man is still a first-class journalist, he lives only for Fleet Street. He has given his life to Fleet Street. I demand that he be allowed his typewriter, his telephone, and his desk, until the day he dies there. Retire him and you'll kill him – and you'll be b----y murderers.'

He won the fight. And he caught a much later train to Brighton. He was alone in the railway carriage, and apparently he must have felt ill, for he put his head out of the open window to get some air. He was a big man in stature, as well as genius, and he struck his head on a projection.

Reporter Anthony Hunter phoned me and said: 'Lindon's dead.'

Seeking comfort I fled to Fleet Street.

The famous Fleet Street taverns were crowded but quiet. The men and women of Fleet Street were drowning their sorrow. I saw tough, hardened, news reporters crying like babes.

Tears streamed down the cheeks of colleague Anthony Hunter. The man some reporters said they hated, the man most reporters said they feared, was dead. And Fleet Street wept.

'Never mind, Tony,' I said to Hunter. 'It took a train to kill him.'

But, in the years before, Lindon Laing helped me to become one of Fleet Street's Ace Reporters.

For eight long years I served the *Daily Mail* – eight years packed with colour, adventure, excitement. I travelled Europe. I talked with kings. I met all the famous, and infamous. I drank with murderers, film stars, great statesmen, and dustmen.

They tell me Lord Northcliffe used to say 'My proudest title is *Daily Mail* Reporter.' This was a title I bore with pride. I do not think I ever disgraced it.

Now my exclusive 'beats' against the opposition were matters for genuine pride. Sex came certainly third-place on the *Daily Mail;* the solid, vital, important news, was the life-blood of this great newspaper.

A private aeroplane was my taxi now, whenever the news required it. If the news was worth it, the *Daily Mail* would allow me to hire a train, a steamship, or a dog-sleigh.

But one thing the *Daily Mail* would not allow me to do was to buy the news.

This was a wonderful thing. For it meant that I had to rely only upon my skill and initiative to get a story. Later on, when working for the *Sunday Pictorial,* I was allowed to pay out large sums for exclusive information – but there was little personal satisfaction to a reporter who had gained a story by payment.

Lindon Laing understood the promise I had given to the Royal Air Force, he allowed me to become an accredited correspondent with the American Forces.

I shall never forget the time when I first donned the glamorous uniform of an American Army Captain – pink pants and all.

I walked proudly into one of my locals in Notting Hill and ordered a light ale, paying for it with a ten shilling note. The barmaid gave me 2s 3d change.

'What's this, Martha?' I queried.

'Hell!' she gasped. 'It's Harry Procter.' And she gave me the rest of my change.

When President Truman met the late King George VI, at Plymouth, armies of reporters and photographers were sent from London to cover the historic event.

The King and the President were to meet aboard an American warship.

On the day before the meeting a press conference was called, and the press were told they would not be allowed on board the ship. There were thousands of us, it was rightly pointed out. Had we all gone aboard the ship would have sunk.

Only an official American photographer, an official American reporter, and an official American news reel cameraman, were to be allowed aboard. The British press were out.

They would be allowed, if they wished, to board a tender, and be taken to within two miles of the historic event. A great moan went up from the British Press.

But I was delighted. To see the meeting with hundreds of other reporters was unimportant. To see it on my own, as the only representative of the British Press, would mean a scoop.

I racked my brains but could not think of any method of getting aboard. Until about 7pm when I was having a light ale at a bar. An idea came.

'Why not?' I thought. 'Simple ideas are always the best. I'll try it.'

I got the name of the commanding officer of the American warship. I had never yet known a sailor captain who was not as proud of his ship as he was of his wife or fiancée. A man who is proud of his wife likes to show her off, I reasoned.

I went into a telephone box, and dialled 'Telegrams'.

I sent a personal telegram, over the ordinary service, to the captain of the American warship. 'Have heard so much about your wonderful warship,' I said. 'I would love this opportunity of visiting her and seeing her for myself. May I come aboard?' Signed Harry Procter, *Daily Mail* War Correspondent.

Within an hour a message came for me from the American naval shore base.

'Can you come here at once?' said an officer. 'The captain invites you aboard as his personal guest. We are instructed to take you to the warship by motor launch.'

And they did.

The following morning, when my hundreds of contemporaries boarded the tender, they looked for me in vain, and said: 'Old Harry Procter's missed the boat this time.'

At that moment I was aboard the warship having breakfast with the captain.

'Do stay and meet the President,' he said.

I was within a yard of His Majesty and the President when they met, I heard every word they spoke. The following morning all the other national papers carried sulky stories, protesting about the way the British Press had been left out.

The *Daily Mail* carried no such protest. They ran my story of the historic meeting on page one, under the caption 'From Harry Procter. Aboard the American Warship...'

Back home in Yorkshire, my wife, my mother, and schoolboy son were sitting in a local cinema. The news reel was shown. On to the screen came a close-up of three men aboard the American warship.

'Look, Mum, that's my Dad' shouted my son. And he was right. I had stood, smiling, just a yard behind the two great men as they shook hands in greeting. On the screen it looked as though I was in the centre – it looked as though the three of us were talking together.

'A Meeting of the Big Three,' joked my wife.

When the *Daily Mail* sent me to France to investigate the scandal of the NAAFI's missing millions, I got a world scoop which shocked the nation.

The *Daily Mail* led the paper on the story. The same day the War Office officially denied that my story was true. Every paper in the land published this denial.

Editor Frank Owen phoned me: 'Are you happy, Harry?' was all that he asked.

'Perfectly happy, sir!' I replied.

'Then so am I,' said Frank Owen. In the teeth of War Office denials, I wrote another story for the following day, which was also splashed, and still another on the third day. On the fourth day, when the slow moving communications of Whitehall were completed, the War Office received an official report from their own investigation officers in France – the SBI – the Scotland Yard of the War Office.

That day the War Office confirmed that the *Daily Mail* had been right all along.

Of course, no newspaperman can get scoops of this kind unless he enjoys the full confidence of his superiors. Never once did Frank Owen ever doubt a report which came from me.

Frank Owen had his own methods of handling his men – even the ones who got big heads.

One day, believing I had a grievance, I wrote out my resignation, and sent it to Frank Owen. Then off I went to the London Press Club to soothe my tuppenny dignity.

A phone call came for me.

'The Editor would like you to come back to the office and see him.'

'I will not,' I replied, like a sulky schoolboy. 'Tell the Editor that I have resigned from his staff and am no longer obliged to carry out his instructions...'

The phone rang again. It was Frank Owen himself.

'Now look here, Harry,' he said. 'If you're not in my office in five minutes I'll come over there, clout you round the ear-hole, and drag you back by the scruff of your neck.'

I went back. I stood before him and tried my darndest to cling to my stupid dignity.

He gave me one glance, screwed up my resignation, threw it at me, and said: 'Now clear off and don't be such a b----y fool'.

What could a reporter do with a boss like that? Other than work like hell for him?

Frank Owen sent me off one day to cover a strike at Smithfield Market. I could not find a line in it worth writing about. I adjourned to The Clachan in Fleet Street, where several of my opposition were drinking.

Bill Jones, of the *Daily Herald,* was telling an amusing story of what he had seen in Smithfield Market. It was a funny incident about a scene when the troops moved in to get the meat moving. A young, haughty captain had shouted to a corporal: 'Corporal, handle that cow!'

'But Captain,' pleaded the corporal. 'That cow ain't dead, it kicked me.' The other reporters laughed. I returned to Smithfield Market, checked the story, found it to be true, and wrote: 'This is the story of the Captain, the Corporal, and the Cow.'

The nation laughed so much that the strikers blushed, and the strike ended. No industrial dispute can survive being laughed at.

Herald Editor Percy Cudlipp asked Bill Jones why the *Herald* did not have the story.

'But honestly,' said Bill, 'I told Harry Procter that story, and I can prove it.'

'It was my reporter who told your reporter about that story,' said Editor Cudlipp to Frank Owen.

'Maybe,' said Frank Owen. 'My father was a preacher, and one day he had a sailor for his guest. The sailor heard my father's sermon and protested that somebody else had written it. 'Maybe', said my father, 'but I preached it!' '

'You see,' added Frank Owen, 'my reporter published it.'

Bill Jones still buys me a drink.

Bill Jones even gave me another story.

It was about an incident at his home, involving his little daughter.

One night, he said, he and his wife sat round the fire discussing money – the rent, the butcher's bill, the most economical methods of buying groceries. They did not realise that their tiny daughter overheard some of the conversation.

With damp eyes Bill told me of what happened the following morning.

Mollie, his wife, and he were having breakfast when down the stairs came the kid. She had several sheets of copy paper in her hand, she had stitched them together at the left hand side. The pages were full of printed words, it must have taken her hours to do the job. She must have sat up all night.

'Daddy and Mummy,' she said. 'You have no need to ever worry about money again. 'Cos I have written a book. Here it is. I want daddy to take it to the men who make books, and the men will give Daddy lots and lots of money...'

She gave Bill the stitched copy paper. On the first page, in large, printed letters was scrawled the title of his little daughter's first book.

The title was *Jumbo goes round the World,* by Pamela Jones.

'I went and locked myself in the bathroom,' said Bill, 'holding her book in my hands. I promised her I would take it to the men who make books. I assured her it would be a best seller and that we would have all the money we could ever want.'

I went back to the *Daily Mail* office and wrote the full, rich story of the small child who wrote the book *Jumbo Goes Round the World.* No newspaperman can claim exemption when he or his become news!

Our Chief Sub was delighted with the story – there are lots of Mr and Mrs Joneses in London, and he did not ask for the occupation of the Mr Jones mentioned in my tale. The story was set up in type. Of course I gave the correct home address.

That night, when Bill Jones answered a ring on his door, he was amazed, as a *Daily Herald* reporter, to find a *Daily Mail* photographer on his doorstep.

'Can I please take a picture of the little girl who has written the book, *Jumbo Goes Round the World?*'

The story was crowded out of the *Daily Mail* through shortage of space, but it was featured in the *Continental Daily Mail.*

What I did not know at the time was that Pamela had been given six months to live because of a 'blue-baby' heart condition. Six months later she was operated on, survived, and while she was in hospital she asked for her book *Jumbo Goes Round the World.*

Pamela is now not only alive and kicking, but later won a ballet

Scholarship to the Royal Academy of Dancing – nursery for the Royal Ballet at Covent Garden.

When I spoke to her over the phone after her operation, she told me she was dedicating her 'book' to me.

Chapter Nine

So now, at long last, the former errand-boy who had dreamed a great dream in a cellar basement, was seeing that dream come true.

This was journalism at its very best, its highest. This Fleet Street really was a Street of Adventure.

I was important – not important as an individual – but I was doing a job which was vitally important to the nation.

When Sir Ben Smith, Socialist Minister of Food, refused to see an official deputation of housewives at the House of Commons on the grounds that he was 'too busy' the *Daily Mail* sent me to find out 'how busy'.

I swept into the House of Commons, on through the sacred corridors, until I found the Minister of Food sitting in an alcove, drinking tea, his feet stretched out on another chair.

'But you are not too busy, sir,' I protested. 'As a *Daily Mail* reporter, I insist that you see these women who have waited on you all day.'

He did as I told him. He returned with me to the lobby, where a private secretary was busy apologising to the housewives.

My great thrill, my great sport, was 'beating' the opposition on every possible occasion. In those days my chief opposition was the *Daily Express.*

This healthy rivalry was exciting, exhilarating, but it was as clean as the new-mown hay. Arthur Christiansen, a truly big man in the Chesterton sense, took such an interest in my defeats of his own fine reporters, that he gave me and one of my stories a complimentary mention on his own daily 'editorial bulletin'. But his News Editor could never forgive me.

Later, when 'Chris' wanted to hire me, his staff said 'No'.

The opposition reporter I respected most in those days was Frank McGarry, *Daily Express.* He was the most formidable opponent I ever knew. He was a really wonderful reporter, and he always worked as a lone wolf.

I beat Frank on important stories many and many a time. And just as many times he beat me. Never once in our lives did we ever work together, or co-operate together. When we met on an assignment we eyed each other ruthlessly; we both knew that we had to work like blazes against each other. Both our newspapers benefited. And Frank and I always had the greatest admiration and respect for each other.

I always remember my pleasure in hearing a comment made by Robert Glenton *(Sunday Express)* to an opposition news editor who was condemning me.

'It's all right for you to belittle Harry Procter,' he said. 'You've never had to work against him, I have.'

He certainly had. I remember, when he was a *Mirror* reporter, he was placed in charge of a story which had been bought up by his newspaper.

A GI Bride in England heard that her American husband was stowing away aboard a liner; it was a good romantic tale. The *Mirror* kept the bride all day at their office, but at night she had to be returned home to feed her baby.

The *Mirror* knew that I was waiting in the house next door for her to return to her home.

The *Mirror* paid me the compliment of sending a staff of six back home with the girl to prevent me from getting her story. In the *Mirror* office, the GI bride was fully informed about how enthusiastic I could be.

When she arrived home with her guards, they made a tent of coats in which she travelled from their car to her door-step – this was to prevent our photographer getting a picture.

The surprise they got was when I never showed up! I was peeping at them from the window of a darkened room. I let them get her safely installed in her home, I let them relax.

Then I knocked on her door. Foolishly they allowed her to open it – a thing which took me completely by surprise. I had prepared no plan for such a piece of good fortune.

'Come at once next door,' I said. 'Your husband is on the telephone.' She came. As she picked up the 'phone, my photographer took a perfect picture.

She said: 'But what do I do? The *Mirror* has paid me in return for my promise that I would not talk to you.'

'Tell me your story, and in return I promise not to tell the *Mirror* you've talked to me.' She agreed. Ten minutes later she was back in her home.

When the *Mirror* saw the *Mail's* first edition, with my front-page story and picture, they were somewhat dazed.

Assistant News Editor Nobby Clarke phoned Bobbie Glenton and told him of the *Mail* story.

Said Bobbie: 'Well, Procter must have flammed the story, because we can swear he has never spoken to her.'

'All right,' said Nobby Clarke, 'come back to the office, all of you, and explain how he's flammed the ruddy photograph as well.'

Bobbie Glenton certainly remembered this, and some stories later, on a murder hunt, he gave me the tanning of my life.

In those days I often worked as a team with my colleague, room-mate and friend, Anthony Hunter, a reporter I had been able to advise, when he crashed into Fleet Street, from a small provincial weekly.

Tony and I were a formidable pair when working as a team. They called us 'The Terrible Twins', and the sight of the pair of us together on a job was never a welcome one for our friends the opposition reporters.

We had our successes. But, while sharing a flat in Notting Hill we also had our humiliating failures. Like the time when 'Russian Robert' was murdered in a car parked smack outside the door of our flat.

That morning Tony and I were both on at 11am. We rushed out of our flat, passed the murder car, got in to the *Daily Mail* office, to be greeted fondly by assistant news editor Jerry Mellor, who said: 'Good! A murder on your own doorstep. I know you boys can write the best story of your lives...'

We did not know a thing about the murder on our own doorstep.

We had to return at once to our doorstep to get the story.

To my relief, I discovered that ace reporter Duncan Webb had got the story Tony and I had slept through. He gave it to us.

When the *Mirror* 'bought up' a story about a child who was loved and claimed by two mothers, they put a dozen men on the job to assure its exclusiveness.

The great exclusive was to be the tale and the pictures, the child being handed over from one mother to the other – later, on the

Sunday Pictorial, I was to give a label for such children the world over when I wrote my article 'Shuttlecock Kids'.

For the great swap the *Mirror* had to bring one mother to the other, a distance of several hundred miles. To defeat the opposition, they arranged the meeting in an independent town, 'somewhere in Britain'. The *Mail* asked me to try and defeat this attempt at exclusiveness as they thought, rightly so, the story was legitimate news.

I asked for the help of Tony Hunter. First of all he and I studied a map of Britain, and asked ourselves the question, 'If we were the *Mirror* where would we arrange the meeting?' We drew several rings on the map.

He took one town. I took another. We phoned up public houses, restaurants, hotels, places where we knew pressmen in those towns might go.

Two hours later, we knew not only the name of the town chosen for the secret meeting, but the name of the hotel, exactly who were the *Mirror* reporters and photographers on the job, which rooms they were sleeping in, which rooms the mothers were occupying, the very hour the child was to be 'passed to you please'.

It must have been horrible for the *Mirror* team to see Tony Hunter and myself walk boldly through the lounge doors of their hotel about five-thirty that evening. The team were sitting there relaxing, the two mothers with them, the child who was to be the pawn in this newspaper stunt, was playing on the floor.

The *Mirror* team grabbed their human charges as though they were parcels.

'To your rooms, to your rooms,' thundered a *Mirror* reporter. 'This is Harry Procter of the *Daily Mail*...'

He spoke of me as though I ate toasted new-born babies, with mushrooms, for my breakfast.

They notified London that I was in the hotel, that Hunter and I had booked rooms. London sent up reinforcements. The new orders were that the two mothers and the child were not under any circumstances to be allowed out of their bedrooms.

Somebody ordered a meal for the mothers. Waiter Harry Procter arrived with the trolley. Bell-boy Tony Hunter arrived later with a requested tray of light ales.

It was a state of siege, a war of nerves. But the *Mirror* were confident that, by having greater numerical forces, signed contracts, and the keys to the bedrooms, they would win.

Mirror Day News Editor, Kenneth Hord stayed on duty that night because of the emergency.

By sheer chance I picked up an extension telephone and overheard reporter Joan Reeder saying to News Editor Kenneth Hord: 'I assure you everything is all right. Harry Procter knows it's impossible and has given up...'

'You're mistaken Joan...' I could not help calling into the telephone. Then I could have bitten my tongue off.

There was a silence. Then Kenneth Hord: 'Joan! Joan! That was Harry Procter's voice!'

'No! No, Ken! It couldn't have been.'

'But I know his voice. I heard it distinctly. Good gracious, he must be in the room with you.'

I am told that Joan Reeder, a girl whose good fellowship and comradeship I enjoyed for years after this, looked under the bed, peeped behind the curtains.

The story told later was that I must have been in the headquarters of the GPO at Oxford, and an investigation was made. The GPO was honourably vindicated. Some swore they had seen me swarming a telephone pole, tapping the wires.

Anthony Hunter and I did a hard, accurate, and full story for the *Daily Mail,* which was published on page one and which, we are still certain, was every bit as good as the *Mirror* story.

How did we get the story?

I am sorry that is a secret I cannot reveal, for it is not my secret, it is the secret of my Fleet Street friend and colleague, Anthony Hunter.

But it was a team job. It most certainly was! But the best team job Tony and I ever did was when we stormed our way into a foreign embassy and made the foreign ambassador confess he had tried to shoot one of his staff.

When he was Chief of the Kent County CID Superintendent Frank Smeed went to Canterbury on a big murder investigation. A Canadian bride was found murdered in a lonely lane.

Superintendent Smeed refused to see the press. I worked on the investigation on my own, took my report to Sir Percy Sillitoe, the Chief Constable of Kent, before I phoned it to my office, saying I thought there were facts in it the police ought to know. The Chief Constable took me himself to see Smeed.

Superintendent Smeed was grateful; he gladly accepted my offer of help. He and I worked on several murder investigations after this, always as good friends, always as a helpful team.

Any good CID man knows that it is folly to ignore the Press. The crime reporter investigates dozens of murders every year, the CID man in charge perhaps only one. Usually the police chiefs and the Press work in full harmony, in complete trust, and in this way justice is well served.

In *Lilliput* magazine, I once wrote: 'When I can't sleep, I don't count sheep, I count the murderers in my life.'

Every newspaper I worked for wanted me to specialise in crime – I always refused. Some of the biggest scoops of my life have been murder scoops. But I never wanted the crown of 'crime reporter'.

There are more important things for a journalist to write about than murder.

Crime and murder are fascinating sometimes, particularly when you have the opportunity, as I often had, of meeting the murderer personally and getting to know him.

Writing the life story of a murderer – and I have written dozens – is intimate work. When you have finished you feel you know the killer better than you know your own brother. By the time you have talked to his wet-nurse, his school-teachers, his friends, his employers, his parents, his aunts, you know him so well that you cannot help but feel upset when they hang him.

I met Neville Heath one lunch time in the City Club, just off Fleet Street. It was on a Wednesday, the day before he murdered Marjorie Gardner at Notting Hill in a room only a hundred yards from the flat I then shared with colleague Anthony Hunter.

I had loaned a free-lance journalist £25. The journalist wanted the money to pay Heath, for Heath had promised to fly him to Copenhagen on the following Saturday. He wanted me to OK 'Colonel Heath', who had, in fact, as we afterwards discovered, several convictions for fraud.

I liked Neville Heath from the very first beer we had together. He was without doubt one of the most handsome men I ever saw, and he had great personal charm.

One thing – and one thing only – made me suspicious of him. He carried a leather flying helmet, which he swung to and fro as he talked to me.

'Why?' I asked him. 'A doctor does not carry his stethoscope with him when he goes for a drink.'

I bumped into him again in the evening at the Nags Head in Kinnerston Street, Knightsbridge, where 'Acid Bath' Haigh had also been a customer.

Heath bought me a pint of bitter, but before I could finish it he was called to the telephone. It was Marjorie Gardner, making a date with him which ended in her death. I said: 'Have one before you go?' But he was in a hurry. We arranged to meet at my friend's house at Stanmore, Middlesex, on the following Saturday.

On the Friday I was at Oxford, covering an inquiry into alleged cruelty to cats. I came back in the evening and, on walking down Notting Hill Gardens, saw a small army of reporters near my flat.

'What's happened?' I asked. 'A murder or something?'

'Looked like a murder,' said Sydney Brock, a reporter-colleague. 'But it turns out to be an abortion.'

That night I went into one of my locals, the Sun and Splendour, where I met a policeman friend.

'On the murder, Harry?' he asked.

'It isn't a murder,' I said. 'Just an abortion.'

'An abortion is it?' said my policeman friend, eyeing his glass of beer. 'Then it's the queerest abortion I ever heard of. The dead woman has seventeen ugly whip-marks on her back. And her ankles are tied with a handkerchief.'

I stared straight ahead, and thought quickly. My friend was a man whose information could be relied upon.

'Repeat one thing to me,' I said quietly, through the corner of my mouth. 'Forget the whip-marks for the moment. Are you sure her ankles were tied?'

'Sure!'

Then it must be murder, I decided. For no abortion could account for tied ankles, let alone whip-marks.

I went off on the trail. An hour later I phoned the *Daily Mail* with the greatest crime scoop of the year. I had the full, and the first, story of the most sadistic murder of the century. I dictated.

The Night Editor said: 'You must be wrong. The Press Association and every other reporter in Fleet Street say this is an abortion.'

I almost went crazy with rage. I raced to the office, and shouted my anger at every executive I could find. Lindon Laing had gone off for the weekend.

'Go and have a drink,' they urged. 'You're wrong!'

'If I'm wrong I'll never show my face in Fleet Street again.'

On the following Sunday they were so abject, they would have given me the bust of Lord Northcliffe from the hall had I asked for it.

Of course, at this stage, I did not know that Neville Heath was the murderer. And on the Saturday I went to Stanmore to keep my appointment with him.

But by this time the evening paper bills were screaming 'Notting Hill Murder. Police Seek Man'.

At Stanmore, Heath never kept the appointment.

'I'll phone him at his room,' said my friend. 'He lives in Notting Hill Gardens, just near you...'

'In where...?'

I phoned Scotland Yard. They sent CID officers racing to Stanmore to interview my friend and me. We gave them a full description of Neville George Heath, 'Wanted for Murder'.

While on the run Heath phoned me at the *Daily Mail* office. He said he was speaking from a remote spot in Surrey. Would I bring him £50? I promised to dash down at once by car, and I did, but I phoned Scotland Yard first.

I arrived at the place, walked down the road, and was immediately arrested by two plain-clothes men. My hair, eyes, and complexion, were the same as Heath's and the local police took me for him.

I shall always wish that Heath had kept that appointment with me. For a few days later he murdered ex-Wren Doreen Marshall in a lonely chine near Bournemouth.

Just before they hanged him the Governor asked him: 'Would you like a whisky?'

'Can you make it a double, sir?' he said.

Certainly the most dignified murderer I ever met was Thomas John Ley, former Minister of Justice in the Government of New South Wales, convicted in 1946 of the murder of John Mudie, a barman. This murder case, though obscured now by the infamous Christie, Heath, and Haigh cases, was a fascinating one, for both the professional and amateur criminologists.

Thomas John Ley was sentenced to death with Lawrence John Smith, for their part in what we newspapermen named 'The Chalk Pit Murder'.

It was 9.30 on a dark November night when I knocked at the door of No 9 Beaufort Gardens, Kensington, which was opened by the corpulent, immaculately dressed, heavy-jowled, Thomas John Ley. I told him I would like a chat with him about the body of a barman found in a chalk pit in the wilds of Surrey.

The man was marvellous. He never batted an eyelid, he never paled, but he stood at his door with a puzzled, friendly smile.

'But whatever could that have to do with me?' he asked.

He was courteous and friendly. He invited me into the well-furnished flat, and rather ostentatiously asked me what I would like to drink. I am a mild-and-bitter man, but I remember testing his stock by mentioning a few vintage wines. He had them all. He delighted and astonished me when I asked him for Napoleon brandy. He produced a fat, black bottle, and poured it out generously.

It was a friendly visit. Ley had a mistress, aged sixty-six. It was later proved that he had murdered Mudie in the cellar underneath the room in which we drank because he believed his mistress had had an affair with the barman. The former Minister of Justice saw me to his door, shook my hand, and said: 'I will keep your card. If, however, I should need you, I will let you know.'

The day after his arrest I was phoned by his son, Clive Ley, with whom I remained in constant touch throughout the trial, in fact until his father's death in Broadmoor Lunatic Asylum. His wife, a frail, sweet lady, who flew in from Australia, made me her friend, confidante, and protector, during her ordeal in England.

The Wigwam Murder of 1943 was described to me by a Scotland Yard officer as 'the greatest detective achievement of the past century'. But I remember it mainly by my brief friendship with August Sangret, 29-year-old French-Indian soldier, from Canada, who was hanged on 2nd May, 1943, for the murder of his girl friend, 19-year-old Joan Pearl Wolfe.

Before he killed her and buried her in a shallow, lonely grave, Sangret and Pearl lived together in a wigwam made of saplings, near Godalming.

Sangret and I often drank together before his arrest, and as a reporter in search of news, I found him helpful. He hated the police, and said to me: 'They want to get me out of this country, but they never will.'

But the Yard did more. They got him out of this world.

The best crime reporters of Fleet Street spent weeks covering this murder assignment. But Montague Smith of the *Daily Mail*, the old-timer who had worked as a youth for Lord Northcliffe, scooped the lot of us daily, almost all the time.

John George Haigh, the acid-bath murderer, got the shock of his life when I opened the door of his room at the Onslow Court Hotel, Kensington, on the Sunday before his arrest.

'How did you know I was here?' he snapped, for the army of crime reporters waiting for him in the front hall believed him out.

He was a Yorkshireman, and it was my Yorkshire accent which thawed the air, and soon we were chatting over a cup of tea about Leeds, Wakefield, the best pubs in Morley.

'The police are a lot of imbeciles,' Haigh said. 'They couldn't catch colds. They have nothing on me, but even if they had they'd never prove it. To an intelligent man like me these coppers are like children...'

I took a risk and called his bluff. 'You're a dead pigeon already, Mr Haigh,' I said. 'You've told the police you parked your car in the car park behind Victoria Street when you went to meet Mrs Durande Deacon,' (one of his victims) 'but the old man there charges a shilling, issues a ticket, and keeps a record of every car. I've just left him, and you're not on his list...'

Haigh went white. My bluff had worked. Once prove a man a liar, and you pose the question, 'why does he lie?'

I told the police, and on the Tuesday he was arrested.

Haigh had none of the glamorous charm of Heath, but he was a very dapper dresser. On the night before he was executed he requested that his suit, socks, and tie be sent to Madame Tussaud's to clothe his effigy. His last note, written to a friend of mine, made the following comment about his execution: 'I go forward to find my mission in other forms.'

In the beautiful village of Pratts Bottom, Kent, where I now live, and write this, lives a neighbour who spoils my Saturday evening drink at the Bulls Head by repeating to me a great truth: 'Remember Haigh? I used to sleep with him when I was a kid of eight.'

My neighbour knew Haigh and his family intimately. He tells me

114

that few men could have possibly had a more religious upbringing than Haigh.

His parents were good God-fearing people, who read their Bible every day. Daily they taught their son the Ten Commandments.

I spent long weeks compiling the life story of Haigh.

Chapter Ten

It was while I was on the *Daily Mail* that I discovered a murder.

The body of a baby had been washed ashore from the Thames, and nobody was interested. The police at first believed it to be 'just another still-born'.

But when I discovered that the baby had a piece of sticking plaster around its arm, I decided at once: 'This must be murder.'

As a father who had sat sweating in maternity hospitals, I knew that, in hospital, as soon as a baby is born, they write 'Baby Smith' on a piece of sticking-plaster and secure this to the arm.

Lindon Laing agreed with my theory. He and I worked all day, phoning up every maternity hospital in the Greater London Area, asking if a baby had been born with the name on the plaster.

We drew blanks. So I decided to try the maternity wards of the big general hospitals.

Yes, a baby of that name had been born, said a matron. Some weeks before, to an unmarried girl. She gave me the girl's name and address. I saw the girl's mother.

Within a few hours I knew the name of the murderer, and I knew his motive.

Laing and I wrote the story together, it was a difficult story to get through legal channels. We sent a copy of our story to Scotland Yard who immediately began a murder hunt on the strength of it.

The *Daily Mail* splashed my story. When I arrived in the office about noon, Mr Sidney Horniblow, at that time the Editor, sent for me, said he regretted he must fire me.

'A man is suing us saying that today you have accused him of murder. I have decided to pay him substantial damages.'

In the room was Mr Donald Geddes, the most brilliant newspaper lawyer in Britain. Geddes knew my work well, and silently he awaited my comments.

'Fire me, sir,' I said, 'as you please, but don't pay this man one single penny, or you'll regret it when they hang him.'

'What?' said Editor Horniblow. 'Do you mean this man may be proved guilty of murder?'

'I am certain he will be hanged.'

Said Lawyer Geddes: 'Procter is perfectly right. The *Daily Mail* cannot pay money to a murderer. If Procter is right – and I believe him to be – we must refuse to pay, and support our reporter to the hilt.'

I was not fired. The man was hanged.

I was in Paris, having a wonderful time, when I got a dramatic plea from Lindon Laing.

'Please catch the next plane back. There is a first class murder, and the *Express* have beaten us every day for a week.' I flew to London at once.

For a week the *Express* had really cleaned up in Fleet Street.

Said Lindon Laing: 'I leave it all to you. Do what you want, but beat them, mister!'

I went to a remote town in Wales. Here I found that the *News of the World* had bought up exclusively the life story of a girl who was to be jointly charged with an American soldier, of a terrible murder.

The *Daily Mail* did not buy news. They depended on the skill of their reporters to get it.

The *Sunday Pictorial* also developed the highest degree of skill amongst its reporters, by recognising that adventitious aids might also be necessary to loosen tongues which would otherwise refuse to wag.

But this girl's life story was one that fascinated me.

Within a few hours I got it all. I obtained an astounding diary, the girl's own diary, which told me everything about her I wanted to know. I sent it at once by registered post to Lindon Laing, who copied every page by Photostat, then took it personally to Scotland Yard, who were most grateful to receive it.

The girl's parents gave me the rest of her story.

Said the delighted Lindon Laing: 'The girl's diary alone is worth £1,000.' I got it for free. I am not mentioning the girl's name for, after a long prison sentence, she repented and reformed, and she is now a good citizen.

The last time we met I was glad to observe that she was a further proof of my theory that all criminals can, with training and treatment, be restored to society as honest, law-abiding people.

I have always written against the death penalty, I have lectured against the death penalty. My experiences convince me that at least two men, innocent of murder, were hanged during my years in Fleet Street. I am thankful that the death penalty, in most cases, has almost been abolished in Britain.

But the close contact which men of Fleet Street must keep with tragedy and crime does not mean that their lives are continually doleful and depressing. The rich humour, which abounds in Fleet Street, is never absent.

I shall never forget 'The Mystery of Whalebone Corner', when the skeleton of an old lady was found in a lonely cottage near Colchester, because on that assignment, Bill Jones of the *Daily Herald* was in his best form.

Bill has left Fleet Street now, but the place is the poorer without him. Although a good reporter in every sense, Bill was always the court jester of the band of top-line Fleet Street men who for years followed the big news.

When I arrived at the tumbling-down cottage, I found that Bill had, without police permission, more or less installed himself as its inhabitant. He had discovered that the creaking door was swinging open, and had gone inside. He was digging among rubble and debris, sorting out old books, old papers, eagerly searching for some clue which might help solve the mystery of the missing occupant of the cottage and, also, provide him with a story.

'So YOU have arrived,' he muttered. 'Well, seeing you're here, take your hands out of your pockets, and help me search.'

We were hard at it in silence, then a dark shadow loomed over us. It was a police constable.

'Now then! Now then!' he said.

This was most unfortunate, I decided. At the very best we were trespassing. And at the very worst…? Well, I dared not think.

Bill looked up, pushed his glasses from the end of his nose.

'Hello, constable, and a very good morning to you,' he said. 'So glad you came, for I was just going to come to your house.'

'And why?' asked the constable, dryly.

'To show you one of the most remarkable things, constable, I ever saw in the whole of my life. A thing which will interest you, fascinate you, and which you will always be grateful that you actually saw. Here, just look at that!'

Bill handed to the constable a dusty, thick, very ancient book. Whether it was a first edition of the *Pickwick Papers,* or a collection of the *Dead Sea Scrolls,* I had not the slightest idea. I just hoped that it was something interesting, and decided to leave our unenviable situation to Bill.

The constable took the old volume in his hands, and opened it. 'What might it be?' he asked. 'Arabic?'

Solemnly Bill shook his head. 'It is a Bible in shorthand, constable. Just think, what a fascinating thing. There are people, constable, who go to colleges, universities, and evening classes, hoping to acquire the art of writing shorthand.

'Some may spend years battling to grasp the mysteries of wiggles and waggles, thick lines and thin lines. And, perhaps, after years, they are only able to write an odd line or two in shorthand. Yet look what you have in your hand. Some great man must have been so accomplished that he has been able to write down the entire book of Holy Writ, and in very good shorthand, too.'

The constable was thawing a little. I hoped he had stopped jingling his handcuffs. He looked at the open page with interest.

'So this is shorthand,' he mused. 'It just looks like scribble to me. Tell me,' he said, with respect, 'could you sir, read these wiggles, just as I read printed orders?'

Now we are sunk, I thought, for despite what Bill might say to the contrary, I have always maintained that – apart from a strange concoction of abbreviated writing of his own – he can neither read nor write shorthand.

'Pass me the book, constable,' said Bill.

And he began to read.

The Lord is my Shepherd, I shall not want. He leadeth me into green pastures. He taketh me beside the still waters. He restoreth my soul...

It was so impressive that I thought the constable was going to remove his helmet. He looked at Bill with profound respect.

'Amazing, sir. Really is amazing.' He looked lovingly at the dusty, tea-stained volume. 'Do you think, sir, it would be all right, sir, if I took it along to my missus, just to let her look at it?'

Bill made a gesture. 'My dear constable,' said Bill, 'not only would it be all right, but it is your duty. You cannot leave such a valuable book to lie here, in a deserted cottage, where the lock has fallen off the door. You must guard it constable, guard it.'

'I'll take it to my missus at once,' said the constable, and left us.

'Come on Harry,' said Bill. 'Let's beat it from here, quickly, before the CID arrive.'

We were told so many stories about the lonely cottage and its vanished occupant that, despite their colour, all our news desks eventually pleaded: 'Please send no more.'

I had a whole column running in the *Mail,* and I decided it was time I went off to the village tavern to relax over a glass of beer.

Said an old inhabitant. 'I'll tell you a remarkable thing about that old cottage. An' you can publish it in your paper, for it be true.'

It would have been rude not to listen, but I swore I would not add another line.

'Behind the old cottage stands a giant oak,' said the local inhabitant. 'Black George, the pirate, was hanged on that spot, just 200 years ago. And, as was the custom, they buried him there, placing, as they always did, an acorn in his mouth, and from that little acorn that mighty oak tree...'

Wearily I decided I must add a few lines about the pirate, the acorn, and the mighty oak. I did, and it was accepted.

'But,' said the night news editor to me later, 'the Chief Sub says I have to tell you, Harry, that he doesn't believe the acorn was placed in the pirate's mouth...'

The police and the press hunted for days for the body, or the person, of the missing old lady.

Eventually they found her skeleton, just underneath the pile of old books and debris which Bill and I were sifting when the constable called. Had we not been interrupted we might have solved the mystery sooner than the police.

In the beginning 'The Mystery of Whalebone Corner' was an official murder investigation, but later the murder theory was abandoned.

Chapter Eleven

Obviously my eight years as a *Daily Mail* reporter had many exciting and fascinating moments.

One of these was when I was a guest at the 'stag party' of the Duke of Edinburgh, then Prince Philip, held at a Park Lane hotel on the night before he became the husband of Princess Elizabeth, later to become Queen Elizabeth II.

It was a private party, a secret party, but news leaked to Fleet Street about it, and reporters and photographers were hurried to Park Lane. They got no further than the entrance hall.

I was the last to arrive, but I, too, was refused a step further than the hall.

I went into a telephone kiosk, phoned up Lord Louis Mountbatten, who was with Prince Philip and his friends in a private banqueting room.

'Sir,' I said. 'I am a *Daily Mail* reporter. May I present the compliments of my editor, Frank Owen. My editor believes, sir, that this private party is a great naval occasion, and has sent me here to ask if we may have permission to take a photograph of Prince Philip, yourself, and the other naval gentlemen present.'

Lord Louis talked it over with Prince Philip, then phoned me back.

'Come up, *Daily Mail*,' he said.

Arrangements were made to pass photographer George Elam and myself through the security ring. Prince Philip welcomed us and gave us a drink.

George Elam worked quietly, but he was excited. This should have been one of the greatest picture scoops of his career.

But there are few fools in Fleet Street. The other boys downstairs sensed what had happened and they all made a joint protest: 'Why should only the *Daily Mail* be allowed to take pictures of this historic occasion?' They had a point. Their point was communicated to Prince Philip. Right at the end he allowed a few other photographers in. George was heartbroken. For his work, and mine, had rewarded all. The decision meant his pictures were not exclusive.

It was a jolly party. Prince Philip went to George Elam and asked permission to borrow his camera. 'You've had your fun,' he said. 'Now let me have a go. I will take a photograph of the press to let them see what it feels like.' He pushed us all on to a settee – by this time we were roaring with laughter – and after a little instruction from George Elam, he took our picture with George's camera. George Elam treasures that photograph – a photograph he did not take. It was the only time I had ever seen George Elam trust his beloved press camera to an amateur.

George Elam had taken many photographs, and he had left a small pyramid of used flash bulbs. Prince Philip seized on these with delight – he was in a light-hearted mood. He began to pelt George Elam and me, playfully, with our own flash bulbs and George and I discovered that the man who is today perhaps one of the world's most popular men, was a darned good shot with a flash bulb.

As a *Daily Mail* war correspondent with the American forces, I roved France, Germany, Holland, Belgium. I ignored the hard war news – this was churned into every Fleet Street office by the agency tape machines.

I searched for the light, bright, story-with-a-difference.

Like the one about the soldier who was sent with important papers to deliver to an officer in a pill box. Politely he knocked on the door of the pill box. A German officer opened it, and stared in amazement. Our lad had gone to the wrong pill box. 'I turned and ran like 'ell,' he said.

With Morley Cassidy, of the *Philadelphia Tribune,* I ran into a grim tale in France. German soldiers, dressed in American Army uniforms, were filtering through our lines. They were walking up to American soldiers on lonely lanes, saying: 'Give me a light buddy,' and shooting to kill at close range – inches close.

This was not war! This was murder!

The censors would not pass our story. I took a jeep and drove non-stop to Paris, where I saw, for a few minutes only, General Eisenhower.

'Sir, this story must be told,' I requested.

He saw to it that my story was released.

I flew with the Royal Air Force on several operations.

Apart from the stories flying with the RAF got me, it was a great personal satisfaction to me to realise that at long last I had joined an air crew – even though it was only as a guest.

I was chosen to represent the *Daily Mail* and fly with the RAF on the Rhine crossing, one of the biggest allied air operations of the war. It was an unforgettable experience. It frightened me to death.

For two weeks I lived with the boys who were to do the job, in a sealed camp 'Somewhere in England'. I was not allowed to communicate with my office – nor they with me. We lived with the crews of the bombers, with the crews of the gliders, due to be towed across the Rhine. We ate with them, slept with them, drank with them. What a glorious bunch they were.

Each reporter was allowed to pick, for himself, the bomber crew to whom he would trust his life. All the skippers were keen to have us as their guests. They coaxed us, argued over us, even played cards for us.

One night I was having a beer in the officers' mess, when a voice at my elbow said: 'Move over lad, and let's get t't' bar.'

Thrilling at the sound of my native accent I turned to see a big, burly RAF skipper at my side.

'Where does thar come from?' I said. 'Pudsey?'

'I do an' all,' he grinned. 'And thar's a Yorkshireman, isn't thar? What the 'ell is a Yorkshire lad doin' in a monkey suit like thine?'

I wore American uniform.

This great, boisterous, Yorkshireman was a former Pudsey bus driver. Now a commissioned officer in the RAF, he was a veteran bomber pilot. At once I decided that, if he would have me, this was the man with whom I was to fly across the Rhine. I have every confidence in Yorkshiremen.

'Thee come wi' me lad,' he said, as though he were inviting me to go with him on a charabanc trip from Leeds to Scarboro'. 'I'll look after thee.'

He certainly kept his promise.

The following day, high over Germany, with anti-aircraft guns pounding below, with flak peppering on our starboard wing, with the air dense – above, below, on both sides – with hundreds of allied bombers, I looked at him. My heart, it seemed to me, was noisier than the engines. He gave me a Yorkshire grin.

'By rights lad,' he said, 'we should turn left 'ere an' go back on't same road we came in on. But I'm goin' up if it's all t'same to thee.'

And up he went, zig-zagging his huge bomber through the maze of other aircraft, up and above the flak.

Ahead of us a British bomber burst into flames.

It was the bomber carrying the *Daily Express* reporter, Geoffrey Bokhor.

'I'll get yer 'ome, lad,' he said.

And I wondered if, perhaps, when he was a Pudsey bus-driver, he might have promised the same thing to my brother, who lives in Pudsey.

We had dropped our glider, 'Gertie', but we were trailing our tow rope. This had to be dropped off where we could be sure it would not damage other aircraft.

The flak rose high, other bombers burst in the air. I thought of the wing commander, who had called me over at five that morning.

'Why aren't you shaved?' he said. 'Go and shave at once, you must be ready to present a clean-shaven face to the enemy if you don't get back.'

The Pudsey bus-driver and his crew got me back all right. It was a Saturday; I had decided to give my story to our Sunday paper, the *Sunday Dispatch*. My full, descriptive story of the Rhine crossing took up most of the front page that Sunday. And I got a full first edition beat on the other Sunday papers.

Charles Eade, then *Dispatch* editor, gave me his personal thanks.

The *Dispatch* used my photograph on page one with my article. This photograph was the only one they could find. It had been taken several weeks before, after I had attended a hectic Fleet Street party, by a photographer who merely wanted to test out a new type of flash bulb.

My mother wrote to me from Yorkshire: 'I could see by your photograph, son, what a terrible ordeal you had gone through,' she said.

Chapter Twelve

Journalists hate to write about each other. They rarely do. Perhaps as a race they are too self-centred, or too mean to say something nice about a rival writer. Usually, reporters wait until a colleague is dead before they write about him; then they give three endearing paragraphs in *World's Press News* (the trade paper of the newspaper world) to a man who has spent his life writing millions of words about other people.

I refuse to wait to write about those two naughty gnomes of Fleet Street, Maurice Fagence and Paul Bewsher, both still all-round active and first-class reporters after Lord knows just how many years.

Maurice Fagence and Paul Bewsher are the two original Northcliffe imps. They worked for the famous Lord Northcliffe when they were young, cheeky, and irresponsible. And, like all the old Northcliffe boys of Fleet Street, Maurice and Paul always refer to 'The Chief' in the present tense... I secretly think they don't believe he's dead.

To them, working for Northcliffe was similar to robbing orchards – never dull. They adored it. They heard every word the great man spoke to them and to others, and with their tape-recorder minds they have stored up the lot.

They rarely get together. I am certain they love each other like brothers, but I am just as certain they would rather stand barefoot on a hot stove for an hour than stick an hour of each other's company. All those who know them understand why.

You see MF and PB are the giants among the raconteurs of Fleet Street. Pint-sized giants maybe – Paul is small and thin, and Maurice is short and podgy – but no man ever lived who could successfully challenge them in bar-room talk. People never talk to Paul Bewsher. They just listen. People never talk to Maurice Fagence. They just listen. So how on earth could you ever expect to see Paul and Maurice in the same bar or café?'

I saw them together only once – and I have known both for years. That meeting took me three days to plan.

That night I saw the battle of the giants. Forty reporters sat in silence for eight hours, listening to them fight each other with words, with a swash-buckling eloquence which I swear would have kept anyone but Churchill in awed and envious quiet.

It was a gentlemanly contest. Maurice would bow to Paul, Paul would bow to Maurice, then Maurice would choose his weapons.

'Did I ever tell you the story behind the kidnapping of Charlie Chaplin?' he would inquire, looking not at his audience but at his glass. 'You did,' Paul would say, with an honourable doff, 'but do tell me again.' And then, with only words for weapons, Maurice would enter the ring like a toreador and tell… and tell, oh such a tale! When it was ended Paul would smile his appreciation and wait until the tumult of applause died. There would be no attempt by Maurice at a second tale. With fairness verging almost on fanaticism each gave the other, in turn, the floor.

'I say, old man,' Paul would then come in (he has never been known to tell one story yet without this introduction), 'do you remember…'

This great feast of conversation which took place at the Queen's Hotel, Folkestone, went on until long past dawn. Sitting at the feet of these great masters of tale-telling, time meant nothing, to any of us – none of us were tired.

The following night each maestro was holding court at different pubs, each with his own flock of adoring reporters, there to do two things only – drink and listen.

When I was younger, even less wise than today, I now and again made the mistake of trying to tell a Paul Bewsher story, or a Maurice Fagence story. If I could really tell them I would write them all down, I would make the greatest book of stories in the world, and I would make my fortune. But the 'Bewsher story', and the 'Fagence story', are things no one can steal – not even one from the other. The PB stories are distinct from the MF stories, they have different melodies, different octaves, and they need different instruments. No one could play Bach like Bach.

They call Paul Bewsher the Peter Pan of Fleet Street – he's the reporter who never grew up. He must have told me a hundred stories. He is in his best form about two in the morning – 'My eyes could never stand the daylight.' At dawn he gropes his way to bed. 'Nothing is worse on the eyes than daylight,' he perpetually complains.

Which is his best story? One of his fifty or so Lord Northcliffe anecdotes? Or one from the series about the terrible things which have happened to Paul Bewsher in every corner of the globe? Or one of the many classical fictional pieces, which he has told again and again to the same audiences right over the years; audiences who can never tire of hearing the Bewsher tales.

Ever heard the story of the Wooden Bayonet? Unless you heard Paul Bewsher tell it you haven't heard it at all – it was just a bloodless echo that you caught. Or the story of the Man Who Caught the 10.30 train from King's Cross to Newcastle? Or the one about the little man who spoke a language no one knew? Or the Bengal Cycling and Tourists' Club? Sit down, clever Dick, on the front row, for I tell you, you never really heard one of these tales unless you heard them told by PB.

Shall I tell them to you now? Shall I blazes! I know when I'm licked.

Paul Bewsher, the mischievous, delightful imp. A hundred times have I been green with envy at his eloquence. But I'll never forget the night when sixty people at a Park Lane party stamped their feet and thumped their hands demanding that he tell them the story of the Bengal Cycling and Tourists' Club. He refused. And then, just as I thought they were going to call the fire brigade, Paul climbed on to the table, and told them the story of why he could only tell that tale once every seven years. That story was almost as good as the original tale. And it was new.

Maestro Maurice Fagence is different. Not for him the classic joke. To Maurice, conversation is religion, and not a word must be wasted. All his tales are from life.

Most of his stories begin with a reference to Lord Northcliffe. 'I remember the Chief once telling me...' he will begin, and every ear tunes to his wavelength. I never knew Northcliffe in the flesh, I wish I had, but I feel I know the man intimately from the many wonderful stories about him told to me by Maurice Fagence.

Down at Seaton, Devon, on a murder assignment, Maurice and I stayed at the Beach Hotel. Maurice was the star turn – once-nightly and all-nightly, at the centre bar there. Visitors and residents would flock into the bar shortly after opening time, to look sheepishly around for Maurice. I have watched them arrange their chairs in the large bar as seats are arranged in cinemas. And they would wait in silence, drinking, but not talking, even amongst themselves.

Maurice would enter. The crowd would part like the waters of the Red Sea, to allow him to get to the bar. Then the breathless hush, the rippling tense excitement, as they watched him taste his first pint of bitter. For a moment or two he would tease them all, me included, by his silence. And then with the gay twinkle I suppose you would see in the eye of every confident knight going out to battle, he would say:

'I remember the chief – Lord Northcliffe, of course – calling me into his office when I was a raw recruit in Fleet Street, and saying to me "Fagence"…'

From then onwards it was Sunday Night at the Palladium for me and the rest of Seaton.

Again I wouldn't dare to tell you a Fagence story. But for me his best ever is the story of 'Lord Northcliffe and the Pimple-Faced Boy'. I am willing to give you the skeleton plot, bare, fleshless bones which have earned me many a free pint in all parts of Europe. I am unable to supply the meat.

Lord Northcliffe, according to Maurice, put up a notice on the board, saying that if any member of the staff was in any personal trouble he had to apply for help to his immediate superior. This notice was read by a little red-haired tea-boy, whose face was one mass of pimples – a kid who had worked for the *Daily Mail* for two weeks only.

The kid read the notice, then went over to the man in charge of the tape-room and asked: 'Please sir, could I have the loan of three pounds ten shillings?' The *Daily Mail's* humblest executive stared at the pimply-faced boy in horror, clouted him round the ear for his impudence, and told him to be off and wash the teacups.

Then he went to the Assistant News Editor and said: 'By the way sir, have you heard the latest? Cheeky young kid, face full of pimples, only worked here two weeks, comes up to me as bold as brass this morning and says to me…'

The Assistant News Editor roared with laughter, told it to the News Editor. The News Editor told it the Chief Cashier with embellishments. Up, and up, and up, went the story of the Pimply-

Faced Boy, until the tale reached the ears of the Assistant Chairman. By this time the entire building of Northcliffe House was rocking with laughter at the brass-faced impudence of the lad with the pimples on his face.

The Chief arrived! The Managing Editor said to him: 'By the way sir, I heard a very funny one this morning, you'll like it... Boy in the tape-room, red-hair, only so big, pimples all over his face... Makes you wonder what the youngsters are coming to these days sir... The kid had the audacity to...'

The Chief did not laugh. He asked a question.

'Why did the boy want to borrow three pounds ten?'

The Managing Editor did not know. But the Chief wanted to know so the Managing Editor sent for the Editor who had told him the story. The Editor didn't know either, so the News Editor was sent for. Eventually every executive, big and small, was lined up in the Chief's room. All had enjoyed the funny story about the Pimply-Faced Boy, but not one of them could tell the great man why the kid was so damned impudent.

So, before the great desk was brought the Pimply-Faced Boy himself. Shivering with fear, crying and snivelling, he told the Chief he was sorry, but his father died last week, and unless his mother could raise the mortgage money due, three pounds ten – all would be flung into the street.

The Chief told his giants what he thought in Saxon English. And before the day was over, the mortgage was paid in full.

Maurice never told me what became of the Pimply-Faced Boy.

I wonder where, and who he is today? I wonder...

I remember meeting Paul Bewsher on that terrible night in Le Havre, the day the great liner *La Liberté* capsized and sank in Le Havre harbour.

I was shot from the *Daily Mail* office like an arrow from a bow. The office car hurried me to the French Embassy to get my visa stamped on my passport, our private plane, engine running, waited for me at Croydon.

The man who stamped the passports at the French Embassy had gone to lunch – could I come back at 3.30pm?

And there was this great French national disaster! And there was I, the man who had to get this important story for the *Daily Mail!* So the world had to wait until some clerk ate his egg and chips.

'I'll go without a visa,' I decided, raced to the airport, and an hour later I landed at the airport behind Le Havre.

I talked my way through. I ran out on to the French country road, hoping to thumb a lift to the harbour.

A car pulled up. 'Most certainly,' said the driver, in flawless English. 'I know just where the *Liberté* lies, I will take you there...'

Of all the millions of motorists in France, I had to pick on this particular one for a four-mile lift.

'I'm grateful,' I said. 'I'm in such a hurry. I am a reporter on the London *Daily Mail* – I want the story. Had a terrible job getting through the security here – you see I didn't have time to get my passport stamped...'

'How interesting,' said my good Samaritan. 'Here is my card...' I was suitably impressed. He was an Inspector of the French Surete – the French Criminal Investigation Department.

He drove me to Le Havre, handed me to the local gendarmes, who locked me in a comfortable cell.

Later on two plain-clothes members of the police came along.

'How sorry we are, Monsieur Procter' one said. 'But it is only for tonight. Tomorrow I shall fine you a few francs, and you will be free.'

I couldn't have cared less if tomorrow I was to be thrown into the Bastille. It was tonight I was worried about, tonight, the wrecked *La Liberté,* and the first edition of the *Daily Mail.*

They brought me in some good coffee and rolls.

'We are sorry we cannot give you a good meal, Monsieur Procter. There is a delightful restaurant across the road, and if you or I could afford it we could all go over there and have an excellent dinner. But, as we cannot afford...'

A nod is as good as a wink to a dying mule.

'You can take me over to the restaurant for a meal?'

'Yes, sir, if you can pay the bill.'

I bought them an excellent meal and some excellent wine. I took a taxi to the docks, got my story, phoned it over to London, and was back with my gaolers before they had finished the packet of English cigarettes I had given them.

'You are an English gentleman, Monsieur!' I could not return a similar compliment.

Paul Bewsher, I discovered on the phone to London, was in a

nearby hotel, phoning over a longer, more detailed story for the later editions.

My friends of the French police came to friendly terms. They took me to an office, stamped my passport, with a receipt for a few francs, recording my offence.

Then they led me to Paul Bewsher, to the very bar from which he was dictating his story.

'Monsieur Bewsher! Your friend Monsieur Procter is a nice man, a good man.' They could have added that I was a slightly poorer man, financially.

Chapter Thirteen

One bright sunny day my wife and I strolled out of Charing Cross Station and turned to walk to Fleet Street.

We had returned from Rye. Lindon Laing had sent me to Rye the day before to cover a row about French fisherman poaching on British fishing grounds and, because it was my day off, and because my wife had to cancel her plans, he'd said:

'Take the missus with you, give her a nice day out, and charge it on your expenses.'

We'd had a very pleasant time in Rye where we stayed the night at an old fisherfolk tavern, and we were feeling on top of the world.

In the Strand I glanced professionally at the news bills.

One read: 'Lord Haw Haw hanged.'

My wife stopped dead in front of the news bill, went suddenly white.

'Are you ill?' I asked.

She stared at the news bill. Then she pointed her gloved finger at it.

'Do you know what I read when I looked at that bill?' she said. 'I read "Harry Procter Hanged".'

I was going to make a joke, but I saw that she was badly shocked. I led her to a bar and bought her a brandy.

'It is the only secret I have ever kept from you,' she then said. 'But I suppose I might as well tell you now. You might have been Lord Haw Haw...'

My wife is, and always has been, a quiet, undramatic sort of person, not prone to exaggeration. And so, coming from her, this shattering statement was immediately accepted by me.

I believed her, and was astounded. 'Tell me all,' I said.

And she told me about an incident in my past which I had forgotten completely.

One lunch-time in 1938, I was in Whitelock's bar, off Briggate, Leeds, with a crowd of reporters and sub-editors. We were discussing Dr Goebbels and his newspaper the *Völkischer Beobachter.*

'Why don't you apply for a job there?' joked reporter Vincent Hartley. 'You are always boasting you have a Christian grandmother.'

'And I'd get one,' I said.

Back in the reporters' room, flushed by three light ales, I pushed a sheet into my typewriter, and wrote to Dr Joseph Goebbels, asking him for a job writing for his newspaper.

'Write it and post it!' challenged Hartley, jovially. 'Go on, see what happens.'

Some weeks later I got a reply from Berlin: a brief letter written by a secretary, thanking me for my application which had been read with interest, and would be considered should ever a suitable vacancy arise.

I had a good laugh, my colleagues had a good laugh, then I forgot it.

'About six weeks before the war,' said my wife, 'when you were in London and I was in Leeds, a parcel arrived by post one morning. It had a German stamp on it. Hitler and the Germans were unpopular in Leeds in those days, and I wondered whether the postman had seen the stamp and might tell the neighbours. I wondered what was in it.

'I was going to post it on to you, unopened, but I got one of the strange intuitions which you know I've experienced all my life. I opened the parcel.

'It contained a copy of Hitler's *Mein Kampf,* printed in English. There was a railway ticket from Leeds to Berlin. And there was a letter from Dr Joseph Goebbels offering you a highly-paid job in his Ministry of Propaganda. The money was mentioned both in marks and in pounds, and I remember it was quite a lot.'

I jumped in delight. 'Incredible!' I said. 'Quickly, where is the letter from Goebbels? I'll get that letter on the front page of the *Daily Mail* tomorrow – this is news!'

My wife smiled sadly, and shook her head.

'No you won't,' she said. 'I burned that letter, I burned the book, the tickets, everything. After I burned them I worried, thinking I might have done the wrong thing, thinking that you might be mad. But today, when I saw that newspaper bill, I knew I had been right.'

'You see,' she went on, 'I know you so well, I know how foolish and headstrong you can be.

'I know that once you get an idea into your head – no matter how crazy it might be – no one can stop you from carrying it out. And when that parcel came from Goebbels I was expecting my fourth baby, and my sister Rene was staying with me. She and I talked all night about what I ought to do.

'We were frightened about anybody seeing the things – our neighbours hated Hitler and Goebbels and all they stood for. And I told my sister that I was afraid that if I sent them on to you, you might be crazy enough to go off to Germany and take the job.

'My sister Rene understood. "If I were you I'd burn them," she advised. So one night, as we both sat round the fire, she brought the parcel to me. I put it on the fire, and was glad to see it all blaze...'

My wife and I were silent for a while.

Then she said: 'Are you cross with me?'

'I am absolutely furious,' I said. 'Let me catch you opening my private correspondence again, my girl, and I'll put you over my knee.'

I bought her a first-class lunch.

Across the front page of an evening paper I read the banner line: 'Lord Haw Haw Hanged'. I shuddered.

I felt my wife's hand press my fingers.

'You know, you're a lad who needs some looking after, aren't you?' she said.

It was while I was on the *Daily Mail* that I won the national competition organised by *World's Press News* for an essay on journalism.

It was there that I came second in a competition organised by *Associated Newspapers* among their staffs, called 'How would you improve the *Daily Mail?*'

My entry made the suggestions for changing the *Mail's* attitude towards women readers – they gave me a generous cash prize and adopted my suggestions. The winner was Michael Christiansen, son of the editor of the *Daily Express.*

It was while on the *Daily Mail* that I wrote a news feature about a pair of hands. A pair of hands shown to me by a young gentleman who refused to go down a coal mine in the cause of national service.

My story about that pair of hands was said by a writer for *World's Press News* to read like a page from Dickens.

Later in this book I will tell you about another pair of hands. After the death of Lindon Laing a great change swept through the *Daily Mail*.

Frank Owen left what Fleet Street then called 'the hot seat' – the editorship of the *Daily Mail*. The new editor was my old Leeds boss, Guy Schofield.

A prophet is never believed by his own people, wrote somebody, somewhere. Although we were both from Yorkshire and had both worked together in Leeds, Guy Schofield and I did not begin our working day with a fond embrace. Never once did we quarrel, never once did he and I have even a difference while we were on the *Daily Mail*.

Shall I put it this way? If Editor Guy Schofield loved me, he never revealed it.

Down from Manchester swept an ambitious band of men, who for many long years had served the *Daily Mail* in the North. They had a motto which to this band was almost a religion, 'All for One and One for All'. But the rule did not apparently extend to us poor 'Southerners'.

John Hallowes, from Manchester, was appointed London News Editor. The Manchester Editor, Elvered Reed, was appointed Assistant Editor in London. They brought with them from Manchester their own reporters. Naturally we London reporters began to wonder what on earth was to become of us all. For one thing the Mancunians were all quite clear about, they had no time for 'Little Laings', a nick-name given to the old Lindon Laing boys.

They had never loved Lindon Laing, these Manchester boys; for he'd had rather a naughty habit of sending his Little Laings up into northern territory when he wanted stories the Manchester lads could not get.

They had long memories, these Mancunians. They recalled to me, with little enthusiasm, how Lindon Laing, a few years before, had sent me into their territory because they were not getting the results he required on the amazing story of Doctor Clements, the wife murderer, at Southport.

When I had arrived at the Manchester office, nobody cheered.

A Manchester executive handed me a money wire from Lindon

Laing. It was for £50, to cover my Northern expenses. 'There's a message on the telegram,' said the Manchester executive, with an accusing sneer. 'We have read it with amusement.'

Lindon's message was brief. 'Harry; Get Dr Clements's Last Note Or Bring The Money Back, Regards Laing.'

Dr Clements committed suicide shortly before the police could arrest him.

'Well, Page-One Procter,' said the Mancunian, sarcastically, 'we'd like you to show us how to get it. Our best reporters – better reporters than you are – are in Southport, and they can't get it. So just you show us how.'

'I will,' I said. And I did.

At Southport the most farcical position I had ever seen awaited me. My bitterest opposition were the reporters from my own newspaper.

A colleague from Manchester brought the police chief to me in the bar of an hotel and said, sarcastically: 'This is the great London reporter who has come to show us poor mugs how to get the last note of Dr Clements.'

The policeman grinned scornfully. 'Well, he'll have to be a ruddy safe-breaker,' he commented, 'for that last note is locked up in a safe at police headquarters.'

'Thanks for the tip.'

A few hours later, when I got, verbatim, the message Dr Clements had written on his death-note, I phoned it direct to Lindon Laing in London, deliberately snubbing the Manchester office who had so rudely snubbed me. The first Manchester heard of the dramatic message was when it came to them from London on the wire machine.

The next day I got an exclusive interview with a woman who was one of the last people to see Dr Clements and Mrs Clements alive, and this made scoop number two from Southport.

Another reporter was so annoyed that he organised a Press petition to the woman's solicitors, asking that an official denial be made of my story which had appeared in his own newspaper.

The solicitor agreed to see him and all the other reporters.

'I have this statement to give you,' he said. 'Please copy the story by Harry Procter in today's *Daily Mail* as my official statement. Every word of it is true.'

I mention this to illustrate what the effect of Manchester virtually taking over London meant to me. I mention it to explain why, after eight very happy, very successful years, on a newspaper of which I was proud, I decided to resign.

Of course I was not the only London reporter affected adversely by the new regime – most of my old colleagues were unhappy.

Anthony Hunter was the first of us to decide to move – he resigned to join the *Sunday Dispatch,* making it very clear that he was leaving because of the new set-up. I went round with the hat and we poor Southerners, as we called ourselves, then, bought him a watch and solemnly presented it to him.

'I have never worn a watch since I was a prisoner of war in Germany,' said Tony solemnly. 'When I swapped that watch for one loaf of bread I took a silent oath never to wear another on my wrist.'

'Then don't swap this for five small fishes,' quipped a colleague, Jerry Mellor, so robbing Anthony Hunter perhaps of one of the greatest moments of his life. This remark brought to an end what might have been a long and brilliant oration.

Lindon Laing, Frank Owen, and now my dear friend Tony had gone. I was feeling rather lonely in that huge reporters' room inhabited mainly now by Mancunians. Their hour of power on the London *Daily Mail* was a very brief hour indeed. But, unfortunately for myself and my future, I could not sit it out.

Before Frank Owen left us, Richard Dimbleby and a BBC team organised a real-life television play about a newspaper. On the original script Frank Owen was Editor, I was the reporter.

Frank Owen's role was now taken over at very short notice by Guy Schofield, and, naturally, this meant revision and rewriting.

My best line in the original script was when I appeared in a telephone kiosk, excitedly talking to the News Editor.

'It's murder,' I had to say. 'A barmaid's body in a bloodstained bedroom…'

Schofield changed this, first suggesting I should report a flower show. Eventually, when I did appear on television, the viewers heard me give a report of a house fire.

The end really came for me when, one night, I took a rowing boat out on the dark River Thames, acting on a hunch. I came back with an exciting story. A number of frogmen, on a secret exercise, had been killed by Father Thames.

I phoned my story over, confidently expecting a front-page lead.

Said one of the new executives: 'This story seems too good to be true.'

They did what Lindon Laing or Frank Owen would never have done. They sent another reporter out to check my story. This was a blow to my pride, indeed.

The reporter phoned to say he could not get any evidence to support my story – instead of rowing out on to the ink-black Thames he had called at a police station. Dennis Fisher, Night News Editor, threw my story into the waste-paper basket.

As I watched this first-class news story screwed into a ball and flung contemptuously away I decided I would leave the great newspaper which I had been so proud to serve. I could tolerate personal humiliation. But I could not forgive an insult to my work. Two hours later I was at the bar of the London Press Club when the night news editor, Dennis Fisher, phoned me.

'This will be balm to your soul,' he said. '*Press Association* have now confirmed that you were right. Will you phone your story over again?'

It was not balm to my soul, I refused to phone my story over a second time. They had to go on their knees and rummage in the waste-paper basket, find my crumpled copy, smooth it out, re-type it, and send it to the subs.

I wrote to Guy Schofield and told him I wished to resign. He accepted my resignation.

I began to earn my living in Fleet Street as a freelance journalist, for me a new and challenging experience. Freelancing is hard work indeed, but I made a living. I found that my best markets were the Sunday newspapers. I worked mainly for *Reynold's News* who splashed, front-page, most of the stories I did for them – using my name.

'Sir' Hugh Cudlipp, undoubtedly one of the most vital newspapermen of our times, had now returned to Geraldine House from his years of exile on the *Sunday Express*. At that moment he was Editor of the *Sunday Pictorial*.

One Friday I was in the office of *Reynold's News* when the telephone rang. It was Harold Barkworth, the most gentlemanly gentleman in Fleet Street.

'Hugh wants to see you, Harry, can you come right away?'

I had known Hugh Cudlipp for years; never well, but we had

always been on nodding terms. He was glad to see me. He came at once to the point.

'Would you like to work for me, Harry?'

'Yes, sir, I would. I've already applied to your News Editor, Fred Redman, for a job, several times.'

'Have you, I did not know. But I'm so busy these days Harry – I'm writing a book about the *Daily Mirror*. When can you start?'

'Any time you wish, sir.'

'Well, there's no hurry, is there? Let's see, today's Friday, start tomorrow morning at 10 – Saturday's always a busy day on the *Pic*.'

He rang for Fred Redman, the News Editor, and told him of his decision.

'In that case,' said Red, 'you'd better come over to Number Ten and meet the boys.' 'No. 10' is a small public house in Fetter Lane, also known by *Pic* people as 'the branch office'. It certainly is that.

As Red led his newest reporter across the street to No. 10, neither of us realised that before the year was out the *Pic* would have a new name in Fleet Street – *'The Sunday Proctorial'*.

Red introduced me to his reporters, bought me a beer. 'Harry,' he said. 'You're going to have fun on the Pic You're going to have a hell of a time!'

Was he a prophet?

Chapter Fourteen

When I joined the *Sunday Pictorial* I joined the most efficient newspaper-team the world has ever seen, or probably ever will see. And this newspaper, with its mammoth circulation, was run, I was amazed to discover, by a small handful of hand-picked journalists.

To this small team of men everything was possible, nothing was impossible. Each week they went out for what 'they' wanted in the pages of their newspaper, and what they wanted, they got.

There may be many who may not approve of the adventures I had on the *Sunday Pictorial* – adventures I shared with the brilliant men I worked with, adventures I shall now relate.

There are many who do not approve of all-in wrestling – who cry 'shame' when they see a wrestler receiving heavy punishment in the ring. But the professional wrestler knows what to expect when he climbs over the ropes.

The *Pic* reporter knows, when he starts his working week on a Tuesday morning, just how tough and arduous might be the tasks he will have to perform before 2am the following Sunday. The blows fall thick and furious, but he never expects picnics. He never gets them.

For five long years on the *Pictorial* I was billed as 'Harry Procter, Special Investigator',' and the slug-line below usually read 'Another Pictorial Exposure'. Exposure was the bread and butter of this giant Sunday newspaper. And the *Sunday Pictorial* made me into their expert.

I exposed, and exposed, and exposed. I exposed the London Call Girl Syndicate, crooked financiers, white slavers, phoney doctors, peddlers in vice or drugs, unscrupulous landlords, swindlers, confidence tricksters; I exposed vile slums, black-marketeers, crooked politicians, dishonest officials in high places. I exposed husbands who deserted their wives, and wives who deserted their husbands.

My exposures became so widely known that a new phrase began to be used up and down the country, which replaced the phrase, of twenty years ago, 'Write and tell John Bull about it'. Now people were saying: 'Write and tell Harry Procter about it'. And they wrote to me in their thousands.

To carry out these exposures I used the skill and the methods taught to me by Lindon Laing; and even the seasoned *Pictorial* team were surprised at the success of these methods. Before, the *Pic* exposures had been done by a group of reporters working as a team by a method of careful, diligent enquiry, which might take weeks, months, or even a year.

I introduced the new method which gave them the exposure story usually within two days. This method completely reversed the old one. Instead of preliminary inquiry I went straight to the fountainhead of whatever we wanted to expose – struck immediately at the heart of the matter. The best way to burst a balloon, I told them, is to prick it with a pin; the best way to floor a scoundrel is to knock him down at the beginning.

My first big *Pic* exposure, in my early days with the *Pic,* was of a man who was taking sums of money from old age pensioners, working-class married couples, and others, promising that he would build them houses and arrange them mortgages.

Assistant Editor Fred Redman, himself one of the best *Pictorial* reporters there ever was, joined me on this assignment because he sincerely believed I should want him to show me how to do the job.

We went straight to Camberwell and called in at a public house only a short distance from the house where the man whom we believed to be a heartless scoundrel, lived. Red began to consider his plan of campaign.

'Red,' I said. 'Will you take a risk on me? Will you give me five minutes – the first five minutes – with this crook? If you think I'm flopping, you take over, I shan't mind.'

'Certainly, Harry,' said Red. 'I'd like to see how you tackle him.' Red was my immediate boss, and naturally he was curious to see me in action. He did not even ask me my plans.

He now knows that I never make plans. I bank on seizing by the forelock whatever opportunity fate presents me with – making my decisions in the split seconds in which a door is opened and slammed in the reporter's face.

On exposure stories the reporter cannot lie. He can bluff, and bully, coax and persuade, but if he lies, his exposure will not be legally water-tight – the exposed will be able to hit back hard. He cannot lie, he cannot say something which is not true. But he can omit! He can leave something out.

'My name is Harry Procter,' I truthfully told the crook. 'I want to inquire about one of your houses. Will you tell me just what you can do for me, how much money you want from me, how long it will take you to build me a house. And, as I want to think carefully over what you say, do you mind if my friend here, who can write shorthand, takes it all down?'

Of course he did not mind. When I knew that we had a shorthand note of facts which I knew, and could prove there and then were utter and complete lies, I said to the man, quietly, unexpectedly: 'You are a liar!'

At first it seemed he had not heard me. Everything had been so quiet, so charming, so friendly. Then he blinked, looked just a little anxious.

'You are a liar and a crook and a swindler. We are from the *Sunday Pictorial* and this week we are going to expose you. If you take my advice you will make a full confession to us and we will publish it – it is the least you can do to make amends to the innocent people you have so mercilessly swindled.'

I glanced at Red. I wondered whether he was going to stop me. He did not. The man broke down, and gave us a complete confession. And no man was happier about my success than Red.

Fred Redman is an unusual man. Although he has a fine wife and a fine family, he is a man who seems to live mainly as a living piece of the *Sunday Pictorial;* it is as though he had no reality apart from the *Pic*. He works harder than any man on the staff – perhaps with the exception of Editor Colin Valdar. He never appears to really want to leave the *Pic* building – in fact he only leaves it to get a few hours sleep and then he is back. He puts the *Pic* first, foremost, last, then first again. He expects every other member of the staff to feel the same way, and of course he is disappointed.

But he was – and is today as Assistant Editor – a powerful member of the *Pic* team.

He decided on that first job that I was a man who could be of value to the giant newspaper he lived for. He made plans for me. From this night on, he gave most of the big exposures to me.

Colin S Valdar, the young, brilliant journalist, took over the *Pic* Editorship when Cudlipp was appointed editorial director of the *Mirror* group.

Harold Barkworth was acting editor – 'Harold is always the bridesmaid but never the blushing bride,' quipped Hugh Cudlipp. There was much speculation in Fleet Street as to who would be the new *Pictorial* Editor.

Reg Payne, Fred Redman, and I were together at the Press Club bar when Reg asked me: 'Who do you think will get the editorship?' I had no idea but, on the basis of strict form study, just as a punter fancies a horse, I personally believed 'Sir' Hugh would choose Colin Valdar.

'Colin Valdar...'

This was the first time Valdar had ever been tipped inside the *Pic* circle. Red confessed that he had never heard of him. Reg shrugged; obviously he had no interest in my 'tip'.

On the following Tuesday, when it was officially announced that Colin Valdar was to be editor, everyone thought I'd had inside information. I hadn't. It was just my personal hunch.

In his first week there Colin Valdar announced: 'Exposures sell the *Pic*. We must be the first with every important exposure – but they must be genuine.' One of the best headlines I ever saw was 'Old Boots from Dustbins Sold as New'.

But he wanted many other things besides.

The power of exposure on a big Sunday newspaper is a weapon to be used, I think, with every care.

I have not turned squeamish in my middle-age. News is news, and I believe that real news should be pursued ruthlessly, accurately, speedily, and completely.

But to be exposed in bold headlines is a terrible thing for a victim – far worse than a heavy prison sentence. By it, lives are completely ruined – not only the life of the subject of the exposure – but of his wife, his children, his parents, his friends.

Exposure of poverty, injustice, crime, is a good thing: but if this weapon is used carelessly and ordinary innocent people become its victims, then this is a terrible thing indeed. To focus the spotlight of publicity on the dark shadows of misery, despair, and injustice, is a noble task for a newspaper to perform – Charles Dickens was the first exposist in Fleet Street.

But when the headlines hit the innocent, a great crime is committed.

I now found that I had a bigger platform to shout from than I had ever even dreamed of. The power the *Pic* gave me could be used by me – and was – as a blessing to thousands. I played a large part in launching the scheme for getting every orphan in the land an 'aunt and uncle' and a personal present at Christmas – this idea of mine has been successfully repeated every Christmas since.

R T Payne, Deputy Editor, developed the idea of the famous '*Pic* Crime Strip', planning that every week the '*Pic* Detectives' would help the police solve crime. But out of this I discovered that runaway brides, runaway husbands, and broken homes, not only provided great human stories, but sometimes we were able to reunite one family. It is true that one runaway wife, who left her husband and many children, confessed to me that her real reason for running away was to get her photograph in the *Pictorial* – but on the whole this scheme was good.

I met Diana Dors, I met Marilyn Monroe. On the *Pic* I was able to scoop the world on the terrible flood disasters at Lynton and Lynmouth. I travelled abroad; I had some very pleasant assignments.

I had some very tough assignments, too, and it is some of these I am now going to tell about.

The new *Pic* team, headed by Colin Valdar, of which I was now a member, was out to build up the circulation by millions, in the shortest possible time. The team had no illusions about how this was to be done.

Sex, scandal, surprise, sensation, exposure, murder. And as many pictures of half-dressed, big-bosomed damsels in distress as possible.

I shall always remember a Fleet Street journalist who moaned to me a few weeks after abandoning a solid post in serious journalism to join the popular Sunday press. He made the change because they doubled his salary; within a month they broke his heart.

Within a month of his entry into popular Sundayism he sadly told me: 'Harry I have suggested to the editor six solid, good news feature ideas this week and all have been turned down. I think I know why! Because all the men in the stories I suggested had two -----. Had they had but one ----, or three -----, they'd have all made page one.'

He went off to write an article about a man who had changed into a woman, grumbling that only a few weeks before he had written an article about a woman who had changed into a man. The next time I met him he was a little more seasoned.

'I'll make page one this week,' he said. 'I've been tipped off about an employee at the London Zoo who has been fooling around with the lions. Think of the headline, chum, 'Britain's Bravest ------' .'

I do not write this as a joke.

On the *Pic* I never knew what would happen next.

Once we ran a weekly series about a beautiful coloured girl brought to Britain by a young British seaman. The *Pic* chased enthusiastically after the story, secured it, paid for the marriage of the girl and her boy friend, then flew them by specially chartered plane from the provinces to London.

The copper-coloured beauty and her sailor were married in the North of England on a Saturday, and Editor Colin Valdar decided that, because the ceremony in the provinces had not been as exclusive as he had hoped, I should be sent to the airport to meet the honeymooners and prevent the opposition Sundays from getting either pictures or interviews of the bride or her groom.

Such a task is not a simple one, it is a major operation in which every second is important – the *Pic* has no time for failures.

I went early to the airfield, and a quick reconnoitre revealed that photographers and reporters from other papers were hiding in old hangars, in bushes, around corners. The positioning of our car and chauffeur was vital. I used a dummy car and chauffeur in another position to confuse the 'enemy'.

I was glad to hear that colleague Madeline McLoughlin, the *Pic's* girl reporter, was on the plane with the bridal couple. She and I worked together scores of times; she and I always worked in perfect harmony as a team and we had pulled off dozens of big exclusives for the *Pic*.

Madeline and I liked each other. She is small, plump, attractive, has a gay sense of fun, and she and I experienced one of those rare relationships – a deep friendship between a man and a woman which was entirely platonic.

'I love Harry,' she often quipped, 'but I think it is most unfair that he never makes a pass at me. Every girl likes to say no.'

We understood each other so completely that, when on a difficult assignment, we knew each other's minds and anticipated each other's actions, usually to the sorrow of our rivals.

Madeline, as the plane began to land, quickly took in the position below. She instructed the pilot to taxi the plane to a suitable position, and then gave me a signal to come and collect.

I flung a blanket to Madeline. From all corners opposition photographers left their hiding places and hurried towards us. Madeline handed me a parcel wrapped in a blanket, which I carried to our car. It felt lighter than a shopping basket.

As the car got on its way to Fetter Lane, I unwrapped the parcel and out popped the pretty pocket-sized bride.

She was still wearing bridal clothes; she looked radiant.

'Hope I was not too heavy,' she smiled.

She was a pretty, trusting creature.

I got the bride and the bridegroom safely into the *Sunday Pictorial* office, where the girl squatted on her haunches close to Madeline's desk. She squatted there for days afterwards, sitting in enraptured silence, her large pretty eyes watching the strange and interesting events which happened every hour in the *Pic* editorial room.

Chapter Fifteen

The *Pictorial* believes that one of the biggest scoops I got them was on the girl who married her brother.

Her name was Anne Hughes. The best way to begin telling of my amazing experiences with this girl is to quote page one of the *Sunday Pictorial,* February 20, 1955.

The headlines announce: '*Pictorial* exclusive, chance-in-a-million girl tells her own tragic story'. And the bold banner-line in two-inch high letters announces 'I MARRIED MY BROTHER'.

The story which I wrote for Anne leads off:

> 'I am the girl who married her brother. Yes, the handsome man who is the father of my two darling baby boys is my father's child, my mother's son. Now that the tragic truth is out I have decided to tell my full story – if only because it might prevent such a terrible thing happening to anyone again.

> 'It is the story of years of happiness as man and wife. And it ends with the most terrible day of my life – the day, four months ago, when we realised that we were the son and daughter of the same mother and father. As all the world knows by now, my brother Geoffrey and I were parted as children by our mother's death. He went into a home, and I was adopted by a couple from the Midlands...'

The story filled the front page and ran over on to the back page. It ended: 'I am still young. My life is before me. But I know that my future must not, cannot, include the man I love. Because the man I love is my brother.'

I ought to have read her palm for her. Because on the evening of the day that story was published, I introduced her to a young soldier, and twelve days later she married him.

I gave the bride away.

But for me this astonishing story really began on the Friday evening when I went into the *Pictorial* 'branch office' to have a drink before driving home to Kent.

Red was there with the 'Redman school' gathered about him as closely and contentedly as chickens about a hen. Throughout Fleet Street there are similar schools, usually formed around an executive by men who believe that diamonds shine from the button holes of his waistcoat. Red and I always liked and respected each other, but I was never a member of his school.

I always considered him a magnificent journalist and news editor.

On that Friday night I gave my customary, friendly nod to all the 'Redman school', and ordered a small beer. The telephone rang, for ten minutes Red had his ear to the receiver.

He beckoned me over. 'Off you go, Harry,' he said. 'Just your meat, this. In the Midlands there's a happily married couple with two children who've just discovered they're brother and sister. Call at the cashiers, I'll sign you a chit. And get there as quickly as you can.'

This was a normal Friday night occurrence for a *Pic* reporter – an occurrence which never failed to give me a thrill. Ten minutes later I was in my car and heading for the place.

It was a terrible winter night. I had a large Humber car, but no heater. Past Oxford I ran into a blizzard. On a lonely stretch of road, I ran into another blizzard, so thick that it was impossible to keep going – although I had told myself for two hours 'keep moving and you'll be OK'. But now I was stuck. Frozen with the cold.

I wrapped an old coat from the boot about me. I hunted for the small, 6s.6d. bottle of brandy I always carry in a car for emergencies. I was there alone for two hours.

As soon as the blizzard thinned I continued and arrived at about 4am cold, shivering, wretched.

Fortunately Red had booked my hotel. A worried porter who was expecting me opened the door, and gave me hot milk and brandy.

'Call me at 7am,.' I requested, as I went to bed.

I woke up at 9am. Fully refreshed and fit after my warm sleep, I hurried off without breakfast, drove at once to the dreary, dismal hostel on the outskirts, where the Girl Who Married Her Brother – according to Red – had been taken.

I was about the last Sunday paper reporter to arrive.

The hostel where Anne and her baby son Robert had been taken the night before was a depressing, slum building, with virtually no furniture.

In a large room on the ground floor I found about a dozen reporters. They were gathered round an unshaven, shabbily-dressed man. He was auctioning the girl and her baby to the highest bidder, some reporters were haggling with him about price.

This man, who, I am glad to say, had no connections with newspapers, had heard the day before that Anne Hughes and her story might be worth a fortune to the Sunday press.

He had sought her and found her when the poor young mother was searching for somewhere to sleep for herself and her little boy. He took her, by bus, to the hostel, and told the sad, bewildered woman to leave everything to him.

Now this man turned to me: '*Sunday Pictorial?* I've been expecting you here,' he grinned, showing yellow teeth.

'Well, everybody's here now, so we can really get down to business,' he said. 'Now, as I've told these reporters here, I'm strictly a business man. I've got the girl, and I've got the baby. And I'm out to get the biggest price I can. The Sunday paper that bids the highest will get her story.'

I felt sick with anger. I could have cheerfully seized hold of him and broken his neck.

'So you're conducting an auction,' I said. 'What do you think this is, a cattle market?'

'What's your bid, mister?'

I paused. Bids, all of them offering three figure sums, came from the circle of reporters. Said one reporter: 'If you'll just wait until I can speak to my editor at 10.30 and get his OK, I'll double all these bids...'

'What's your bid, *Sunday Pictorial?*'

'I'll pay more than the *Pic.*'

'A hundred quid, straight down in cash...'

'Will you take a cheque?'

'Just let me talk to my editor, first...'

What a scene! Cringing, pleading, whining. And somewhere in this foul slum was a mother and a child, friendless, miserable, bewildered. I looked on this scene, and I thought of Thomas A Stott, of Lindon Laing, of Frank Owen.

'Come on, *Sunday Pictorial,* make your bid! Or have you got to ask your boss first?'

I walked towards him, slowly. 'No, I don't,' I said. 'I can make

149

you my bid without consulting my editor. Not one blasted ha'penny! And do you know why? Because I don't believe in buying or selling human flesh and blood! So just count me out of your auction.'

I turned and left the room.

Out in the bare corridor I listened. The haggling, the noisy bidding, continued. Good, I thought, that will keep them all occupied for a while. I began to make a search of the hostel.

In an upstairs room, with orange boxes for seats and tables, with a drab, iron-framed bed, I found pretty Anne Hughes. She sat frightened, hopeless. The tears flowed down her cheeks, as she rocked to and fro, the baby son upon her knee.

I stretched out my hand to her at once, and smiled.

'Anne,' I said, 'don't cry. Now look, downstairs are a bunch of newspaper reporters, bidding for you as though you were a pound of sausages. I am a reporter too, but I refuse to take part in such a disgusting affair. Now I'm not going to promise you any money. But, right now, this very minute, I will take you and your baby son out of this black hole into a decent hotel room where you can both have a nice warm bath and a meal. And then, when you feel better, we'll talk. What do you say, Anne?'

She smiled through her tears, and nodded.

'Yes, please.'

I took her crying baby son into my arms, I signalled to Anne. She picked up a paper carrier bag, containing all her worldly possessions.

'Just follow me, Anne, quietly. And, no matter what happens, just keep moving.'

We tiptoed downstairs, tiptoed along the corridor, rustled past the open door of the room in which the auction in human souls was still continuing. And within seconds, Anne was seated at my side in my car, her baby on her knee.'

I pressed my starter button, began to turn the car round in the muddy drive.

Like a pack of yelping puppies whose bone has been taken away, my friends, the opposition, rushed outside. Cameras flashed. Voices shouted in anger. One reporter came to my driving seat window.

'OK Harry!' he whispered. 'But just to cover me can I tell my office how much you've paid for it – can I say you've given £1,000, because they won't go higher than £500. Just to cover me.'

I revved my engine, and flung my car into gear.

'You can tell your office I got it for free,' I said, as I drove away. Shaking off the opposition cars was, by this time, child's play to me. It was taught me by a coloured Weymouth taxi-driver, who, in my *Daily Mail* days, shook off six opposition Rolls Royce cars by his superb driving of an Austin 12, when I had Anne Davison, the girl who lost her husband and her ketch off Portland Bill, scaled the cliffs there, and later sailed the Atlantic alone, in the back.

Three times around the centre of the town and we'd lost them, and I set off at eighty mph on the road.

At the next town, I booked a suite of rooms, gave Anne her keys, coaxed her into sipping a stimulant, and told her to relax.

Then I phoned my office, which by this time were wondering just what on earth could have happened to me, and told them:

'I can give you the exclusive story of the girl who married her brother, signed by her. I think you will want to use it page one.' They did.

I went out and bought Anne a change of clothes, bought baby Robert a small suit and new underwear.

After a nice bath and a good lunch they appeared two different creatures to the mother and child I had found in the hostel. I let Anne relax, and told her that, if she wished, I would like her to tell me her story.

'But I want you to know it, Harry,' she said. We were friends by this time, and had been joined by a photographer from London. 'I really want to get it off my chest.'

I wrote her story, and the world read it. Pictures of the lovely Anne and her baby son were wired to London, and an excellent picture, a credit to the skill of photographer Percy Bosher, appeared on page one.

Then we all relaxed. I took Anne and her baby out for a drive. I was pleased to see that both were now happy; the gloom of their morning had gone.

The mother and child went to bed early.

Fred Redman phoned me from the *Pic* office. He had received a visit, he said, from an officer from Snow Hill police station. Friends of Anne Hughes had complained to the police that I had kidnapped her and her baby against her will and was holding her a prisoner. Would I give the matter my attention?

I phoned the police. I explained to them that the so-called friends of Anne Hughes were in reality newspaper contacts who were trying to make money out of the girl's misfortune. She was willing to let the police know where she was, she was willing for the police to come and see her, on condition that her whereabouts were not revealed to the opposition reporters.

Two police chiefs arrived at the hotel later, and one policewoman.

I took them up to Anne. 'I do not wish to be present at this interview,' I told the police. 'I will wait downstairs. If you find there is anything unsatisfactory I am sure you will advise this young mother to leave this hotel. Before I go I might say that the best advice I can give her is for her to accept *your* advice.'

After two hours the police came and shook my hand.

'We are perfectly satisfied,' they said. 'We shall not reveal her whereabouts to her so-called friends.' The police kept their promise.

This story sold furiously on the following Sunday. I drove Anne and her child down to London, and all the way we stopped at newsagents and tried to buy a *Sunday Pictorial.* But that day the *Pic* sold out. It was selling out most weeks, in those days.

My success on the *Sunday Pictorial,* if measured by material standards, was considerable. But it endeared me to few – success is like that. Fleet Street loves failures, but it cannot tolerate success.

If anyone takes the trouble to look through the back numbers of the *Sunday Pictorial* for the five years I was there, they will see that I had my fair share of space and success and of front page stories. There were few members of the staff – few reporters on any newspaper – who were more prominently featured.

And yet, when my star was high in the heavens, and when Reg Payne came from the *Sunday Express* to join us as Deputy Editor, he called me to his desk within the first week.

He made it clear to me that there was much about my work that did not meet with his approval, and that he apparently thought I was too big for my boots. I never had any quarrel with him before and had a respect and admiration for him that made me ponder over his words and wonder what it was that had inspired this hostile viewpoint. Perhaps I wasn't sufficiently self-critical, because I never found the answer.

For long years following he was my Deputy Editor. In this period he certainly made the fullest use of my professional ability – when the Editor was away and he was in charge he would depend on me pulling out for him a Page One exclusive, which I usually did.

But I never got his wavelength. The man who was all for me, who had every confidence in me, who wanted me to be given the biggest stories, who continually congratulated me on my work, the man whom I knew instinctively liked me personally as well as professionally, was the *Pictorial* Editor, Colin Valdar.

To me, it seemed, this fact was all-important. For not only was Colin Valdar a brilliant editor, the most brilliant projector of ideas we had in Fleet Street, Colin Valdar was also a powerful man.

However, these things did not trouble me as I drove Anne Hughes and her baby towards London on that Sunday when my efforts were selling *Sunday Pictorials* by the million.

What did worry me was the pretty young mother at my side and her baby son. What of their future?

Anne was a nice, intelligent girl, who had recently known great sorrow. She had pleaded with me not to leave her at home where she would be pointed out forever in the streets as the girl who married her brother.

She asked to go to London where she could lose her tragedy among the hundreds which London bears in her great heart every day.

I told her that I would see that the *Sunday Pictorial* gave her a sum of money sufficient to help her make a new start in London. I took her to a respectable hostel in Earls Court organised by the Army Welfare services, saw her into a clean cosy room, with a decent bed.

When I shook her hand she began to cry, she was lonely and sad. I did not want to leave her, but my own wife and children were waiting at home for me.

I led her into the canteen lounge and bought her a cup of tea. At the piano a young Army corporal was playing *Little Things Mean a Lot.*

He looked up and saw Anne was crying. He came over and asked if he could help.

He was Corporal Donald Anderson, son of a Hull railway worker, the man whom, twelve days later, Anne was to marry in church.

I liked Anne. But I think she was extremely fortunate in finding, so quickly, such an excellent young man for a husband as Donald Anderson. I sincerely hope that neither Anne nor Donald have ever regretted their marriage.

When Anne phoned me a few days later at the *Sunday Pictorial* office and told me she was going to be married, I got quite a shock.

I went to see her at once, and talked the whole thing over with her and handsome Donald Anderson. My first reaction was to try and talk them out of it, for I felt that it was not wise for two young people who had known each other only a few days to join themselves in holy matrimony. I was also concerned about the parents of this most respectable young man – they were in Hull, and I felt they should be fully, and thoroughly, consulted.

I returned to the office and made my personal views known to Editor Colin Valdar.

Colin did not agree with me. He said, and most emphatically, that if Anne and Donald were in love and wanted to marry, it was none of my business.

What was my business, he said, just as emphatically, was to ensure that, if they did marry, the *Sunday Pictorial* should have the story of their wedding – with pictures – exclusively.

He gave me authority to pay the expenses of their wedding, to organise it, to buy for Anne a wedding trousseau second to none.

I decided, then, that if I was to organise this wedding, I would organise it properly, and do my utmost to make both young people realise the solemnity of such an occasion. I told Donald that if he and Anne wanted to marry without my help they were perfectly entitled to do so. But if the *Pic* paid for their wedding, and the reception, the *Pic* would want the story, exclusively.

Both he and Anne accepted my offer.

The next few days were extremely anxious ones, and busy ones, for me. By this time Anne and I had grown fond of each other in a father-and-daughter way, and I wanted her wedding day to be a happy one. I arranged for baby Robert to go to a first-class nursery school in the country, I advised Donald Anderson to write fully to his parents, ask their advice, and invite them to the wedding, I saw the parson, I fixed the wedding arrangements at the church.

I went shopping with Anne, helped her choose her white gown, her veil, her shoes, her bouquet. I ordered a magnificent wedding cake. And I made plans for a secret wedding reception at a Kensington hotel. The invitations to the wedding were few; Mr and Mrs William Anderson, bridegroom Anderson's brother Gordon, and two *Pictorial* photographers.

With all this hustle and bustle Anne and I completely forgot about another man who had played an important part in her happiness and her sorrow before she met me: tall, lean Geoffrey Hughes, her brother, father of her children.

But my colleagues at the *Pic* office did not forget.

Anne asked me whether I would 'give the bride away' and I agreed. She wanted a bridesmaid, she had no friends in London, so she asked my teenage daughter, Phyllis, to perform this office. Phyllis agreed, and I was glad for, although young, my daughter was a trained junior reporter, and I was expecting trouble from my old friends, the opposition.

The wedding of the Girl Who Married Her Brother was big news which interested the whole of Fleet Street and already, despite my care, news of it had leaked out.

I decided that to keep the wedding out of the evening and morning papers would be impossible, but I depended on the secrecy of the reception to provide my inside story.

It certainly did.

On the night before the wedding, Phyllis and Anne shared a twin-bedded room at a West End hotel. The bridegroom's parents, a nice, kindly couple, arrived from Hull, and I installed them at the same hotel.

Mr and Mrs Anderson were proud of their young son, and were naturally anxious about the wedding. They asked me to tell them all I knew about Anne. I told them all I knew.

They were good, respectable people, and they told me they did not want the wedding to be like a peep-show in a circus. I told them frankly of the arrangements I had made for an exclusive story and picture in the *Pic,* but promised them I would do my utmost to see that the wedding got the minimum of publicity in other newspapers. This was a promise I certainly intended to fulfil.

A *Pictorial* reporter came to see me and told me he was to meet the bride's brother in London the following morning.

'My instructions are to take him to the wedding, let him mingle among the crowds on the outskirts, and write a story about the lonely man who watches it all from afar,' he said.

'That is your worry, not mine,' I told him. 'I have too much to worry about. But keep him out of the church for the sake of the bridegroom's mother and father. I have promised them this will be a serious, nice wedding, not a peep-show. And I'm keeping that promise. For my part I shall tell neither Anne, the bridegroom, nor his parents, about this side-shoot.'

'We shall keep in the shadows,' he said. 'None of you will know that the brother and I are there. But it will give the story a good twist,' he commented.

'Twist or no twist,' I told him, 'these are nice people. Tomorrow is a solemn and important day in their lives. I will not have it made into a stunt.'

The following morning, as I went to buy myself a red carnation for my button-hole, I spotted opposition reporters and photographers hiding about the hotel.

I made a phone call to a friend on a rival newspaper, and he told me the plan.

'They won't worry you when you go off to the wedding,' he said. 'But they plan to crash in on the reception – there'll be hundreds there.'

'Thanks!' I said. The radiant bride and her bridesmaid were waiting for me. I led them into the Rolls Royce car and drove off with them to the church. I did not worry the bride with my problem – it was my problem. I had to prevent a fiasco at the reception for two reasons. Firstly, I had promised Mum and Dad a nice, quiet wedding, and secondly, I wanted the story and pictures – especially the pictures – exclusive.

On the journey I made up my mind. I scribbled a note and gave it to the car driver. 'Tell the other driver to cancel the wedding reception and collect the wedding cake. Tell him to follow our car with the cake.'

I led the lovely bride through the battery of press photographers into the church.

It was a beautiful service. I kept my eye on the bridegroom's parents, and when I saw they were happy about it, I was satisfied.

Outside it took me seconds only to get the newly-weds and their relatives safely into our two cars. I led slowly, knowing the opposition would pretend to chase us.

I knew, and I was right, that they would hurry to the Kensington hotel to gate-crash the reception, but they did not want us to know yet that they knew about this.

For ten minutes I circled around Knightsbridge. Then I saw an imposing restaurant with a notice outside 'Weddings and Parties Catered For. Private Room'.

I told the driver to stop.

'Can I book your private room for a wedding reception?' I asked.

'Certainly, sir. What will be the date?'

'Today, right now, this very minute. The best wedding reception you've ever put on.'

While he stared at me, doubting my sanity, I hurried out and returned with the beautiful bride. He blinked.

Then he bowed, and said: 'This way! This way!' and led us into a luxurious private reception room below his restaurant.

My bridal party were obviously a little flustered at this sudden change in plan. But I called for champagne.

'To the happy couple.'

We drank. The champagne corks popped, the waiters bustled round, a magnificent four-course lunch was provided. And everything was exactly as it should be. The bridegroom's father made a speech, the bridegroom's brother made a speech.

Then the bride, herself, made a speech. And she finished with a special toast.

'To Harry Procter,' she said, and I was glad to see that all drank.

I began to relax. Two *Pictorial* photographers pictured every moment of this happy reception. Like a delighted, radiant schoolgirl, Anne cut the cake.

Everything was warm, friendly, and nice.

Then the telephone rang. It was my Editor.

'Good work, Harry,' said Colin Valdar. 'I'm pleased! But there is just one thing. There is going to be an uninvited guest at the wedding feast.'

I gasped into the telephone. 'Not the brother...?'

'How did you guess? Look, the brother is upstairs, just above your heads, having a drink. I want a picture of him congratulating the bride and bridegroom.'

'It is impossible, Colin! It can't be done! The young couple, perhaps, might allow it. But what about mother and dad?'

'That's your problem, Harry,' he said.

I drank off my champagne, filled up my glass, returned to my place at the wedding feast.

I looked around at the happy faces. I determined I was not going to spoil this day for them. If the uninvited guest had to join this party I was determined that he would, at least, do so decently.

If it had to be, it had to be, but nicely…

It was up to me.

I asked the waiter to serve brandy all round. I stood up, raised my glass.

'Now,' I said. 'I have a very special toast to give. I want us to drink to a man who has suffered great sorrow, a good, kind man, who might feel very lonely today. The older ones among us here, who watch the happiness of this wonderful young couple, know that fate plays many strange tricks on men and women as they make their winding journey through life.

'The older folks here, I do know, would want me to make this toast, just to show that, in the hearts of none of us here, lingers the slightest ill-feeling or hostility to the lonely man who, though he is not in our presence, must surely have been today in all our minds. Ladies and Gentlemen, I give you a toast to the brother of this lovely bride – to Mr Geoffrey Hughes…'

They all drank. And I certainly joined them.

'What a wonderful thought,' said the bridegroom.

'To her brother,' cried the bridegroom's mother. 'We certainly bear him no ill-will…'

'To my brother Geoffrey,' said Anne.

I signalled to the waiter to fill up the glasses, and he must have sensed that this was very necessary for he did so at once.

I had remained standing.

'It is indeed a great pity,' I continued, 'that the brother of the bride is not with us here to day. I am certain that all of us here would have been willing to let him share a little of our happiness, if only he could have been present. I am confident that there is not one person in this room today who would not wish to seize his hand firmly, and wish him well…'

'I wish he were here so that I could shake his hand,' said the bridegroom.

'So do I,' said the bridegroom's mother.

'So do I,' said the bridegroom's father.

'And so do I,' said the bridegroom's brother.

I looked at Anne. Her eyes seemed to say to me 'I know, I know.'

'Well, he is here!' I said quietly. 'At this moment he is upstairs wishing his sister and her bridegroom the very best of luck. He hopes to be allowed to catch a glimpse of the happy couple as we leave – just a glimpse from across the street.'

I sat down. In the words of Robert W Service, it was the 'silence you could almost hear'.

The bridegroom's mother broke that silence. 'Mr. Procter, I think you ought to go upstairs and bring him down...'

'Fetch him down...'

'Go and get him...'

'Yes, please do...'

I went upstairs, beckoned the reporter and brother Geoffrey Hughes.

'Will it be all right?' asked Geoffrey. 'I would not hurt her any more for all the world.' There were tears in his eyes.

He was warmly, fondly, welcomed. He shook hands with his sister, the mother of his babies. He shook hands with the bridegroom. Somebody gave him a glass of champagne and he drank the couple's health.

The flash-bulbs flashed, the cameras clicked.

The best, the newsiest, the most story-telling picture of the year, had been obtained for the *Sunday Pictorial.*

It was splashed the following Sunday – the picture of the uninvited guest at the wedding of the Girl Who married Her Brother.

I went off into a corner with the reporter.

'Get me a pint of nice clean beer,' I said. 'I've got a nasty taste in my mouth.'

Chapter Sixteen

There were many stories I got and wrote for the *Sunday Pictorial* which I shall always remember with pride – the *Pic* with its mammoth circulation can do, and does do, a power of good. I derived a great deal of personal satisfaction when the *Pic* allowed me to go to Folkestone and try to solve a human triangle – a husband, a wife and mother, and a girl. A divorce had been granted, the husband had left his wife and children and was going to marry the young girl. But by all getting together and talking it over we were able to persuade the husband to return to his wife, the wife to forgive him, and the girl to promise she would try and forget. It was a story well worth printing.

But there were other assignments I covered for the *Pic* which I tackled with less relish.

One of them was the investigation into the story of the Black Prince of Oxford. It will be obvious why I do not mention names in relating this.

News came to the *Pictorial* office that, in a small bed-sitting room at Oxford, the student Prince of a well known African nation lay dying of a Ju-ju spell. He was a wealthy young man, a well educated young man, a handsome young man, a very fit young man, bodily, but he fearfully believed he was going to die.

An Oxford psychiatrist, really concerned about him, had done everything in his power and skill. An Oxford priest of the Church of England had visited the young prince many times, had remembered him in all his prayers, but to no avail.

The young prince lay alone in his small room, his curtains drawn, crippled with fear.

It took much time, tact and kindness, for me to win his confidence and get him to tell me his story.

He was the nephew of the King of this African nation, he explained, and in that country the King's nephew is heir to the throne. He had been given a first-class education in his homeland,

and the elders of his tribe regarded him with pride and admiration. Then one day he announced to his people that he had decided to go to England, to become a student at Oxford University, and to study and live with the white men for five long years.

The elders had been angry at this decision, so had his uncle, the King. First they had tried gently to persuade him against going to Oxford, but he remained firm, and when they began to threaten and bully, he became more determined than ever.

He went to England, against the wishes of his King and his people. Also against the wishes of the most powerful men of all among his own people – the Witch Doctors, the Black Magicians, the Ju-ju men.

At first he was happy in Oxford, he was keen on sports and games, he worked hard at his studies, he was a popular student. Then came a letter from Africa, telling him that the witch doctors were very angry about his leaving his people. They had placed upon him a Ju-ju spell.

This may seem a childish, trivial thing to many a man or woman living in Britain, brought up in the healthy atmosphere of an intelligent Christian home.

I have little personal knowledge of the seriousness of Ju-ju to those who are reared under its black, threatening shadow. But enough to make me realise, when I talked to the Prince, that despite his bodily fitness, mentally he was a very sick man indeed.

A problem of journalism the whole world over is that it is the people in the office who have the final say about how a story many miles away from them should be treated and presented. The reporter on the spot should always be the man to pass judgment on a story; he has lived a part of it, he has seen the people, he has actual contact with the real facts.

I left the young Prince and went to see the priest.

He pleaded with me not to publish the story.

'If you publish it, it will jeopardise his life,' he said. 'Promise me here and now you will not publish this story.'

I told him I had no powers to make such a promise, that all I could do was report the facts fully to my Editor, making all the recommendations about it I felt I should make.

'Then I shall phone your editor myself and beg him not to publish,' he said. He did.

The psychiatrist I saw told me that he had grave fears for the life of the young Prince.

'Ju-ju's a grim business to many African people,' he said. 'I really think that the only hope he has got is by getting the spell removed. People in Oxford are now in touch with his uncle the King. If things are left alone I think this will be possible. But if you publish this story it will anger the King, make him determined not to forgive his nephew. Then there will be no hope of getting the spell removed.'

It was a tremendous story. It was also a tremendous responsibility for a reporter to have to shoulder. But the decision was not mine to make.

I phoned London and discussed the thing thoroughly with my editor. He was gravely concerned.

'Return to London at once,' he said. 'We shall have to discuss this story very fully.'

Back in London, I was asked to write the story, giving every detail in full, also to write the full recommendations of the priest and the medical specialist.

I had a long conference with Editor Colin Valdar about it. I recommended that, despite its excellence, it should be scrapped.

This was certainly a moment in my life when I did not envy my editor his job. For, after all, an editor has a duty to his newspaper, to his readers. The suppression of news is a thing despised in Fleet Street. And, let us be honest, this story, with its big names, was BIG NEWS.

On the Saturday morning I went in to see the editor to ask his decision. He was busy planning out the lay-out for Page One of that week's issue. He was mapping it out on paper with a thick, black pencil. Although the letters were upside down they were so big I could easily read them.

THE BLACK PRINCE OF OXFORD

'I have thought the thing over very carefully,' he said, gravely. 'This story is too important to be suppressed. How can we know we are the only newspaper to have it; another paper may print it in the morning. I am going ahead.'

'Decisions are for you to make, sir,' I said.

But I felt most unhappy.

Later in the day the editor sent for me. He picked up the Page One lay-out of the Black Prince of Oxford story, glanced at me, flung it into the waste-paper basket.

'Stop worrying, Harry,' he said. 'I have decided not to publish the story. I received a telephone request from an Oxford clergyman who assures me that its publication may be dangerous to the young man, and from his point of view, thoroughly undesirable. In the ordinary way news can't be suppressed, but it can, I think, be suppressed when its publication may do personal injury.'

I don't think anyone in the world was less likely to suppress a story than Colin Valdar, but in this instance his infallible judgment was again entirely right. This was a story that should have been suppressed and the suppression of which was creditable to everyone concerned with the matter.

We talked about it a little longer. Years later, I learnt that there was an office legend that Mr Cecil King, chairman of the *Mirror* Group, had been travelling in Africa at the time and the story had been suppressed because he was or might have been the guest of the King of the -----. So do myths originate.

But I was very pleased this story was not published.

Chapter Seventeen

Exposure is work for the expert. Very few can do it. It is a gift, an art, plus many long years of training and experience. The reporter who can do it has an elusive something for which I can give no name. Duncan Webb of the *People* has it and uses it in a truly masterful way. Lindon Laing had it.

Tricky work. Not only have you to get your facts, break down your villain and either bully him or trick him into a full confession of his villainies – there should be no holds barred when fighting scoundrels – but you must prepare and write your story in such a way that it becomes legally unassailable.

When amateurs try out this exposure business the results are terrifying, dramatic, and expensive – so far I have never lost a case for libel in my life. I saw a reporter try to unmask the bearded stall-holder of Salisbury market who hoaxed millions over television by pretending he was a Hollywood beauty specialist. I winced with pain as I watched – all that was gained was that the bearded stall-holder got angry and somebody got a punch on the jaw.

When I took on the bearded stall-holder at Salisbury market, I told him immediately that if he was looking for a bout of fisticuffs, he must count me out; I told him he was much too big for me to wrestle with.

But twenty minutes later I had him completely unmasked and pleading: 'Please don't print it.'

We printed it!

When I exposed a young scoundrel at Bristol, who was taking fees from teenage working girls with stars in their eyes, promising them stage and film careers, I refused to have another reporter near me.

'Be my agent,' I urged the scoundrel. 'Get me on the stage; I can do tricks.'

'But what kind of tricks?'

'Tricks such as exposing you in this week's *Sunday Pictorial* for the young scoundrel that you are.'

His bubble burst like a bomb, at once. On the following Tuesday he phoned me.

'Where are you, Johnnie?' I asked. 'In your Bristol office?'

'Not ruddy likely, Harry,' he said, 'not after your page-one last Sunday. I'm on the run. But do you know, I phoned you to tell you I think you wrote a damned fine story about me. It was fair and it was true.'

He told the police the same after his arrest. He went to gaol.

When exposing a phoney Harley Street doctor, I went in on my own, genuinely offering myself as a patient. He wrote down my name.

'You're not Harry Procter of the *Sunday Pictorial?*' he asked, startled.

'What if I am?'

'Are you here to expose me?'

'Why, have you anything about you which ought to be exposed?'

And he was in the bag.

But when I exposed the infamous rogues of Rogate school, I made the mistake of taking one of them back to the *Pic* office and allowing colleagues, who just did not have a clue about exposure work, to take a hand.

The results were almost disastrous. And we almost lost the story. Never again did I ever allow a colleague to interfere with my own plans of campaign on these difficult, exacting assignments.

No one admires the efficiency of the *Pictorial* organisation more than I – no one admires more, the *Pic* team.

But that team, that machine, has one weakness – a weak link I have often noted with anxiety. If any staff reporter walks into the *Pictorial* office with a first class front-page story in his note-book, everybody else tries to get in on the act. The results can be chaotic. I watched it happen when I made the suggestion – the most worthwhile suggestion I ever made in my life – that our readers should adopt orphans for Christmas; my colleagues rushed in where the angels feared to tread. The same weak link almost cost me the greatest crime scoop of my life – the Christie story.

The same weak link cost the *Pictorial* thousands of pounds over the terrible tragedy at Canvey Island – 'The Houseboat Twins' tragedy.

It is a weak, dangerously weak, link, and it could be removed. That is my advice, offered with respect, to Editor Colin Valdar – and he can have it for free.

On 12th June, 1955, my name appeared above a front-page story, with the two-inch-high headline EX-JAILBIRD RUNS FLY-BY-NIGHT SCHOOL, Fake Doctor Headmaster exposed by the *Pictorial*.

I wrote:

> The *Pictorial* today unmasks two ex-jailbirds who have been running a boarding school for eighty boys at Stow-on-the-Wold, Gloucestershire.
>
> Worse. This fly-by-night school has decamped – with the eighty boys – twice in six months. And a trail of unpaid bills and dud cheques is left.
>
> And this, at a time when the Ministry of Education is busy proclaiming the triumphal success of moves to tighten up control over private schools – moves urged by the *Pictorial*.
>
> How did this extraordinary school come to be missed?
>
> Look at the details. The Headmaster: 'Dr R Barrington Davies', claims to be a Doctor of Philosophy of London University, and also a Bachelor of Science. His real name is Ronald Sampson Davies. And he is no Doctor of anything. London University has never heard of him. He has been a street musician, chauffeur, handyman, RAF corporal, and therapist at a colony for mental defectives.
>
> He admits to the *Pictorial* that he has had five convictions for fraud.
>
> When he was made a bankrupt for £11,174 in 1953, it was said that he had acquired an interest in a number of schools including Ranksborough College in Rutland.
>
> The Bursar: 'Colonel Edward Whittaker'. This fake 'Colonel' was a private in the RASC who was discharged from the Army with ignominy.

It was a complete exposure, very detailed, very full, and very important.

How did I get it?

Only a week before the exposure was published, I received a letter from a reader complaining of dud cheques and unpaid bills left by a school which had moved rapidly from Brill, Bucks, to Aylesbury, and then to Stow-on-the-Wold.

'Apart from tradesmen needing protection, it is time someone took an interest in the pupils, who have had three school premises in three months,' the reader wrote.

I was at once intrigued by this letter although then, of course, I knew nothing about the two ex-jailbirds who were running the school. But on the Tuesday morning, determined to have the full facts in time for publication on Sunday, I left by car to follow the trail, starting at the beginning.

At Aston Clinton, Aylesbury, villagers told me many intriguing stories of the learned-looking headmaster, 'Doctor Barrington Davies', and the dapper, dashing Bursar, 'Colonel Whittaker'. I discovered, for they had regularly attended a nearby hostelry, that the two men were certainly not *too* pedantic. Sometimes boys, in their bright school blazers, had been sent to the hostelry with a note requesting a bottle of Scotch. This much I already knew about the headmaster and the bursar; they were not dull. They were a couple of gay dogs!

I made a detailed list of their many creditors in Aston Clinton – mostly small trades people. My list gave Name, Trade, Amount Owed. Then I turned the nose of my car towards Stow-on-the-Wold.

Cotswold College, latest abode of the Rogues of Rogate, certainly impressed me, as I drove along the winding drive to the front-door of the impressive mansion. Boys played cricket on the spacious lawn, boys peered from every window. The head boy answered my ring at the bell, and I asked him at once for 'The Head'.

'The Doctor, sir?'

'Yes!'

'Doctor Barrington Davies' bade me to a seat with a majestic wave of his hand. He looked magnificent in his mortar-board hat, his black gown, with his tall, broad, erect figure.

'I have called to discuss with you the possibility of sending a boy to your school,' I began.

'Ahem!' said 'Doctor' Davies, in a most scholastic way. 'Well, you realise it's difficult to get in here, very difficult you know, no vacancies for two years. Still, I will do my best to help you, providing of course, you have references. I insist on first-class, impeccable references.'

When I look back upon him sitting pompously at the great desk that sunny June morning – look back upon him with all the knowledge about him I now have – I must hand it to him. He was a rogue, but a marvellous, superb rogue. None of your small-time petty-crook, or pick-pocket about this magnificent specimen of the criminal classes.

As Lindon Laing would have said: 'You're a champion, mister, a champion!' He was.

This man was certainly a worthy opponent to any skill I might have as an exposist.

'Has anyone recommended us?' he then asked.

I took out my list of his creditors.

'Yes, doctor. You have been most highly recommended to me. Not by merely one person, or even two, or three. But by many! I have a list here of about thirty people who have strongly urged me to call and see you. Shall I read it to you?'

He beamed. 'Most certainly…'

'There is Mr Jones, the grocer, who recommends you to the tune of £24 4s. There is Mr Smith, the butcher, who recommends you to the tune of £8 12s. And they all live in Aston Clinton…'

He looked me straight in the eyes. He never blinked.

'Shall I go on, doctor?'

'Who are you?'

'I am Harry Procter, of the *Sunday Pictorial.*'

'Oh! The man who does the exposures?'

'That's correct.'

He rose like a monarch rising from a throne. He rang the bell for his head boy.

'Would you please escort this gentleman beyond the precincts of our school,' he said. Then he spoke a motto in Latin, which I could not understand. Now I know that he could not, either.

'Leave,' he said, 'please leave my school.'

But he had overplayed his hand. No genuine headmaster of a public school could ever look as much like a headmaster of a public school as he did. My suspicions were aroused. I made some telephone calls to educational contacts in London. And I found, to my joy, his degrees were phoney. I also discovered his criminal past.

That night I sat up late typing out everything I knew about the phoney headmaster. Next morning I again drove down the winding drive and rang his bell. He appeared at the large door in person, in all his scholastic splendour.

'I will not invite you in,' he said.

'No, don't!' I said. 'This is just a courtesy call. I have written my story exposing you and your partner, and it will be published on Sunday. But I want to be fair, so I'll let you have a preview – you can read it now...'

I handed him my typed story. He whitened as he read it – it was only a quarter of the full story, but there was enough to worry our 'Doctor'.

'Come into my study,' he said. Inside he flung off his mortar board cap, and his black, scholastic gown, opened a drawer of his huge desk, and took out a bottle of whisky.

'Have one?' he said. 'I need one.'

'No thanks,' I said. 'But you have one, a large one, for you certainly need it.'

He drank it off, lit a cigarette, puffed furiously.

'Look!' he said. 'I'm prepared to make a bargain with you.'

I smiled, remembering Lindon Laing, fondly wishing he could be present.

'Impossible, doctor,' I said. 'I'm an honest journalist and I cannot make a bargain with a rogue.'

A prefect entered with a pile of exercise books. He waved him out. His head flopped into his hands. He began to cry. 'What can I do?' he asked.

'Let's get out of here for a start,' I said. 'The best thing you can do now for the sake of the boys and their parents is make a clean breast of the lot.' He did, and he signed it.

I had got one bird. And I was determined to get the other.

I phoned over his confession to London in full. They were jubilant. But they asked me to bring my bird back to the office, and foolishly I agreed. I never did this again.

In London he was taken into an executive's office where a number of my colleagues fired questions at him. I remained silent – this was not my way of doing things.

I asked: 'Can I now take him back to the school? I have my other bird to pluck, remember – "Colonel" Edward Whittaker, the Bursar.'

Once again I was on my own. And I was glad. I took with me a young freelance journalist to act as witness to my conversations. But I told him, 'Please say nothing yourself. Just sit tight and listen.'

It was late when we arrived back at the school. In a well furnished lounge I found 'Colonel' Whittaker', the Bursar, and a lady.

He was drinking. Davies introduced me: 'This is Harry Procter of the *Sunday Pictorial*. He wants to ask you questions about the school.'

'Get out!' cried Whittaker, angrily. 'I am an officer and a gentleman, and I will have nothing to do with the yellow press.'

I stood up and faced him. 'You are neither an officer, nor a gentleman,' I told him. 'You are a liar, a thief, and a rogue.'

An hour later my investigations were complete. I returned to London and wrote my article.

As a result of the story both men were sent to gaol.

Chapter Eighteen

The life story of John Reginald Halliday Christie, the Monster of Notting Hill, the man who – in my opinion – murdered at least seven victims, has been told fully to the world. That story was obtained and written by me, exclusively, for my newspaper; it was told in full to a horrified world. I am not going to tell it again here.

Christie wrote his life story for me in his cell at Brixton prison and the Christie papers, written in the ostentatious handwriting of this most infamous murderer of our times, are locked in the safe of the *Sunday Pictorial.*

I met Christie personally, twice. I discussed the subject of murder. I spent weeks investigating his early life in the north – I talked with his relatives, decent, respectable people, who can never fully recover from the grief his terrible deeds caused them.

I am convinced, and I have said so in public, that it was Christie who murdered both Mrs Beryl Evans and her baby – and that, therefore, Timothy Evans, who was hanged for those murders, was innocent. But, let me emphasise strongly, this is only my private opinion.

Christie confessed to me that he murdered Mrs Evans, but when I asked him he denied murdering the baby. I have always held the view – and I always will – that the reason he would not confess to the baby murder was because he was ashamed of it. He was proud of the unfortunate women he murdered – like a seducer is proud of his conquests.

I knew the mother of Timothy Evans, a mother who never for one moment doubted the innocence of the son who was hanged. In the final days of Christie's life I did all in my power to wring from him a confession which I believe would have cleared the name of the man who was hanged as the murderer of his own child – a child he undoubtedly adored.

My editor, anxious to help in every possible way, sent to the Home Secretary Christie's written answers to the questions I asked him about the murders of Mrs Evans and her baby. Sir David Maxwell Fyfe, then Home Secretary, was glad to have Photostat copies of the original Christie writings, and he placed them before the official inquiry into the Evans case.

I maintained then, and I still do, that if I had been allowed to see Christie on the night before he was hanged I could have obtained from him a written confession to the murder of baby Evans. Hanging is, unfortunately, irrevocable; so nothing can ever be done about this terrible question now. But relatives of Evans will be, privately, thankful to know that I am still convinced that Timothy Evans was innocent of murder.

Christie told me himself that he murdered Mrs Evans – it was a typical Christie sex crime. I believe that he murdered the baby later because the crying infant was a threatening embarrassment to him – he feared that its living presence would reveal the sinister secrets of his miserable, sordid life.

Sir Linton Andrews, now chairman of the Press Council, agrees with my theory.

But the story I wish to tell here is how Christie affected me as a Fleet Street reporter – a story which has not been told before.

When the bodies of the murdered women were first discovered in a small alcove in the back kitchen of Christie's home, No 10 Rillington Place, Notting Hill, once again the cry was heard in Fleet Street 'Abortion!' Once again Fleet Street was wrong.

Twice before I had refused to believe when told, at the beginning of a murder investigation: 'It's only an abortion'. I was determined not to be caught napping a third time. And on a Wednesday night in March 1953, when no other Fleet Street man was interested in the gruesome remains found in Rillington Place, I drove my car towards Notting Hill.

Reporters who are constantly travelling the country are constantly getting that feeling, 'I have been here before. Why, when, and what for?'

And as I turned my car into dismal Rillington Place, I began at once to wonder why I had been there before. It was not until I stood before No 10, and wondered again, that it all came back to me.

I had first knocked upon that door about four years before, when I was a *Daily Mail* reporter investigating the murders of Mrs Beryl Evans and her baby.

172

It was unfortunate indeed that at that time we, in Fleet Street – I was just as mistaken as the rest – regarded the Evans murders as what we professionally call 'fish-and-chippy'. By that phrase we mean, dull, sordid, unglamorous, dreary. None of us realised then that we were literally on the doorstep of the most horrifying crime story of the century.

Consequently the trial of Timothy Evans received very small publicity – the Press box was empty for most of the trial. Had it received the spotlight of publicity which the average murder trial gets, there might have been a different result. The public, who didn't read about it then because it was so meagrely reported, might have sat back and wondered why the unfortunate Evans, who could not read or write, should have wanted to harm a wife and child he had always loved.

Star witness for the prosecution was John Reginald Halliday Christie, who wept in the box as he gave evidence – poor fellow, he was so upset. He took off his glasses and wiped away the steam of his tears when Timothy Evans shouted from the box that Christie was the murderer, that he was innocent. The judge expressed sympathy with the 'respectable' Mr Christie who had had to suffer such an undeserved ordeal – had that jury known what was at home in Christie's kitchen cupboard they would certainly have acquitted Timothy Evans.

But that night, when Christie opened the door for me, of No 10, Rillington Place, I regarded my call as routine inquiry.

Christie smiled his thin, suspicious smile, and invited me into his kitchen.

Christie was anxious to talk, but he wanted to know exactly who he was talking to. In the dimly lighted hall he asked to see my reporter's card, and he held the card close to his horn-rimmed spectacles.

Then he became quite friendly. He smiled, a sickeningly, silly smile, and he gave me an unforgettably repulsive handshake, damp and limp.

'It was like shaking hands with a snake,' I wrote later.

'Sit you down,' he said, in a slow rasping voice, as he filled a tin kettle in the kitchen where (although I did not know it then) he had murdered at least five women. 'I know you reporters like something stronger, but I can only offer you tea.'

He poured out two cups. Then he took off his spectacles and wiped them.

'You're a Yorkshireman, aren't you?' he said. 'I was born in Yorkshire, many years ago, but you never forget the accent, do you?'

His manner was peculiarly servile. He told me his version of the Evans murders, the same version he told the police. He talked to me about how a second-hand furniture dealer had bought the Evans furniture, of how Timothy Evans was missing.

And then, nervously, he asked me: 'Who do you think murdered Mrs Evans and her baby?'

I am not going to pretend to be wise after the event. At that time it never occurred to me to suspect Christie – I offer no apologies for myself, but I think, with all my training and experience, it should have. This night, professionally, I regard as the flop of my life. I too made the mistake of thinking it a 'fish and chippy' murder. Had I given Christie 'the treatment' I would have got somewhere. I ought never to be forgiven for my failure on that night. Because fail I did. And it is no balm to me to know that others also failed.

We met again in the corridor of the Old Bailey when Evans was tried for the murder of his baby and was sentenced to death. Again Christie was wiping his spectacles. He appeared to be very upset because Evans had told the jury he believed Christie to be the real killer.

'What a wicked man he is,' rasped Christie.

I next met Christie when he was in the dock at the West London Magistrates' Court, and he smiled at me as a proud son might smile at his parents on speech day. While details of his atrocious crimes were being read out he was busy writing me notes. He thanked me for sending him a shirt, but politely complained that it was half a size too big. And he did not like the colour of the tie I bought him.

From the day of his arrest to the night before he was hanged, I remained in constant, daily touch with Christie, through his solicitor, one of my oldest London friends. The many letters and notes Christie wrote me are all preserved.

I next got an opportunity of talking to him when his case was transferred to the Clerkenwell Court where he was committed for trial. Then, Derek Curtis Bennett took me into Christie's cell.

By this time, Christie regarded me as his friend and champion.

'Tell me one thing,' I urged, 'one very important thing. Did you kill Mrs Evans and her baby? It is best for all concerned if you tell the truth.'

He said: 'Mrs Evans, yes. I had an affair with her. But not the baby.' He turned away. He was ashamed of something.

The day following I was flown to Calvi in Corsica, to write a story about an ex-debutante who had married a handsome Corsican fisherman. It was an island of enchantment, the bay of Calvi was like something from a picture postcard, but I could not enjoy it. I was worried about Christie and the man whose bones lay rotting in a felon's grave. I did my story – it went Page One – and immediately flew back to London and contacted Christie's solicitor.

I pleaded, 'do get this man to confess to the murder of the baby. Honest, I don't ask for it as a newspaper story. You and I must get the truth.' The solicitor, charming, bearded, courteous, wise, did his very best right to the end.

When I first realised that Christie was one of the most infamous murderers of our times, and set out to buy up his exclusive story for my paper, I met a problem I had never encountered before. Reporters on some other Sunday papers faced the same problem.

'Who shall we offer the money to?'

There was no wife of the killer to offer the money to this time – she'd been murdered and buried under the floor boards at No 10 Rillington Place. There was no mother or father; thank God, for their sakes – for they were decent, religious people – they were dead. There was a brother and sisters in the North of England, but they had not heard of John Christie for seventeen years.

Who could we offer the money to?

Christie was missing, sought by the police throughout the land. In London there was not even a friend of Christie's to be found. This certainly was a new and original problem for those of us in Fleet Street who dealt in human souls. By this time I was as expert as any of my Sunday paper rivals in buying up the life stories of murderers. The formula was a known one. First you contacted a friend – 'No intrusion on private grief' says the rule book of the National Union of Journalists – through the friend you contact a relative, preferably a husband, wife, mother, or sister. Then you talk, and talk, and talk, and talk …

I know. I have done it so often.

Or failing that you go in officially through the solicitor of the man or woman you know will eventually be charged with murder.

Sit down there, you, that man on the back row. I'll have no hypocritical comment! How many murderers' stories have you read, sir, in the Sunday papers? If you've never read one, then I'll listen to you. If you have read one, then shut up! We poor slaves are your servants, sir, not your masters. We give you what you want because you want it!

Let me tell you, sir, before you throw your back-row seat at me, it was tougher for me to do than it is for you to hear about it. But you, sir, you were the boss.

The Ruth Ellis story was straightforward. I knew exactly where I stood.

But my editor, and my fourteen million readers, wanted the life story of John Reginald Halliday Christie; I was paid to get it. And I was a Fleet Street reporter.

Also, you in the back row there, the local butcher, baker, and retailer of electric bulbs, were paid by me out of what Fleet Street paid me.

While Christie was still missing – 'police believe he may be able to help them in their inquiries' – I made a quick, indirect check of all his relatives in the North.

I met most of them, later; they were all good, respectable people. I refuse to mention any of their names, for they all suffered grievously from the notoriety of their infamous brother; they must not suffer from anything I write here.

But I think they would all like me to say that not one of them was ever even slightly interested in cash offers from Fleet Street for Christie's story. They wanted nothing to do with him. Some were offered money by Fleet Street, not one accepted a penny.

But their honesty and principle did not help Fleet Street to get the Christie story. We were all running round in circles.

Eventually I was informed that one Christie relative in the north was willing to discuss it with me. This relative, although he knew that some Sunday papers were willing to pay up to £5,000 for the Christie story, was not interested in money.

Fortunately, knowing by uncanny instinct that to offer money would offend the relative, I did not do so.

But I did point out that the relative – all the relatives – had a duty to this monster-like creature to whom they were related. It might be, I said, that he was a mentally sick man. Then it would be their duty to get him the best medical help, and the best defending counsel at his trial. I would pay for all this, I said, in return for an inside story to be published after the trial. To this the relative agreed.

Christie told the solicitor that he remembered me and said: 'I want Harry Procter to have my story.'

From that day I knew I had secured a world scoop in crime, knew that I would be the man to write the life story of the most infamous murderer since Crippen. I took my success calmly as I always have done. My plan now was to go quietly about the job of organising the Christie story.

But my colleagues in the *Pic* office were far more excited about this beat than I was. It seemed that everybody wanted to give me a hand. Some of them began running round in circles, dizzy with enthusiasm.

R T Payne, the Deputy Editor, announced that he wanted to attend the preliminary police court proceedings with me, 'in case there are difficulties'.

A reporter cannot give orders to his Deputy Editor. There were certainly difficulties.

When we arrived at the West London Police Court we were amazed to find representatives of two different firms of solicitors seated in the well of the court; both claiming they were there to represent Christie. One was the man I had already met as representing Christie. The other solicitor had been told by reporter James Reid of the *Sunday Dispatch* that his newspaper was willing to pay for the Christie defence.

It was a macabre situation. There in the dock sat a man who had taken the lives of at least six people; who was to stand his trial for murder. In the well of the court were two solicitors who both believed he was their client. And two great, national Sunday newspapers believed that, in return for paying for the man's defence, they would have his exclusive story.

The two solicitors requested a private meeting with the magistrates, and the door was closed upon a crowded, excited, court. Most of the crowd inside the court were newspaper men.

In the same small dock where, a few years earlier, I had watched Neville Heath doodling with pencil and notebook, sat John Christie, completely relaxed, his arms crossed upon his knees. He nodded and smiled at me, just as though we were meeting on a Number 9 bus.

He wrote out a note and held it up for me to see.

It read: 'Thanks for the shirt.' I nodded.

It was a grim, tense atmosphere. It was a moment in crime. It was also a moment in newspaper history.

From across the court, James Reid of the *Sunday Dispatch* looked at me. He allowed himself a half-smile.

'Reid is smiling,' said a reporter next to me.

'I don't think he will smile for long,' I said. I certainly hoped he would not.

My Deputy Editor was white with suspense.

It was terribly hot in the small crowded court. We stepped out into the hall for a smoke.

James Reid crossed over to us and made some attempt at conversation.

'Anyhow,' he said. 'This is a moment we shall all remember when we write a book...'

'Maybe,' commented Reg Payne, drily. 'But I'm not going to write a b-----y book.'

We tip-toed back into the court. Christie gave me another smiling nod – as though he had missed me. Minutes ticked torturously by.

Then the little door opened and Reg Payne and I were told that Christie himself had been taken from the dock, down to the cells, and asked to choose. He made no change.

'You can get the Christie poster ready,' I told Reg Payne. Outside the court in the street James Reid was shouting out 'I shall protest, I shall protest ...'

'I wonder what's got into that chap?' said my Deputy Editor.

'I haven't the vaguest idea, sir.'

Up north, I saw some of Christie's relatives, and was able to assure them that he was to have the best defence possible. Publicity, I told them, would be most regrettable so far as they were concerned, but it was inevitable. They understood. None of them wished to attend the trial.

After his sentence, Christie sent me word that before he was hanged he would like to see one of his sisters. I passed the message on to her.

She said that she was willing to agree to his request providing there was no publicity about her visit to him. I promised her there would be none. I kept this promise.

On the night before the execution she went to see him. She was surprised, she said, that he was in such good spirits.

'Don't worry about the morning' he told her. 'They won't hurt me. They'll take my glasses off before they hang me, so I won't see much.' As a gesture to his words he took off his glasses, then put them on again.

I know nothing of that morning. But my personal experience of Christie, the knowledge of his life and his crimes which I gained in weeks of hard work and exhausting inquiry, convinces me of one thing – he was mad! He was wicked, he was a monster, but he was mad! Our law at the time said that no man should be hanged for murder if he was not sane.

Was Christie sane?

Let me quote you the private opinion of a very wise man indeed – Colin Valdar, Editor of the *Sunday Pictorial.*

He said to me: 'Had you come to me when Christie did his first murder I would have said: He may be sane.

'Had you later told me of this third murder I think I would have allowed myself a doubt; I might have asked myself: I wonder if a fellow who does this three times has perhaps something wrong with his head?

'But after five sadistic murders of this kind, spread over years, had you come to me and asked me about him I would have had no hesitation in saying: The man is mad!'

My Christie story sold many extra newspapers for the *Sunday Pictorial.* I had no qualms of conscience about taking from them my wages that week. I will not tell you what the story cost the *Sunday Pictorial,* but I will tell you that another newspaper bid £5,000 for it. It cost the *Pictorial* much, very much, less.

I will tell one thing here which has never been told before; I will tell you what caused the burning hatred in the mind of John Halliday Christie resulting in those revolting, cruel murders at No 10 Rillington Place.

When Christie was in his early teens, in Halifax, Yorkshire, it was the custom for youngsters to promenade up and down on a Sunday night on a Lovers' Lane, known as The Duck Walk.

One Sunday night, Christie, the teenage Christie, paraded on that

Duck Walk and met a teenage girl – a mill girl I believe – whose morals were rather free.

She was not a virgin. She was, to an extent, experienced; Christie was shy, nervous, unpractised in love-making, and completely uninitiated in the act of sex.

The amorous adventure which took place that night between Christie and the girl was a failure.

The girl laughed at him, laughed loudly. Throughout his life, her scornful laughter rang in his ears.

This girl had other teenage lovers, and contemptuously she told them about Christie's attempts at love-making. She believed he was impotent, she inferred. Christie's pals ragged him about the incident.

They gave him a nick-name, 'No ----- Reggie.'

Her laughter and their jokes caused Christie to experience a bitter humiliation which he never forgot. It caused his hatred and his fear of women. I believed it caused him to commit murder.

But this is a story not only about me, it is a story about the living, breathing Fleet Street; and it would be unfair if I ended the Christie chapter without paying a well-deserved tribute to the doyen of Fleet Street crime reporters: Norman Rae of the *News of the World* – Jock Rae as I know him.

Jock Rae has many more years of experience in crime reporting than I; I knew and respected his work long before I came to Fleet Street. He is a fine craftsman, he takes crime reporting very seriously, he has no time for sensation or stunts. When Jock reports a murder assignment he reports it accurately, fully, and with a skilled interpretation which is the hallmark of the expert.

He has served the *News of the World* for many years as its crime reporter; his world scoops are many; they include the confession of Dr Buck Ruxton – a man who murdered when I was in knee pants.

Many young Fleet Street men have made the mistake of regarding Jock Rae as belonging to a Fleet Street which is past; but not I. I always thought of him as a skilful, powerful, but scrupulously honest rival. Jock Rae taught me much about crime reporting.

I first ran into Jock at Thetford, Norfolk, in my early years of Fleet Street, on one of my first murder assignments. I was on a daily paper, he was on a Sunday, I had been there all the week, he had just arrived. I was able to give him a little help.

Jock Rae never forgot. And he helped me several times later. Jock Rae, in a bigger way than I, has suffered from the ills of 'Success' – has often been alone at a bar because of an exclusive story.

During the first week of the Christie murder investigation – a week when nobody called it murder and nobody mentioned Christie in print – Jock Rae swept the floor with the lot of us.

When I read, that Sunday morning, his magnificent, detailed, fully-factual report of the happenings in Rillington Place, Notting Hill, I knew twice as much about the murders than when I wrote my story.

I read Jock's story. He was my rival, he worked for the newspaper with the world's biggest circulation, and he had beaten me hollow – he had beaten us all.

Yet I had never admired Jock Rae more than on that Sunday. So I sent my rival a telegram saying 'Congratulations on your magnificent story – you have beaten us all'.

Chapter Nineteen

There is one man in the world who, I know, will never forgive me for a story I wrote as a Fleet Street reporter – a world-wide exclusive story which appeared splashed across Page One of the *Sunday Pictorial.*

That man is Captain Niven Matthews Craig, father of the sixteen-year-old gunman Christopher Craig, the teenager who shot and murdered Police Constable Miles on the rooftop of a Croydon building way back in 1952.

An unforgettable murder with which I was closely associated for long, long weeks; an unforgettable story which I wrote. A story of a murder which will always haunt me because (and again let me emphasise that this is only my personal opinion) it led to another execution in which I believe the man who was hanged was innocent of murder – another hanging where the subject was a man who could neither read nor write. I shall always maintain that Derek Bentley, the nineteen-year-old youth who was jointly charged at the Old Bailey with Craig for the murder of the Croydon policeman, was 'Not Guilty'. Derek Bentley was a house-breaker, a thug, an illiterate; I have never had any admiration for him. But I do not believe he was a murderer. In my view he was 'Hanged But Innocent'.

But first let me tell of my long and warm friendship with Christopher Craig's mother, father, and his beautiful sister, Lucy – a friendship which ended when the father emphatically refused to shake my hand or to speak to me ever again. I can understand the bitterness of Niven Matthews Craig, I always did understand.

A mystifying thing about my experiences with the crime of murder is that the families of those who ruthlessly take the lives of others are usually nice, ordinary, kind people – people like Mr and Mrs Craig and their daughter, Lucy. The Craig family I came to know so well were very much the same as the nice friendly family who live next door to you, decent, honest, industrious.

Captain Craig and I became good friends during the long dark weeks in which we all awaited the trial of Christopher Craig. He was always courteous, helpful, generous. He was a father who dearly loved his sixteen-year-old son, who suffered great grief when the son went wrong.

Niven Craig trusted me. He believed that both I and the *Sunday Pictorial* betrayed his trust. His disillusionment came at the end of a path of duty I found it very hard to tread.

Again let us forget the story of the murder; it was told in many millions of printed words in every newspaper in the world. It was one of many stories I secured for my employers.

When news of this terrible shooting burst upon a shocked world, newspapers, churches, and the government were gravely concerned about a wave of violence sweeping the land; about young teenage thugs, carrying coshes, who were daily finding victims and bludgeoning them for a few pounds, a few shillings, sometimes even for a few coppers. The terror-problem of the times made the Craig murder focus a grave social problem of that day.

Shortly after the murder I went tactfully and gently to inquire whether Mr and Mrs Craig were willing to co-operate with me in throwing light upon the problem of why so many of our teenagers were practising violence and thuggery.

Mr and Mrs Craig welcomed my inquiry, so did eighteen-year-old Lucy Craig. They were deeply shocked by the tragedy, were concerned at the national wave of violence. They wanted to help.

I asked for the help of colleague Madeline MacLoughlin; I wanted her to befriend the mother and the sister. She was certainly a great success and Mrs Craig adored her before the long assignment came to an end.

Madeline MacLoughlin has a quality extremely rare in women; that of being liked by other women. This quality is a great asset to her, professionally.

Almost daily Madeline and I visited the Craigs at their home, spent hours with them, constantly making a gentle investigation into the deeper, hidden cause of the tragedy which clouded their lives. Eventually the Craig family regarded Madeline and me as their truest friends. They gave us all their confidences, they sought our help over every problem. And for weeks Madeline and I, as paid and skilled journalists, had the tough task of keeping away the

183

opposition reporters and photographers. The opposition never allowed us a day or night free from anxiety; but this girl-reporter and I were the perfect team; we succeeded.

When the trial opened at the Old Bailey I had to organise my forces like a military operation. My long experience of the Old Bailey made me realise that the task of taking Mr and Mrs Craig and daughter Lucy to that great court of justice every day for perhaps a week without allowing even a 'Yes' or 'No' for quotes to our friends the opposition, was a formidable one. Madeline and I were determined that it should be done. The ordeal was almost as mentally shattering for us as it was for the tragic Craig family.

Everybody in the road where they lived knew the Craigs; they had been a large, laughing, often boisterous family of three brothers and five sisters. Mr and Mrs Craig had lived for their children; if they had a fault at all it was that they had loved their children too much.

The Craig family, in the last few years, had known several tragedies – tragedies which do not concern this book. Some of the children had married, some had gone away. Now the family's 'baby', the handsome Christopher, was facing the most tragic ordeal any human being can face.

At home the Craig family had been whittled down to three; the tall, dignified father, the still beautiful woman who was the mother, the attractive, immaculately dressed daughter. Lovely Lucy Craig, I understand, has since married and made a new life in a new world; I certainly hope she has found the happiness her faithfulness and loyalty deserve. She was young, then, when the dark clouds of trouble overshadowed the lives of her parents; scores of people offered her quiet havens away from it all but she stayed on in the centre of the tragedy to be with the man and woman whose hearts were breaking.

Early every morning the task of Madeline and I was to take the Craig family by car, from their home in Norbury, South London, to the Old Bailey. We had to guard our professional interests. But, in addition, we had a moral obligation to see that the Craigs were not bullied or tormented by the opposition; it was our duty to try and make their ordeal a little less unbearable.

We succeeded. Not one opposition reporter got one word with either Captain Craig, Mrs Craig, or Lucy Craig during that long and history-making murder trial. One pirate reporter flammed an interview for his Sunday paper with Lucy, but Lucy denied, through a solicitor, that she had ever seen or spoken to the reporter.

Each day, Madeline and I had to see to it that the Craig family ate a good lunch, uninterrupted and undisturbed. We booked a private room at a tavern near the Old Bailey.

Twice every lunch-hour, Madeline and I had to battle our way through a jungle of reporters and photographers with the Craig family nuzzling close to us for protection. To me those short journeys were frightening.

But the trial came to an end. Craig and Bentley were both found guilty of murder; Craig, because of his age, was sent to prison for life. Derek Bentley was sentenced to be hanged by the neck until he was dead.

Allow me just a reference to the story told of the trial, a reference to the most important line of the entire evidence presented. The prosecution declared that Bentley shouted to Craig, shortly before Craig shot PC Miles: 'Let him have it, Chris.' Never were five words in a murder trial so vitally important.

On that dark winter's night when the shooting took place, it was very noisy up on the roof where Craig, holding a gun, was trying to escape from the police who had, in large numbers, surrounded the building. Police constables were shouting information from one to the other, the crowd in the streets were shouting, 'There he goes! There he is.' A real-life game of cops and robbers was being played on the Croydon roof-top – no quiet game of cat-and-mouse.

Derek Bentley was captured, officially apprehended, correctly and legally taken into custody. When the police took that youth by the scruff of his neck and firmly held his arms he was a felon and the property of the law. As matters stood then he would have been charged with carrying burglar's tools by night, with being in possession of an illegal weapon (a knuckle-duster), with attempted breaking and entering. No murder had been committed when Bentley was arrested.

It was after the official apprehension of Bentley that Craig shot and murdered Police Constable Miles – a truly terrible deed.

No one ever suggested that Bentley's finger was ever on the trigger. No one suggested he did the shooting. Everyone agreed that, at the time of the murder, Derek Bentley was under arrest.

But what he did, was to shout out to Christopher Craig, 'Let him

185

have it, Chris...' Because of those five words, Bentley was hanged – those five words made him, legally, guilty of murder.

I talked with Christopher Craig as he lay, propped up with pillows, in the hospital bed of his private cell. This was before the trial. This was long before the sixteen-year-old boy knew anything about what might happen to Derek Bentley.

'Before you shot the policeman, did you hear Bentley shout to you "let him have it, Chris"?' I asked.

'No,' said Christopher Craig. 'He never did. No, he never did.'

'Look, Chris,' I said. 'This is very important. Think about it carefully. Are you absolutely certain that Bentley never shouted to you "Let him have it, Chris"?'

'No,' said Craig, and I repeat this story in young Craig's favour, 'Derek never said it.'

On leaving I again urged Craig to think over this question, and urged that if ever he remembered Bentley shouting these words to him, to let me know. But he never did.

At the end of the trial the great problem for Madeline and me was to get the Craig family away into the country and hide them. Hiding people whose photographs for weeks have been on front pages of every newspaper in the land is not the same as hiding needles in haystacks. We got them into a Rolls Royce car and headed for the country, our destination unknown. I reasoned with Madeline: 'How can the opposition know where we are going if we don't know ourselves?'

Mrs Craig, after her long ordeal, wanted to go anywhere but to her house in Norbury, which held so many mixed memories.

'Do you know,' she confessed frankly, 'I'm excited. Despite all the worry and the trouble I find that I can still be excited – just like a schoolgirl – about going off on a journey and not knowing where we'll end up.' Madeline squeezed her hand.

'You're going with us, love,' she said. 'That's all that matters.'

We ended up at a lovely, old inn at Shepperton, in the heart of Britain's film world. I booked a suite of rooms. And we all relaxed, even the driver of our Rolls Royce car.

It was here that Mrs Craig and Lucy broke through the 'not-a-single-sound' barrier imposed on them by Madeline and me.

Walking into one of the lounges the following afternoon, I found Mrs Craig and Lucy, deeply engrossed in conversation with a handsome stranger. It was film star Alan Ladd. Both mother and daughter were enraptured, spell-bound. He was, it seems, their favourite.

I joined them. 'All right,' I said, indulgently. 'I'll forgive you both this time – seeing as he's better looking than me.'

Now Madeline and I believed that the long hard weeks of night and day work were at an end. We had both written our stories. These were in proof at the office, there was nothing more to do other than guard the Craigs. Or so we thought.

My only problem was the problem of lovely Lucy's panties. To Madeline's amazement, the lovely Lucy insisted that a pair of panties should never be worn twice. Yet, because Lucy did not carry panties by the dozen with her, Madeline ordered me daily to go and buy her a pair.

'Why can't *you* go and buy the panties?' I protested.

'Because a man has always better judgment concerning what a woman should wear,' she bullied. 'Now off you go to Staines and get Lucy's panties.'

That night we all went to a cinema show. We got into the car to return to the hotel, when Lucy remembered. 'I have left my new panties in the cinema,' she announced.

'Go on, Harry,' said Madeline. 'Go and get Lucy's panties.' This was some assignment. Inside the empty cinema I saw the manager.

'Excuse me, but a young lady has left a pair of panties in that row down there. Can I go and get them.'

He remained silent. I spotted the paper bag with the newly purchased panties lying on the floor, picked it up, and waved the bag at him.

'It's a cold night, isn't it?' I said, and left.

On the Friday I took Captain Craig, Lucy Craig and her mother into a private corner, deciding to show them the story I had written about Christopher Craig, the story to be published on the Sunday. I decided to be honest with them.

'I do not know what you are expecting me to write,' I said. 'I know that, despite all, you love Christopher. And the three of you have now become my friends. But you will not like the story I am going to publish on Sunday.'

'We do not expect to like it, Harry,' said Captain Craig.

I decided to be very frank. 'I am going to condemn your son,' I said. 'Not because I bear him any grudge – I don't; I am sorry for the boy, I will do anything I can to help him in the future. But it is my solemn duty to condemn him so that he is not glorified in the eyes of millions of other young boys. In this country there may be many stupid teenagers, reared on crime films, who regard Christopher Craig as a hero – who think he was brave and tough. My duty is to assure these boys that Christopher Craig was a coward. I am going to destroy any Craig legend which might exist.'

Then I gave them all a typed copy of my article, which was published the following Sunday headed 'Killer Craig, a candid pen picture by Harry Procter'.

To the fourteen million readers of the *Sunday Pictorial* I told of a handsome dark-haired youth lying in bed in a small gloomy cell in Brixton Prison.

I told those readers that the youth who lay there appeared to be enjoying the drama in which he had played a principal role since he had shot unarmed Police Constable Sidney Miles.

I told them how his first question to me was whether I had brought him any comics and how all the time I was with him he had expressed no remorse for his action nor shown any sympathy for the relatives of the man he had killed.

My article ran on to tell the life story of this boy who killed a policeman. It contained no glory, no glamour.

I think it is wickedly wrong for any newspaper – particularly a popular newspaper which is read by teenagers – ever to glamorise crime or compliment criminals. It is our duty to write about criminals with contempt; they must be cheapened, ridiculed, never martyred.

Therefore I condemned Craig; and I would condemn him again if it was happening this week. But, because I want to be scrupulously fair, I must say here that the reports I have heard about the excellent moral and intellectual progress Christopher Craig has made in jail have delighted me; I look forward to the day when he will return to the world, as a God-fearing, useful citizen; I believe that all wrong-doers can repent and reform and become the men and women God intended them to be.

But to return to Shepperton. The Craig family did not like my 'candid pen-picture' of their son. But they agreed it ought to be published.

188

On the Friday evening I received alarming news from the London news desk. They wanted another article – a front page lead. They recalled the many comments, opinions, regrets, and other statements Captain Niven Craig had made to me about his son in the many weeks I had known him. They wanted the father to condemn his own son, and to put his own name on the story of condemnation. Would I please go to my room at once, write this second article, and phone it over immediately.

This was a development which Madeline and I had never anticipated.

I went alone to my room, and wrote the story of the confidences Niven Craig had made to me.

I wrote Niven Craig's own story of how he had failed as a father.

The story described how, as the youngest child of a family of eight children, Christopher Craig had had lavished on him all the affection a big family have for the 'baby'.

I told how Niven Craig now realised that, through neglecting to ensure proper religious instruction for his son, and by sparing the rod, he had been to a large part responsible for Christopher Craig growing up to be a thug.

It warned other parents how like indulgence towards their children, under the easy slogan of freedom for youth, could lead to like tragedies.

And much more on these lines.

Fred Redman phoned me back. 'This is a brilliant human document, Harry,' he said. 'But be sure you get Mr Craig to write his name above the story and to sign it on every page.'

Be sure you get him to sign it on every page…

Again, this was my problem, the reporter's problem, the problem of the little chap at the other end of the stick. Back in the *Pictorial* office the executives sat back, smoked cigars, preened themselves on what a wonderful paper 'they' would turn out that week.

'They' are the wonder men, 'they' are the people who make the millions for Beaverbrook, for Kemsley, for Associated Newspapers, for the mammoth *Mirror* group.

Remember the words of that grand old-timer Montague Smith. '…be careful dear. He's only a reporter…'

I remember, much later, when, delighted by a sudden boom in circulation, the paper generously gave an order for a load of champagne to be brought to the office, and 'they' went in and filled their glasses. Not one reporter was invited – not even I.

'...condemned by all, to the uttermost perdition...'

But that Friday night in Shepperton I too drank champagne, and filled the glasses of the Craig family to the very brim.

'Have a good drink,' I urged. 'Here is a story they want to publish page one lead tomorrow. But before they publish it they want you, Niven, to write your name on top of it, and to sign it on every page.'

I handed him a large cigar, the best in the house.

He read my story. 'No!' he said. 'Definitely no! I will not allow that story to go in the paper.'

'Is the story true, Niven?'

'Yes, it is true. I have said these things to you. But I do not want to write them in an article in the *Sunday Pictorial*. Frankly I think you have got enough for your money...'

Lucy Craig read the story. Mrs Craig read it. They said they thought it ought to be published as a warning to other parents.

'Well, I refuse to sign it,' said Captain Niven Craig, and went off to bed. I followed his example.

Much later on a phone call came for me from Fred Redman. Madeline told him, 'Fred, Harry is in bed, fast asleep I hope. He's had a tough day, so have we all.'

'Go and get him out of bed then,' said Redman.

'I refuse, Fred,' said Madeline. 'Let him sleep if he can.'

Fred Redman phoned me early in the morning.

'I phoned you last night, but you were in bed according to Madeline. What the 'ell were you doing in bed?'

'Just a silly old habit I picked up in my childhood, Red.'

'Well, tell me, has he signed it yet?'

'No, not yet. But he will.'

The five of us had a gloomy breakfast. 'I insist on going back to London at once,' said Captain Craig.

'Anything you say. Get your luggage in the car; I'll be ready when you are.'

Later, in the car, Niven suddenly said: 'Give me the story, I'll sign it.' I gave him my story, the story I had ghosted for him.

'Don't sign it unless you are sure it is all true,' I said.

'Oh, it's true enough,' he said. 'If you treat it seriously I do not mind, but do not treat it sensationally.'

The next morning, when he bought the *Sunday Pictorial,* he was angry to read the front-page headline, in black, two-inch high letters:
MY FAILURE: BY CRAIG'S FATHER
The first two words of the headline were heavily underlined. And the story was sub-headlined 'Why Have I Failed?' By Niven Matthews Craig.

Some months later, when we met again, he refused to shake my hand; he told me our friendship was at an end.

I was really sorry. For I liked the Craigs.

Saturday, 13th December did not end there, of course.

I phoned the office, told them the story was signed – signed on every page – and I would send it to them within the hour, which I did.

But the five of us had had a tough, exhausting, anxious week. We felt we must relax.

I took them all into a little Soho club I know, feeling sure there would be nobody there who would recognise the Craigs. We were just beginning our drinks when two reporters from an opposition Sunday paper rushed at us. We left the drinks.

Every Sunday paper in London was hunting for the Craig family that day.

We wanted a good meal, and a little peace, so I decided that it would be best to have dinner at the ancient Prospect of Whitby, by the edge of London's docks.

Both the food and the wine there equals that of many a West End restaurant.

We were eating trout, and drinking champagne, and somebody gave a toast. We had decided to forget the last terrible weeks for an hour; we were happy. We looked happy.

As we drank the toast, the flash bulb flashed.

'This is the end of you and me, Harry,' said Madeline. 'What a scoop this picture is for the *Sunday Dispatch.*'

I walked over to the photographer, determined to smash his camera. We could not fail at this eleventh hour after all our efforts.

'How many copies would you like, sir?' said the photographer.

He was a 'Happy Snap' man.

'Just three apiece,' I said. I did not want to sound anxious. 'What address, sir?'

The photographer walked away not knowing that in his camera he

191

had an exposed negative which he could have sold in Fleet Street, within the hour, for £500.

When I met him later, I bought him a drink.

'I shall never forgive myself for not knowing,' he said. 'I'd got the scoop of my life, and I did not know.'

Chapter Twenty

If there is one place in the whole world where a man is never allowed to doze, even for one hour, upon his laurels, that place is Fleet Street.

'They' considered that 'they' had beaten Fleet Street so completely, exhaustively, and decidedly with the Craig story, that on the following Tuesday morning I was told to write no more about the Craigs.

In fact I did another Craig feature story late in the following January when Lucy Craig was refused permission to go to New Zealand as an emigrant, after her application had been fully accepted and her passage arranged. That headline, above Lucy's picture, asked: 'Must I suffer for my brother?' and in the story Lucy posed the question: 'Am I my brother's keeper?' – but that was merely an echo.

On the Tuesday following my Craig scoop I was asked to turn my attention to the family of Derek Bentley, then in the death cell awaiting execution. From that day I began to see as much of the Bentley family, almost, as I had seen of the Craigs.

The conscience of the country was uneasy about Derek Bentley, and appeals that his life should be spared were made from many quarters. Derek's mother, a sad, bewildered little woman – one of the most pathetic figures to walk on the stage of this great criminal drama – wrote to the Queen pleading for her boy.

I saw Mrs Bentley many times, but her grief was too complete for talk. She was numb with her grief. She was interested in nothing but the flickering hope in her heart that her boy's life might be spared.

One thing I can say, I never blew a breath upon that tiny spark of hope; there were others who did.

The Bentley family, mother, father, and sister Iris, worked night and day organising petitions for his life. Support for those petitions came from all parts of the world.

On the Tuesday before the day on which Derek Bentley was

hanged, I had lunch with his father. I was able to make him an offer on behalf of my employers.

If, on the night before he was hanged, Derek Bentley wrote a death-cell letter, we would pay generously for permission to publish that letter exclusively the following Sunday. Mr Bentley accepted my proposal.

I did not mention it to Mrs Bentley – I dare not have done. Late that night I was drinking in the Strangers' Bar at the House of Commons – and there were certainly many strangers at the bar.

There were Mr and Mrs Bentley, and Iris Bentley. There was Mrs Craig, Lucy Craig. In our party were several MPs whom I knew. I introduced these to the Bentleys and the Craigs.

While we drank, miserably, quietly, in the Strangers' Bar, a great fight was going on in the House for the life of Derek Bentley – 200 MPs were urging the Home Secretary to grant a reprieve.

It was a macabre scene at the bar. There we were, an oddly assorted party of people, inside the very hub of the British Empire, a hub which controlled our laws, our wars, our taxes, our homes, our lives, our dreams. I sat there with MPs who were famous throughout the world and with ordinary people who would certainly never have been there not even for one minute of their lives, had it not been for that second in time when a bullet sped from a gun held by a sixteen-year-old-boy, to the body of a police constable.

Again and again an MP would walk over to me at the bar and whisper in my ear. He would tell me how the debate was going. I would whisper into the ear of Mr Bentley, he would tell his wife and daughter. Then we would call for another round of drinks.

Mrs Bentley, an obscure suburban housewife, sat in this historic building while famous men whose names she only knew by reading her newspaper walked by her or stopped to glance at her in sympathy.

'I wish you would get Mrs Bentley to have a brandy, Harry,' urged my friend Hugh Delargy MP. 'She just sits there, waiting, saying nothing.'

As I paid for a drink for the Bentley family, the Craig family, for the odd MP present, Derek Bentley sat with the death-watch warders in a cell in Wandsworth prison. The hangman watched him through a peep-hole, wrote notes on a pad about his height and his weight, calculated the depth of the required drop.

Derek Bentley did not know that at that moment his mother, father and sister were sitting in the Strangers' Bar at the House of Commons – that 200 MPs were fighting for his life.

But at that moment, while the Bentley family were thinking about their son, he was thinking about them.

We did not know it but he was dictating a letter.

As his mother sat there by my side, Derek Bentley was dictating:

'I told you Mum, it would be very difficult to write this letter. I can't think of anything to say except that you have all been wonderful the way you have worked for me...'

The youth who was to die the following morning did not know that the letter he dictated to his mother and father was the letter I was to buy for a three figure sum a few days later, a letter which was that week to be published in the *Sunday Pictorial.*

Big Ben boomed above us – the hour of midnight; Hugh Delargy MP approached me.

'There is no hope,' he whispered. 'Can you get Mrs Bentley home?'

I broke the news to Mr William Bentley. 'I am going to fight on for the rest of the night...' he said.

'OK, Bill! But I think I'd better take your wife and daughter home.'

'Look after them, Harry,' said Tom Driberg, MP.

I got them into my car outside the House of Commons and drove them home. 'Is there any hope?' asked the mother. She was beyond tears or hysterics.

I just hadn't got the guts to say to her: 'There is no hope at all.'

My silence answered her question.

We arrived at the Bentley home. Mrs Bentley said nothing, she just sat down in a chair. Sister Iris Bentley went and sat on the bottom step of the bedroom stairs.

This was one moment in my professional life when I just did not know what to do.

Iris Bentley's head was in her hands. She was not weeping.

'You can tell me the truth, Mr Procter,' she said. 'There is no hope at all, is there?'

'I am terribly afraid you are right, Miss Bentley.'

She glanced from the stairs, through the open door of the sitting room, to the shelf where a clock ticked. It was almost dawn.

It was very quiet in the house. Neither the mother nor the sister was weeping. Sometimes in life there is grief which is too big for tears.

'I shall go on fighting for him, always,' said Iris Bentley, simply, calmly.

'Shall I stay here? Or shall I go?'

'You may as well go,' she said. 'There is nothing you can do.'

I went home, flopped into bed with my clothes on, and thought about five small words.

'Let him have it, Chris.'

Derek Bentley was hanged on the Wednesday morning. There was a riot outside the prison gates and, when a prison official attempted to suspend the notice board announcing the execution, the crowd seized it from his grasp and dashed it to the ground. The official notice was torn.

On the Thursday morning my office sent me to call on the Bentley family.

'He wrote a letter,' said William Bentley. 'You can have it on the terms we arranged. But I can't lay my hands on it at the moment.'

Mrs Bentley was seated on her chair which had a large cushion. She was silent.

'Call back later,' said her husband, 'and I may be able to lay my hands on it.'

I reported to my Deputy Editor, Reg Payne, 'Bentley did write a last letter. But I don't think his mother wants us to have it!'

On the Friday my office asked me to call again at the Bentley home.

Mrs Bentley was seated on the chair. Mr Bentley said: 'Tell my wife, Harry, that you think Derek's letter ought to be published.'

'I am afraid I cannot advise Mrs Bentley on that,' I said.

'I think,' said Mr Bentley, 'that Derek's letter showed that he believed in his innocence right to the end – that is why it ought to be published. I think his letter should be given the fullest possible publicity.'

Mrs Bentley raised herself slightly from her chair. She put her hand beneath the cushion on which she sat, and pulled out an envelope. 'There is the letter, Mr Procter,' she said, 'the letter from my boy.' Then she burst into tears.

I will not attempt to describe my feelings at that moment.

I read the letter.

This is what I read:

Dear Mum and Dad,

I was glad to see you on my visit today but I was a little disappointed that Rita could not come. I got the Rosary and letter and I saw the photo of the dogs. Iris looked quite nice surrounded with all those animals. I couldn't keep the photo because it was a newspaper cutting.

I told you Mum it would be very difficult to write this letter, I can't think of anything to say except that you have all been wonderful the way you have worked for me.

Thank Rita for writing to me, tell her I am thinking of her. Don't forget what I told you today. 'Always keep your chin up' and tell Pop not to grind his teeth. Oh! I mustn't forget to thank Lil and Bert for writing and coming to see me. Give my love to them both and to everybody else that we know. Tell Ronnie to keep away from the boys and to stay on his own.

I hope Dad has some more televisions in [Mr Bentley was a radio engineer]. I forgot to ask him how things were on the visit. Dad and I used to have some fun on that one of Leslie's, he certainly had some spare parts for it.

Oh, Dad! Don't let my cycle frames get rusty they might come in handy one day 'cause old Sally [a bicycle] has got a cracked frame and I want you to change it before something happens to you, and Dad, keep a strict eye on Dennis [a younger brother] if he does anything wrong, though I don't think he will but you never know how little things can get you into trouble, if he does, wallop him so that he won't be able to sit for three weeks. I am trying to give you good advice because of my experience.

I tell you what, Mum, the truth of this story has got to come out one day, and as I said in the visiting box that one day a lot of people are going to get into trouble and I think you know who those people are. What do you think Mum? This letter may sound a bit solemn but I am still keeping my chin up as I want all the family to do.

Don't let anything happen to the dogs and the cats and look after them well as you always have.

I hope Laurie and Iris get married all right, I'd like to give them my blessing, it would be nice to have a brother-in-law like him, we could have some fun together. We could have gone round the club and drunk ourselves to a standstill on the great occasion of them being married, tell him to lob out my own flower, tell him to keep my mac clean and my tie. Laurie and I used to have some fun up at the pond till four o'clock in the morning, by the cafe. I always caught Laurie to pay for the pies, he never caught me once.

That will be all for now. I will sign this myself.

Lots of love,

Derek.

Derek Bentley was almost illiterate, he dictated his death-cell letter to a warder, but signed it.

This was the letter I took back with me to 'The Street of Adventure' where it was hailed as another world scoop.

It was published the following Sunday head-lined:

BENTLEY: HIS LAST DRAMATIC LETTER FROM DEATH CELL

When this letter was placed in the post the crowd outside Wandsworth Jail were singing: *The Lord is my Shepherd.*

This was one of the longest death-cell letters I have seen. Christie's last letter, written to his sister on the night before he was hanged, was much briefer.

That letter was not published because the sister to whom it was written did not want to sell it to Fleet Street.

Chapter Twenty-one

Pictures, to the popular newspapers of Fleet Street, have become today every bit as important as stories. The news-photographic side of Fleet Street has been developed into a fine, scientific art; and to most papers the cost of maintaining a team of skilled experts, capable of overcoming every difficulty and every problem to get that Page One picture, is equal to the cost of a top-rate team of writers and reporters.

The day will come – and not before its time – when the Fleet Street photographer will be paid as high a salary as the Fleet Street reporter. These wonderful photographic artists deserve an equal financial status with their writing colleagues. Some of them have great genius.

Like the photographer I worked with, mainly for the *Sunday Pictorial,* who undoubtedly – and I could prove this easily, without spectacles – is the finest, THE most skilful, THE most journalistic newspaper photographer in the world.

I mean of course, Frank Charman, that brilliant ace of all ace-lensmen.

To consider Frank as a photographic artist alone is sufficient to award him the Fleet Street Picture Oscar. His photographic technical genius comes out in almost every picture he takes.

It is not so much what Frank Charman gets into his picture that matters – it is what he leaves out. It is his extravagant use of nothing that amazes me; his pictorial 'understatement'.

Frank Charman and I toured Europe together – the *Pic* considered us the best reporter-photographer team they had – we did hundreds of jobs together, we stopped counting our scoops. For a newspaper in which pictures are life's blood itself Frank and I were of great value – for we never thought of an assignment as a 'good story' or a 'good picture', but as a good picture-story.

My only concern about the work of Frank Charman was that I sometimes wondered whether men like him might make reporters some day obsolete. We would return from a job to the office, he would show me his picture, and my whole tale was in it. Frank Charman can usually tell the story in one picture; sometimes he needs two.

I never once knew him use trimmings or trappings when taking a picture – *he* would never perch a budgerigar on balsa wood suspended from a long moustache.

Yet some of his warmly human pictures are world-famous, they have even brought a dampness to the eyes of his boss, Art Editor Jack Crawshaw.

Their sincerity and simplicity make the Frank Charman pictures great. When I launched my plan to provide every orphan in the land with a real-life Santa Claus for Christmas, all kinds of elaborate ideas were suggested as to how an appealing picture should be organised. Many pictures were taken, but most of them were too dramatic, too heart-breaking, in fact just too, too-much.

Frank was given the job to do, and the great picture he brought back is still considered a Charman classic.

It told everything a writer could say in printed words, it assured that the scheme would be successful. It told the millions of *Pictorial* readers all about the loneliness of orphan children on Christmas Eve; it told them all about the joy they could bring into the lives of these children. It told it all in one picture.

Just a picture of a little girl – a very ordinary little girl. On her shoulder was a hand – just a hand. It was wonderful.

Frank Charman's pictures of chimpanzees behaving like chimpanzees are famous the world over.

He could tell anything with his camera. And on the many long drives we made through Britain together I would challenge his genius by thinking up situations and saying: 'How would you tell this story in one picture.' He usually had an answer.

I once asked him, just before a Christmas: 'Let's suppose you were sent off to the land of reindeers to illustrate the lovely old tale of Santa Claus? Supposing I gave you a hundred reindeers, mountains of snow, dozens of children, masses of toys, genuine sleighs with jingle bells. Now, how would you tell this story in one picture?'

He thought it over – he is a man who likes to think things over.

'Well, I wouldn't want your reindeers, or your jingle bells,' he said, 'they've been done a million times over on Christmas cards.

'I would go and get a skier – a really expert skier, and ask him to dress as Santa Claus. Then I'd find a small hillock, just a small hillock, covered with snow, and I'd lie in the snow with my camera, about twenty feet away. Santa Claus would come skiing down the mountain slope, up, over the hillock, and into the air. Santa Claus would leap into my picture. I would caption the picture with two words, 'He's here!' '

When I wrote an amusing story about a housewife who wanted her 'small room' at home to be exactly like a 'small room' at Buckingham Palace, but who could not get permission from the local authorities for a valve system to replace the old ball and chain, they decided it was pictorially impossible – they did not send a photographer with us.

The next day, when I challenged him, Frank said, 'Well, of course I could have told it in a picture. Just a picture of the housewife in her home was all you needed – who wants to see a picture of a brass ball and chain.'

He could get more sex into one picture of one attractive girl than one could find on the entire stage of the Windmill Theatre. When I wrote the life story of Eileen (I Was a Nun) Griffiths, who had renounced her vows and returned to the world after eleven years in a convent, they had her for hours in the office studio, trying to get a glamorous, telling picture. Then they sent her to an expensive West End studio. And still they did not get what they wanted.

So they sent Frank Charman along to join the ex-nun and me – I was writing her life story in the country.

He took her looking at the world she had returned to – looking at the flowers and the trees. He took her relaxing in the world she had returned to, sitting on a farmer's gate.

Frank never needed a studio – the world, just as it is, is his studio.

Yet Frank Charman is not only an artist – he is a first-class, hard news photographer as well – there is usually a whale of a difference.

He went out with me on dozens of hard-news assignments, where he had to get his picture often in the fleeting seconds when a face might appear, and disappear, at a window.

Frank is also an expert with a Hasselblad camera – a Swedish camera which will take a perfect picture of a person or a group from a distance of more than 100 yards. This camera can be the most ruthless instrument Fleet Street ever possessed.

When on assignments where the people in the story did not wish to have their pictures taken – and it is amazing how many such people we newspapermen meet – Frank would keep at least a hundred yards away.

I would knock on the door of the person concerned with the story, I would talk to the person in the doorway. No battery of cameras no blinding flashbulbs. Frank would be in my car, parked 100 yards away. If I could get the person – and I usually could – to step one foot outside the door for one half-minute, the Hasselblad could add another notch to its trusty, telescopic lens.

Our victims were astounded to see their pictures in the paper – they could not work it out.

The Hasselblad is invincible, infallible. With this deadly weapon Fleet Street can get a photograph of any man, woman or child in the world.

Used on crime jobs, used for sporting events, used for hard, vital news, this camera – it costs over £300 – can be a help and a blessing to the photographer.

Also it can be a heartless, ruthless instrument, indeed.

The *Pic* once sent me to a town in the Midlands to inquire into gossip that a forty-year-old Guide Mistress was seeing too much of a tall, seventeen-year-old Boy Scout.

The Guide Mistress was not a terrible woman. She was a spinster, rather lonely, who had worked hard in an office all her life. She was kind and generous to all who came in contact with her – she was approved of and respected in the small provincial suburb which was her world. To me she seemed small stuff, really, far too small to merit the attentions of the mighty Hasselblad camera. But it seems I was mistaken.

I carried out the investigation required by my office into the friendship between the Guide Mistress and the Boy Scout – two very small, very unimportant people. I did it officially, talking to the boy in the presence of his parents, seeing the County Commissioner and getting his co-operation; asking for, and getting the help of the lonely spinster herself.

Very soon I had the full, true facts, about a friendship between the woman and the boy which I do not think the local paper in that town would have deemed worthy of a four-line mention. I was asked to write a full story, which was splashed.

The Guide Mistress was asked for her photograph for publication. She quietly refused this.

She said: 'Because of all this I have resigned my commission as a Guide Mistress, have given up a job which gave me no reward other than the satisfaction of useful social work. Do not publish a picture of me, for it may cost me my job, and I have my aged mother to support.'

The Hasselblad camera took many pictures of this bread-winning spinster from a distance of 100 yards, too far for the photographer to be attacked with a knitting needle or struck on the head with a guide's whistle. To her amazement she saw her picture in that week's *Sunday Pictorial.* So did her friends, her neighbours, her employers.

But I saw the magnificent pictures also, which were taken by the Hasselblad. I helped to get pictures for the *Pic* which the subjects liked when published; which did them a power of good.

When Diana Dors was 'under a cloud' so far as Fleet Street was concerned, I met her at a small hotel on the South Coast. It was New Year's Eve; she was playing in pantomime.

'I'm getting poor publicity,' she told me, frankly. 'In fact hardly any publicity at all. If one Sunday paper splashed a picture of me it might be the turn of the tide. Can you get me into the *Pic?*' I spoke to Mr Norman Hardy, then *Pic* Features Editor.

'No, Harry,' he said. 'Diana just isn't news at the moment.'

'So we must make you news, Diana,' I told her. 'Tomorrow is New Year's Day, the weather forecast says fine and dry. Go for a New Year's Day swim in the sea, and I'll get you in the *Pic.*'

Diana Dors, who never lets opportunity knock in vain, was up early in the morning. The sky was blue, the sea was calm.

'But there is one snag, Harry, that you won't believe,' she said. 'I haven't got a bikini. I haven't even got a bathing costume with me. And I can't swim in the sea in the nude.'

I raced through the hotel, searching for a girl with a bikini – an impossible quest on a New Year's morn. But one of the hotel chamber-maids – about Diana's size – remembered she had a strapless job she bought in the summer, still lying in her suitcase. Gladly she loaned it to Diana. Diana thanked the girl for the loan of the bathing costume, quickly donned it, returned to me with a dressing gown over it, and I drove her to the beach.

I tested the water with my toes.

'It's as cold as ice, Diana' I said. 'I wouldn't go in for a thousand pounds!'

'Neither would I, for a thousand pounds,' she replied. 'But I would for a glamour picture of me in tomorrow's *Pic.*'

Photographer Bill Turner took an excellent picture, it was splashed in the *Pictorial*. That dip in the tide seemed to turn the tide for Diana; immediately other newspapers began to use her pictures. The next picture I saw of her wearing a bathing costume was a two-piece job made of mink. I'll bet it cost more than the one I borrowed for her from the chambermaid.

From Diana Dors to Marilyn Monroe. I rescued Marilyn Monroe when she was a damsel in distress. When she arrived at London airport they led her into a small canteen where an army of reporters and photographers swept towards her like a surging, menacing sea. She retreated into a corner; she was terrified.

'Look, Marilyn,' I said. 'For goodness sake get behind that ice-cream counter there and you'll save yourself from being squashed to death.'

I manoeuvred her, Sir Laurence Olivier, and Lady Olivier safely behind the counter. She thanked me, and gave me a first-class interview.

'Marilyn, You're Marvellous,' I wrote, and meant it, for she is. A picture of Marilyn and me, with our faces inches apart, appeared in the French picture magazine *Paris Match.*

Marilyn who was also born without riches, might have understood my dreams.

Back in Fleet Street, I met *People* columnist Arthur (Follow me around) Helliwell. 'If I died tonight, Harry, what would you write about me?' he asked. 'Seven words. Arthur, under my own byline. I'd just write: Arthur Helliwell is dead, follow me around!'

And then I had to go and offend the Prime Minister of Britain, Sir Anthony Eden.

I went to the Premier's country house, Chequers, and discovered that Lady Eden was objecting to the domestic arrangements of a cowherd's wife, Mrs Butt.

Mrs Butt would hang out her washing on a clothes line in her back garden, and this line of washing could be seen by the Prime Minister's wife. She requested that the washing be removed, and not hung there any more. The farmer, for whom Mrs Butt's husband worked, ordered that a new line should be fixed in the front garden.

'What?' said the cowherd's wife. 'Hang my washing next to the road, to be dirtied by every farm lorry that passes by? Lady Eden may be the wife of the Prime Minister, but she's not going to stop me hanging out my washing in my own back garden.'

The washing stayed. My story appeared. Britain smiled. But Sir Anthony and his Lady did not like the story.

Oh, it wasn't all murder, crime and squalor in Fleet Street. There were moments...

Chapter Twenty-two

My much publicised exposure of the London Call-Girl Syndicate was a difficult and embarrassing assignment – it was a job I did not enjoy a bit. Neither did the man with me on the investigation, who came with me so that I could have a reliable witness to all my conversations.

That man was Mr Leslie Hubble, head of the *Pictorial's* great 'Let Us Help You' bureau. The John Noble bureau is a separate, but highly organised, department of the *Pictorial,* employing a vast staff of experts who can, and do, help readers with every conceivable problem a reader could have. I think it is the best reader's advice bureau in the world.

No man could look – and in fact – be, more respectable than chubby-faced Leslie Hubble, known to millions by his *nom-de-plume* of John Noble. The sensational *Sunday Pictorial* never did a more respectable thing than when they chose this pin-stripe suited cherub to accompany me into an investigation of vice, which, we later found, would have shocked even the most hard-boiled crime man in Fleet Street. It took Leslie and me many long weeks to complete our dossier on the London call-girls, but in the end the dossier was so accurate and so thorough in every detail, that Scotland Yard's vice squad followed it as closely as a sea-captain follows his navigational chart.

For weeks we followed a fantastic trail of intrigue which revealed a sex-for-sale system in London which shocked Britain far more than the 'Jelks' Vice Ring Trial shocked America. The trail led from a luxurious flat in Kensington to an expensive apartment in the heart of Mayfair; to dozens of small flats and rooms where well-groomed, young, attractive women, offered us companionship and amorous adventures – for a fee.

The trail began in earnest when I was given a telephone number and told I could dial 'M for Madam'. I spoke to a madam, gave her the password, and asked for two attractive, well-groomed girls with whom we could have dinner at a West End restaurant with, later, a visit to a night-club and later...

A shocking state of affairs was revealed. But to know it to be true, and to publish and prove it, were different matters.

It was decided that Hubble and I should meet the girls, should have dinner with them, should return to Madam's apartment with them, and, at such a moment as we should both be convinced of the extent to which the girls were willing to offer their favours, we should leave.

'But,' I protested. 'They will be suspicious. Hell hath no fury like a woman scorned – even a call-girl'.

The first investigation went off all right. But at the second, the girls became suspicious when we declined their final favours.

Soon I knew everything there was to know about London's call-girl syndicates; and shocking knowledge it was.

There were, I discovered, thirty-seven separate syndicates in London, and all flourishing. Each was run by a 'madam', and each madam had at least a hundred call-girls on her books. It was a highly organised business – a most profitable business, all the madams were living in luxury. I talked with madams who kept careful account books, indexes, files of photographs and vital statistics. The madams offered me elegantly gowned women: English, French, German, Japanese, or Chinese.

Few of the call-girls were of the prostitute class; the madams did not want these. The high fees being paid were attracting foolish girls who had, until they met madam, been leading respectable lives. Some were young wives, cheating their husbands while the husbands were away at the office.

One call-girl I met was the wife of an army colonel. One syndicate was run by the wife of a peer.

Not only did I get a full list of the names, addresses, and phone numbers of all the madams and many of the call-girls. I got a file of the names of regular patrons of the London call-girls, and the names on this file were astounding. Well known politicians, sporting personalities, men well known on the stage, the screen, the radio.

Many condemned the *Pictorial* for allowing me to make this very full and very successful investigation into one of the darkest evils of the day. I was not one of them, I am not one of them today. I think, that in allowing myself and Leslie Hubble to conduct this great investigation and make this shattering exposure, this newspaper rendered a great service to the community.

For, as a result of the dossier I compiled, which my editor sent to Scotland Yard, every one of the thirty-seven syndicates was closed down, and most of the thirty-seven madams were punished.

Of course we sold papers by this startling exposure which ran for several weeks and was billed throughout Britain. And why not? Selling newspapers to the public is, in the phrase of that famous television team, 'the end product' of the *Mirror* Group; the final act which makes their millions. I agree that some official body should have investigated, exposed and cleaned up this terrible business first. But they didn't. We did.

I hated this assignment, so did Leslie Hubble. We hated mixing continuously with brazen, shameless hussies; we sickened at having to enter scented boudoirs, confirm our suspicions, then beat hasty, embarrassing retreats. It was hard work and it was rotten work. But it was a job worth doing, and we did it.

My stories about the call-girls were splashed across the pages of the *Pictorial* in no half-hearted manner, we gave irrefutable facts which could not be challenged, and we demanded action. We got it.

The *Pictorial* would not publish pictures of the call-girls themselves, but they had to have an illustration to the articles. So they published my picture instead, captioned, 'Harry Procter, the reporter who discovered the facts'.

The investigation was so exactingly successful that eventually my position was so strong that I could contact every call-girl in London and prove her guilt.

One call-girl – a spy sent by a syndicate – came into my office pretending to offer information, but planning to gain it. She gave me a false name and a false address.

I said to her, 'Here is your taxi-fare home. Go home at once, and in thirty minutes I will know your real name and your telephone number – I will phone you and ask for you by your real name.'

I did.

Hugh Cudlipp made me completely re-write one article because he said I had made the call-girls sound exciting. 'I will not glorify sex,' he said. 'These girls are trollops, not glamorous creatures.' This great journalist went up even higher in my estimation. He was right.

One thing which annoyed me intensely about the call-girl exposure is what eventually happened to 'Little Pat'. The bitter fruits of exposure to the exposist is that often his attack is good publicity for the rogue or swindler he writes about; the publicity often is good advertising for the subject.

'Little Pat' was the daintiest and most attractive of the call-girls I met. She was a young married woman, deceiving her husband almost daily. She was one of the most active of London's call-girls, one of the most in demand.

I devoted almost one entire feature to an exposure of 'Little Pat' and her activities.

She moved to the South Coast, accepting only special commissions. And her picture, clipped to my article, was shown to wealthy American visitors. She was now hawked as 'Little Pat, the Call-Girl the *Pictorial* Exposed'. Because of the publicity she was able to get £50 fees. She will, most certainly, bear me no resentment.

Another bitter pill was the fact that, some months later, after Scotland Yard had followed up every clue I gave them, found every fact correct, they were able to issue a detailed story saying that 'Thirty-seven call-girl syndicates had been closed down; thirty-seven Madams punished...'

Our own crime staff missed this story. It was got, and published, exclusively, by my old friend Norman Rae in the *News of the World,* and that paper, naturally enough, did not give a credit to the earlier work carried out by my newspaper and me.

Once, I became front-page news myself – my name appeared in a news story on page one of the *Sunday Pictorial.*

Almost the entire page one was taken up by a dramatic news picture – a picture of three members of the Yard's Flying Squad arresting Peter James Sheppard, Britain's notorious escapologist.

'The Game's Up' read the banner-line. 'Amazing *Pictorial* scoop as "The Thin Man" is caught.'

The story beside the picture announced: 'Minutes before this dramatic picture was taken by a *Pictorial* cameraman, Peter James Sheppard, Britain's notorious jail-breaker, was being driven round London by *Pictorial* reporter Harry Procter.

'Scotland Yard patrol cars were hot on their heels, and "The Thin Man", who had made a daring daylight escape from Winchester jail nineteen days earlier, was recaptured by the Flying Squad.'

It was one of the picture 'scoops' of the year.

For me this dramatic adventure began at 2.30pm on Tuesday, 3rd May 1955. The telephone on my desk in the *Sunday Pictorial* rang, and a voice said:

'This is "The Thin Man", Peter Sheppard. You featured me in your detective strip the Sunday before last. I would like to give you my true story.'

He asked me to go and meet him at once outside the Collin's Music Hall, Islington.

Naturally I expected it was all a hoax.

'I don't believe you,' I said, 'but if you're there in ten minutes I'll come and meet you. My car number is KGF 98.'

Ten minutes later I stopped my car in Islington. A tall, lean, sun-tanned man approached at once, opened the car door, and jumped in.

'Drive on,' he said, 'and keep driving.'

I gasped, and took a quick look at my passenger. It really was 'The Thin Man' – the prisoner on the run whom we had featured in our crime strip. And it was the crime strip which was to lead to his undoing.

'I think you're a fool, Peter,' I told him. 'Take my advice and give yourself up. Every policeman in the country is looking for you and so are the public.'

He smiled knowingly, 'I want to be friendly, Harry,' he said. 'But I don't want to be caught. I'll tell you my story because I want the world to realise I cannot face the prospect of ten years in jail. Reduce it to something more reasonable and I will go back and become a model prisoner. When I've told you my story, drop me off, give me fifteen minutes start and then phone up the rozzers. I know you have to do that.'

I had. It is the duty of every reporter, and of every citizen, to phone up the police if they know the whereabouts of an escaped prisoner. But now I had to keep on driving, I had no option. We twisted and turned about the awkward, narrow, busy roads of Islington, circling. I drove past dozens of policemen on point duty, two or three Scotland Yard patrol cars.

I did not know whether Peter Sheppard was carrying a gun or not; I was certainly not going to ask him. But I knew him to be a non-violent type of prisoner, and I knew he had a record in prison for always keeping his word to his friends. But, of course, I could not be sure. Each time we stopped at the traffic lights I desperately hoped someone would recognise my passenger.

In fact, somebody did.

At 3.20 the telephone rang in the *Pic* room and a message came that Flying Squad cars were hunting a grey Humber saloon, index number KGF 98.

My colleague Tom Tullett phoned the Yard.

'Please be careful,' he said. 'Our reporter Harry Procter is at the wheel of that car.'

This was another occasion in my life when I did not know what to do. I just kept on driving. City workers, shorthand typists, women with shopping baskets on their arms, peeped casually at me as I tried to attract their attention by a wink or a stare. They took no notice.

By this time Inspector Geoffrey Crosbie Hill and Sergeant McVernon, assigned to the case with six other detectives, had been informed that a member of the public had reported seeing 'The Thin Man' being driven round Islington in a grey Humber car KGF 98. Flying Squad cars converged on north London.

Not knowing all this I kept on driving, but kept on urging Peter to give himself up. I looked anxiously at my petrol gauge, and fearfully noted it contained several gallons of petrol – enough for a long drive. Peter must have noticed this too. I watched him turn my driving mirror towards the passenger seat so that, in addition to endangering our safety, he could see all that was happening behind.

I noticed his neat, smart appearance; he was no tramp, this man on the run. His white silk shirt was spotless, he sported a polka-dot tie, a well-pressed grey, bird's-eye suit, a gabardine overcoat and a smart trilby hat. His shoulders and waist were narrow, he had strong, nervous hands, and the overall slimness which had enabled him to climb through an eleven-inch ventilator at a London police station, two years before...

I recalled that this famous cracksman had been sentenced thirteen times. While we drove, he told me the story of his escape.

'I planned it for months – like a military operation,' he said. 'I walked into the trusted prisoners' huts and calmly got out two bed boards and two tables. These I piled up against the prison wall, all the time keeping my eye on the exercising party as it moved round and round.

'In one quick dash I leapt forward, ran up the bed boards and was over the wall without being spotted. I can still see the astonishment on the faces of my mates.

'I landed smack in the middle of a lawn on which the screws (warders) and their wives were holding a garden-party. The screws rushed at me but I ran for it. I jumped on a girl's bike and rode off, abandoning it a hundred yards away. Then I darted into the back garden of a little house.

'I stayed there until it was dark, the rozzers and the screws hunting within a stone's throw of me. Once they had gone I was deliriously happy. I felt so safe that I fell fast asleep. When I awoke it was dark. I left my hiding place, walked quietly down the road.

'Three miles further on I saw an A40 1953 car standing unattended at Harestock Corner. I jumped in and drove off.

'You were dead right in that crime strip of yours about me driving right through the police cordon. A copper stepped into the road, flashing his light with his hand up. I slowed down as though I was going to stop and then suddenly stepped on the gas, and swept by. If I hadn't slowed down I would have got his truncheon through my windscreen.'

As 'The Thin Man' talked he smoked cigarette after cigarette. The Humber was heading for Dalston Junction, and as the fantastic journey progressed, he kept his eyes glued to the rear mirror.

Each time the car passed a policeman he pretended to blow his nose, covering his face with a white handkerchief. In Dalston he directed me to drive the car to Dalston station, and to turn left at Ashwin Street. We passed a dozen taxi-cab drivers, and stopped with the car facing a wall. 'The Thin Man' got out.

To the right was a road down which he could run, or he could have run forward on either side of the taxi-rank. He asked me: 'Telephone a friend of mine for me from the box near the station. I will come in the box with you.'

I made the call, and Sheppard returned to the car alone, telling me to stay near the box.

It would have saved my nerves if had known that at that moment, the innocent-looking Flying Squad lorry was crawling down St Pauls road nearby. It looked like any other transport lorry. Hidden inside were three detectives. Under 'The Thin Man's' very nose the radio operator sent out a call to the patrol car, Squad 5, 'Watching suspect. Await your directions.'

Back came the message. 'Stand by. We are coming in the other way.' Through the busy streets dashed the high powered squad car to a narrow, twisting alley at the back of Ashwin Street.

The detectives got out, and Sergeant McVernon walked slowly along the pavement towards 'The Thin Man'. Inspector Crosbie Hill walked along the other side.

A colleague arrived in time to see Sergeant McVernon walk up to Sheppard and take off his trilby hat.

'Sheppard, you're off!' said McVernon. He had recognised Sheppard by his shock of wiry black hair.

After his capture Sheppard said he got his idea for the escape by watching the film *The Colditz Story* – the story of escapes from a prisoner-of-war camp.

Chapter Twenty-three

But though I was big-time in Fleet Street, I was unhappy. I did not like some of the stories I was writing.

A man can have too much of murder and crime, of spending his life with members of the criminal classes.

I wrote 'corn' stories, also, for the *Pictorial,* but these I liked doing. They were not deathless prose, but they were doing a lot of good. They were bringing in letters to me from every part of the country, warm, friendly letters which told me the readers liked this stuff. They brought in far more letters than my crime stories.

COME HOME ALL IS FORGIVEN, was the headline on a two-page feature I wrote, urging dozens of runaway wives, runaway fathers, runaway children, to come home to those who missed them.

Most of them did. I wanted to abandon crime, murder, yes, and even exposure. I felt strongly now that I must write to make people happy.

It became my hope that colleague Tom Tullett, himself a former policeman, and a journalist who liked crime reporting and preferred it to all else, could take over crime entirely and leave me to my 'corn'.

I told the office my health was dithering a bit – which was true – and I asked if I could be relieved entirely of murder assignments, crime assignments, and exposure assignments.

But no one would take me seriously.

'What do you want to do, then?' quipped Reg Payne. 'Edit the What the Stars Foretell column?'

I was now living in one of the loveliest spots in Britain, just on the edge of Pratts Bottom, Kent; my wife and I were making delightful friends – people who had never walked down Fleet Street, people who could live without the popular press.

Early in 1956 my wife had said to me: 'I wish you would resign from the *Sunday Pictorial.* I don't like the stories you are writing for the *Pic.* I hear comments in the village about your stories; comments

I don't like. I wish you would leave and join some different kind of newspaper.'

I remember flushing angrily: 'I've got to live,' I told her. 'I've got to think of you and the children.'

My wife, who attends church each Sunday morning, said: 'I want you to think of me and the children. If you get a job sweeping leaves we can be proud of you. I do not like these stories you are writing.'

She added: 'I got a letter from your mother, back home. She says she too does not like the stories you are writing.'

'But they're all going Page One lead!' I protested.

I was now troubled by an acute physical pain. I went to a Harley Street specialist. Then I went to my local village doctor, Dr G A Brooks.

In a small village like Pratts Bottom, everybody knows everything about everybody.

'So you're not sleeping at nights?' he said. 'Well, I can give you something to help you sleep. But if I were you I would change your job.'

In May of that year, a fire broke out on a houseboat moored in a creek at Canvey Island. Two bonny baby boys, aged three, were burnt to death in that fire. After their death they became known as 'The Houseboat Twins'.

The whole country was deeply shocked at the terrible fate suffered by these small, innocent children. Their mother, Mrs Violet Wright, known as 'Nylon' Vicki, became a woman who was discussed by every mother in the land.

She was brought to trial at the Old Bailey, London, and charged with the murder of her twin sons. She was acquitted of the murder charge and found guilty of manslaughter. She went to jail.

When I first read, in a Midlands town, about the terrible death of the 'Houseboat Twins' I never realised how personally and professionally involved I was to become with their tragedy. And how their tragedy was to force me into making grave decisions about myself and Fleet Street. I never realised then that this news would lead to the most sickening assignment of my career. An assignment I was to hate, and would never forget.

In the *Pic* Fred Redman and I discussed the Canvey Island fire – in the beginning, for Fleet Street, it was no more than a tragic fire.

Fred Redman asked my professional opinion about the tragedy.

215

Fred often did this – no man has ever had more respect for my journalistic ability, for my news sense, than Red.

'I think this is the beginning of the biggest story of the year,' I said. 'It will end at the Old Bailey.'

Nobody else agreed. My colleague Tom Tullett had no professional interest in the fire. Editor Colin Valdar was far too busy – Friday is a busy day for a Sunday paper editor – to discuss it with me.

But Fred Redman, whose faith in my news sense has never once wavered, said: 'If you think there's something in it, Harry, then off you go and have a look at it. Off you go to Canvey, stay the night, but keep in touch with the news desk.'

By lunch time the following Saturday I was convinced that the 'Houseboat Twins' fire was a very grave matter indeed. I was also convinced that it would eventually be necessary for Mrs Vicki Wright to tell her story of the fire to an Old Bailey jury. I was convinced that within a few days the big Sunday newspapers, and some of the dailies too, would be offering four figure sums for a 'tie-up' with Mrs Vicki Wright.

At six that night I phoned up Fred Redman. He was very busy running the news desk – on a Saturday this becomes the busiest job of the week. But he listened to me carefully.

'Frankly, Harry,' he said, 'I can't get them interested in it at all here. But if you feel we ought to buy up Mrs Vicki Wright I'll give you the OK up to £100 for a start. I'm willing to risk a hundred quid on your opinion.'

That night Red was scorned by other executives for giving me this instruction. Ten days later he was laughing his head off in the faces of his critics.

Through a friend I sent a message to Mrs Vicki Wright that I could pay her £100 for a story about the fire, an exclusive story. The message came back that she would see me on the following Tuesday and discuss the matter.

On the Tuesday, armed with the normal Fleet Street 'buy-up' contract, I went to see Vicki at the home of her sister, Florrie, in Southend. She was a small woman, pretty in a sort of way – her large dark eyes were attractive. We shook hands and were left alone to discuss our business.

For the rest of that week I barely left her. I ate all my meals facing

216

her, for hours I drove about the countryside with her sitting at my side.

She was most unhappy, she told me at that first meeting, because if she walked into the street, women called her names and shook their fists at her. She agreed to sign my contract and to receive a sum of £100 for her own, exclusive story, and to allow me the first option on any future stories, should there be future developments.

'But there is one thing else I want,' she startled me by announcing. 'I have lost my best clothes in the fire. You must also buy me some clothes.'

I agreed.

On the Wednesday morning I called for her early, prepared to help in any way I could a bereaved and tragic mother. I found her fully dressed and waiting for me.

'Drive me to London,' she said. 'And buy me some clothes.'

Sister Florrie said: 'First I think we must all go to Southend and make arrangements for the funeral tomorrow. If Mr Procter will buy you clothes today, they must be black clothes, for the funeral.'

'I agree with your sister, Vicki,' I said. 'Tomorrow you must wear black.'

I drove Vicki and sister Florrie to a florist, chased all the way by a car-load of photographers. Inside the florists I suggested simple posies, floral crosses.

'I want two chairs of flowers,' said Vicki. 'Today is the twins' birthday, and I had promised them two chairs as presents.' I ordered the two chairs, showed my press card, promised to be responsible for the bill.

I was now out of money. I drove to London and asked for sufficient money to pay for the funeral clothes.

My paper, however, would not agree to my spending any further money on this assignment. 'It isn't worth tuppence, Harry,' they said. 'And already you've wasted £100. She must buy the clothes out of that £100 – not one penny more will we give. We are not a philanthropic institution.'

Within a fortnight, one of them was daily making a car journey – a chauffeur-driven car journey – to Southend and Canvey Island, and offering a four figure sum for the Vicki Wright story, and the story of a man friend. By that time I had gladly handed over the tiller and my contract, signed by Mrs Vicki Wright, offering her story for

£100. By that time the sky was the limit, and the paper was willing to spend thousands.

But when, in the *Pic* office, he and I discussed buying Vicki Wright her funeral clothes, they placed a different value on her story.

I went to see the Editor, Mr Colin Valdar. 'It may be that I have made a mistake,' I said, 'but I have promised this woman black clothes for the funeral tomorrow. I have promised this as a member of your staff – my promise must be honoured.'

'How much?' asked Colin.

'I'm not sure. But at the most, £12.'

'Oh, I don't mind that.'

Twelve pounds allowed by a Sunday newspaper for clothes for Mrs Vicki Wright. A week later some newspapers in Fleet Street would have clothed her in mink and sable.

'Can I have Madeline MacLoughlin to help me? I'm sure, Colin that this story will prove a big one in the end – I'll stake my reputation on it despite what anyone else tells you.'

'Then yes, Harry,' said Colin. 'Take Madeline with you.' And again this Procter-MacLoughlin team was in operation.

I had got my way. But I had not pleased my Deputy Editor. In Fleet Street, where you have Editors, Managing Editors, Assistant Editors, Deputy Editors, News Editors, it, is so difficult for the reporters to please everybody all of the time.

Madeline, Vicki, Florrie and I, all had lunch. Vicki asked me: 'Would it be all right for me to ask Bill to come to the funeral?'

'Bill' was William Smith, a married man with grown-up children, who later became a central figure in the story.

'I think it would be unwise,' I said.

Florrie and I sat in my car while Madeline and Vicki went into a store. Madeline returned about an hour later.

'Sorry, Harry,' she said. 'But you'd better take over. Mrs Wright refuses to have black. She says she wants a more attractive colour than black.'

Inside the shop, I had my first difference with Vicki, but I was firm. 'You must wear black tomorrow,' I said. 'If you wear any other colour then you'll pay the bill yourself. And that's that.'

Sister Florrie agreed with me.

I helped her choose a black coat, a black dress, a black hat, black shoes. I gave in on the stockings and she chose a flesh-coloured pair of nylons.

On the drive back to Southend, Vicki asked me: 'Can I call and see a friend? It will only take us ten minutes out of our way.'

Sister Florrie advised strongly against this.

Vicki appealed to me: 'You understand, Harry, don't you? Honestly, if I had to go three days without seeing my friend, I think I would go crazy, really crazy.'

I was thinking about the 'Houseboat Twins', the baby boys who died in the fire. I felt depressed.

I also felt that it would not be fair to the babies, to invite Mr Smith to the funeral.

The kindly local police had arranged that the funeral should be held in the early hours of the morning – 7.30 – so there would be no crowds. But the crowds came, and hundreds of reporters and photographers.

Madeline and I left our hotel shortly after 6am and drove to Florrie's house.

There were to be five mourners at the funeral of the 'Houseboat Twins', it seemed – just five people to follow the small, white coffins of the baby brothers. Vicki Wright, her sister and brother-in-law, Madeline MacLoughlin, and myself.

I said to Madeline: 'I am sorry but I don't want to travel in the funeral car. I will drive behind you in my own.'

I did not feel well.

Great crowds were gathered at the small church where the funeral service was to be held. I was last in the small funeral party which followed the small coffins into the church. I walked through a lane of newspapermen. They knew me, they looked at me. None of them spoke.

My colleague Madeline McLoughlin was obviously extremely moved. She was obviously most unhappy.

We all took our seats in that tiny church, we faced the two white coffins. Somebody handed me a prayer-book and a hymn book.

Somebody began to speak holy, sacred words.

I decided I had no right to be there in that church. I decided that my presence there was not a part of my professional duty as a member of the fourth estate. I decided that this funeral service was a private affair.

219

Then suddenly – I just could not help myself – I left my seat and walked out of the church.

I walked through the ranks of waiting newspapermen.

'Harry Procter must be getting soft in his old age,' I heard one mutter.

I heard my friend, reporter Laurence Wilkinson, then of the *Daily Mail* say, kindly, understandingly:

'If you can't take it, Harry, it must be tough.'

'I can't take it, Laurie,' I said.

I got into my car, took out a 6s 6d flask of brandy, and drank it all. Never before had I taken an alcoholic drink so early in the day.

Madeline McLoughlin led Mrs Vicki Wright to the grave-side, stood with the family as the last prayers were said. I stood many yards away.

After the funeral I drove around to collect my thoughts.

'If this is why I came to Fleet Street,' I thought, 'I really wish I'd never done so. If this is Fleet Street, it's time I left it.'

Tomorrow came. One day after the funeral I took Vicki for a drive in the country. She stopped and made a telephone call.

She got back into the car. 'I am going to meet Bill,' she said.

By following her directions I came to a lonely country path, running off an equally lonely country lane. It was a pretty spot, trees hung with May blossoms were all around. The air was clean and fresh.

In this beautiful place a car waited with a man inside it.

He got out of the car.

'Will you beat it?' he said to me. 'Give us an hour on our own!'

I want to a roadside cafe nearby and drank tea with two *Sunday Pictorial* photographers. They had several cameras with them, including the Hasselblad. Their job, was, they told me, to get a photograph.

One of them was my friend and colleague, Frank Charman. I asked him if he would return in my car to the lonely blossom-scented meeting place of Vicki Wright and her friend. He agreed.

Frank Charman was then invited to take a photograph, the day after the funeral of the 'House-boat Twins'.

That picture was published in the Pic on 27th May 1956.

In an inside page I told Mrs Violet Wright's story as she related it to me.

It was the story of a woman who said she would forever afterwards brand herself as a coward for not trying to do more to save her babies.

In the story she denied rumours that she had deliberately let her babies burn so that she could run off with the man she loved; told how she was haunted by the memory of the terrified screams of the twins as the houseboat went up in flames; admitted that she was not a good woman, and had loved not wisely, but too well.

That story of Vicki Wright and the houseboat fire, of course, was published long before the historic trial at the Old Bailey at which Vicki was acquitted of murder and convicted of manslaughter.

On the following Tuesday I went into the *Pictorial* office to discover that 'they' now believed that the 'Houseboat Twins' story was the biggest story of the year – I recalled then that the Deputy Editor had said it was not worth tuppence a week before, but I did not mention this.

This is where I came in, I thought. Once again, everybody wanted to come in on the act. Now that the story was secured, and the preliminary, all-important digging had been done; now that the whole of Fleet Street were after Mrs Vicki Wright, 'they' on the *Pic* were saying what I myself had said two weeks before and I insisted on being released from this assignment. I left the job to my colleagues.

My colleagues spent a very large sum indeed in the next few weeks, but my newspaper did not 'clean up' on the 'Houseboat Twins' story.

Other Sunday papers had good after-the-trial stories.

And I firmly decided that, after my Canvey Island assignment, I wanted no more to do with crime stories. I wanted to get on quietly writing 'corn'.

When Fred Redman complimented me on my exclusive 'I Brand Myself as a Coward' story from Mrs Wright, he commented, 'You see why I can't take you off crime? You are the only man in Fleet Street who could do a job like that.'

But I swore I had finished with such jobs forever. I had had more than my fill of such so-called glory; I had brought home the sensational exclusives which had sold the extra millions. There were younger men on the *Pic* – men with more enthusiasm for such assignments.

I announced that my health was not improving, that my nerves would not stand it, that I simply would not do this type of work any more.

'Procter's getting soft,' said my colleagues on the *Pic*.

Perhaps I was.

Lightning Source UK Ltd.
Milton Keynes UK
UKHW020021280520
363925UK00024B/5720